SOUL OF AMERICA

SOUL OF AMERICA

DOCUMENTING OUR PAST
VOLUME II: 1858–1993

ROBERT C. BARON
SENIOR EDITOR

North American Press
Golden, Colorado

Cover Illustration: From the painting *The Statue of Liberty Unveiling* by Edward Moran, courtesy of the Museum of the City of New York.

Interior Illustrations: page 3, Abraham Lincoln, courtesy of the National Archives; page 25, *Wounded Soldier*, courtesy of the National Archives; page 53, Booker T. Washington, courtesy of the Tuskegee Institute National Historical Site, Tuskegee, Alabama; page 72, Theodore Roosevelt, courtesy of the White House Historical Association; page 102, Franklin D. Roosevelt, courtesy of the White House Historical Association; page 118, Harry Truman, courtesy of the White House Historical Association; page 138, Dwight Eisenhower, courtesy of the White House Historical Association; page 151, Martin Luther King, Jr., courtesy of the National Archives; page 154, Lyndon B. Johnson, courtesy of the White House Historical Association. Excerpt from *Silent Spring* reprinted from *Silent Spring* by Rachel Carson. Copyright © 1962 by Rachel Carson. Reprinted by permission of Houghton Mifflin Co. All rights reserved.

Library of Congress Cataloging-in-Publication Data

Soul of America : documenting our past / edited by Robert C. Baron.
        p.   cm.
    Includes bibliographical references and indexes.
    Contents : v. 1. 1492–1870 — v. 2. 1858–1993.
    ISBN 1-55591-921-9 (v. 1) :   — ISBN 1-55591-922-7 (v. 2) :
    1. United States—History—Sources. I. Baron, Robert C.
E173.S687   1993
973—dc20   93-21115
                                                                 CIP

Printed in the United States of America

0   9   8   7   6   5   4   3   2   1

North American Press
a division of Fulcrum Publishing
350 Indiana Street, Suite 350
Golden, Colorado 80401-5093

TABLE OF CONTENTS

INTRODUCTION

THIS book is about America; it presents the ideas and writings of the men and women who have shaped our nation.

America has always been a special place, a place unlike any other. We are a nation of immigrants and descendants of immigrants. From the villages and towns of Europe, Africa, Asia and the Americas, immigrants sailed and steamed across the ocean to reach this country's shores. And once in the new world, they walked and rode across the continent, heading west, toward new opportunities, jobs and the open land—marching on to the leadership of the free people of the world.

Our leaders have recognized the special place that is America. Included in this book are basic American ideas, eloquently expressed in their words:

Thomas Jefferson in the "Declaration of Independence": "We hold these truths to be self-evident, that all men are created equal, that they are endowed by their Creator with certain unalienable Rights, that among these are Life, Liberty and the pursuit of Happiness. That to secure these rights, Governments are instituted among Men, deriving their just powers from the consent of the governed."

John Adams in his "Inaugural Address": "Employed in the service of my country abroad during the whole course of these transactions, I first saw the Constitution of the United States in a foreign country. ... I read it with great satisfaction, as the result of good heads prompted by good hearts, as an experiment better adapted to the genius, character, situation, and relations of this nation and country than any which had ever been proposed or suggested."

Abraham Lincoln in the "Address at Gettysburg": "That this

nation, under God, shall have a new birth of freedom—and that government of the people, by the people, for the people, shall not perish from the earth."

Herbert Hoover in an October 1928 speech: "And what have been the results of the American system? Our country has become the land of opportunity to those born without inheritance, not merely because of the wealth of its resources and industry but because of this freedom of initiative and enterprise."

Franklin Delano Roosevelt in the "Four Freedoms" speech: "Since the beginning of our American history we have been engaged in change—in a perpetual peaceful revolution—a revolution which goes on steadily, quietly adjusting itself to changing conditions."

John F. Kennedy in his "Inaugural Address": "The torch has been passed to a new generation of Americans—born in this century, tempered by war, disciplined by a hard and bitter peace, proud of our ancient heritage—and unwilling to witness or permit the slow undoing of those human rights to which this nation has always been committed."

Lyndon B. Johnson in his November 1963 address to Congress: "Our American unity does not depend upon unanimity. We have differences; but now, as in the past, we can derive from those differences strength, not weakness, wisdom, not despair."

America is a country born of an ideal, an idea of freedom—religious freedom, political freedom, economic freedom, the freedom to speak and think as one wishes—and the opportunity to grow and change and to provide a better world for their families and for their descendants.

Change has come slowly at times, but it has come. It was more than a century between the time when Roger Williams and William Penn demanded freedom of religion and the time that the Bill of Rights was ratified. The first amendment states: "Congress shall make no law respecting an establishment of religion, or prohibiting the free exercise thereof; or abridging the freedom of speech or of the press; or the right of the people peaceably to assemble, and to petition the government for a redress of grievances."

It has taken time, often far too much time, for woman suffrage and black equality to be achieved, for political and economic rights to be extended to all citizens. But progress has been and continues to be made. This change has occurred because of individuals.

Hear their words. Hear the words of Coronado; William Penn and Roger

Williams; Benjamin Franklin, George Washington, John Adams, Thomas Jefferson, Thomas Paine, Patrick Henry and James Madison; John C. Calhoun, Daniel Webster and Henry Clay; Abraham Lincoln and Robert E. Lee; Frederick Douglass, Booker T. Washington and Martin Luther King, Jr.; Abigail Adams, Elizabeth Cady Stanton, Susan B. Anthony and Jane Addams; Theodore Roosevelt, Woodrow Wilson, Franklin Delano Roosevelt and John Kennedy. Hear their words.

The native people who resided in this land had much to teach us. We have too infrequently listened. Hear their words as well. Listen to Red Jacket and Tecumseh. Let Chief Joseph of the Nez Percé speak: "Treat all men alike. Give them the same laws. Give them all an even chance to live and grow. All men were made by the same Great Spirit Chief. They are all brothers. The earth is the mother of all people, and all people should have equal rights upon it."

In the five centuries since Columbus and his ships sailed on to a new world, in the four centuries since Coronado led an expedition of discovery and exploration across the southwest, in the three centuries since Roger Williams and William Penn wrote so strongly about religious freedom, in the two centuries since Jefferson's immortal words proclaimed our independence, in the century since Lincoln with his courage held the country together and helped heal the nation's wounds, and in this century of wars and depression, economic growth and the movement of the United States onto center stage as a world power— throughout all that time, political and economic rights have been extended to an ever-increasing share of our population.

How did the wilderness described by Columbus and Coronado become the leading nation in the world? How did the dreams of freedom—freedom of religion, of political beliefs, of expression, of opportunity—develop? What are some of the ideals and hopes of this country? What are some of its principles? The documents, Supreme Court decisions, speeches and songs collected here provide some answers to these questions.

The origin of *Soul of America* was in watching television, a rather dangerous pastime for a historian. In noting the anniversary of the death of President John F. Kennedy, each network showed a three-minute summary of Kennedy's life, focusing on his inaugural address and the "ask not what your country can do for you" quote. No television program or, for that matter, any newspaper ever reproduced more than a few sentences from his inaugural address. There were numerous commentaries, reports, historical analyses and opinions about the speech, but only fragments of the actual text.

A few weeks later, the editors and others began to discuss the most important documents in American history as well as some of the most beautiful speeches. Eventually we decided to prepare a book of documents and developed a list of items to be included. We discussed the documents and their influence on people and history.

Sometimes choices were obvious—the Constitution or the Declaration of Independence. Some choices were based on their long-term influence—the Seneca Falls Declaration or Thoreau's speech "Civil Disobedience," which influenced Ghandi in South Africa and India and later, Martin Luther King, Jr., and the civil rights movement. Some selections were made based on the beauty of the language and the expression of major ideas—the selections by Thomas Paine, Frederick Douglass, Sojourner Truth and Chief Joseph.

The volume is organized in chronological order. But certain themes often extend over many decades. A reader can study each document in order or read all writings on a particular subject.

Suggestions were made by each editor, but ultimately, I am responsible for the final selections. I am also responsible for the introductions to all material from the fifteenth century to the early nineteenth century.

I would like to thank the associate editors: Maxine Benson, former State Historian for Colorado, an editor, author and friend who assisted in the organization and editing of this book; Chris Bierwirth of the University of Wisconsin, who wrote the introductions to those pieces from the mid- to late nineteenth century; Cathy Lavender-Teliha of the University of Colorado, who wrote the introductions to the selections from the early twentieth century; Samuel Scinta of Yale University, who wrote the introductions to the selections from the late twentieth century; and Kay Baron, who aided in selecting the material and organizing the book and who typed all the documents. I would also like to thank Carmel Huestis, Karen Groves and Jay Staten of Fulcrum for their editing, suggestions and encouragement.

Robert C. Baron
Winter 1993

VI

CIVIL WAR

"HOUSE DIVIDED" SPEECH

Abraham Lincoln   *June 17, 1858*

Born February 12, 1809, Abraham Lincoln spent his first twenty-one years on frontier farms in Kentucky, Indiana and Illinois. In his young adulthood, he tried his hand at several occupations before eventually settling on the law.

Lincoln first became active in politics in the 1830s. From 1834 to 1842, he served as a Whig member of the Illinois state legislature. His legislative career was mostly involved in the promotion of economic enterprise, but in 1837 he helped draft a protest to an anti-abolition bill, maintaining that slavery was "both injustice and bad policy." Lincoln's distaste for slavery, though grounded in moral objections, stemmed mainly from its divisive effect on national politics. From 1847 to 1849, Lincoln served as the sole Whig in Illinois's congressional delegation. One of the few bills he introduced during his single term was a proposal for the gradual emancipation of slaves in the District of Columbia.

In 1856, Lincoln joined the new Republican Party and, due in part to his moderate views on slavery, soon rose to leadership among Illinois Republicans. He was chosen as the Republican candidate for the United States Senate in 1858. At the close of the state convention, he delivered a speech clearly stating his belief that the nation could not continue to be divided between two opposing economic and moral systems, a speech that has been identified ever since by its biblical quotation (Mark 3:25).

———————————

MR. President and Gentlemen of the Convention: If we could first know where we are, and whither we are tending, we could better judge what to do, and how to do it. We are now far into the fifth year since a policy was initiated with the avowed object and confident promise of putting an end to slavery agitation. Under the operation of that policy, that agitation has not only not ceased, but has constantly augmented. In my opinion, it will not cease until a crisis shall have been reached and passed. "A house divided against itself cannot stand." I believe this government cannot endure permanently half slave and half free. I do not expect the Union to be dissolved; I do not expect the house to fall; but I do expect it will cease to be divided. It will become all one thing, or all the other. Either the opponents of slavery will arrest the further spread of it, and place it where the public mind shall rest in the belief that it is the course of ultimate extinction, or its advocates will push it forward till it shall become alike lawful in all the States, old as well as new, North as well as South.

Have we no tendency to the latter condition?

Let any one who doubts, carefully contemplate that now almost complete legal combination—piece of machinery, so to speak—compounded of the Nebraska doctrine and the Dred Scott decision. Let him consider, not only what work the machinery is adapted to do, and how well adapted, but also let him study the history of its construction and trace, if he can, or rather fail, if he can, to trace the evidences of design, and concert of action, among its chief architects, from the beginning.

The new year of 1854 found slavery excluded from more than half the States by State Constitutions, and from most of the National territory by Congressional prohibition. Four days later, commenced the struggle which ended in repealing that Congressional prohibition. This opened all the National territory to slavery, and was the first point gained. . . .

While the Nebraska Bill was passing through Congress, a law case, involving the question of a negro's freedom, by reason of his owner having voluntarily taken him first into a free State, and then into a territory covered by the Congressional prohibition, and held him as a slave for a long time in each, was passing through the United States Circuit Court for the District of Missouri; and both Nebraska Bill and lawsuit were brought to a decision in the same month of May, 1854. The negro's name was "Dred Scott," which name now designates the decision finally made in the case. Before the then next Presidential election, the law case came to, and was argued in, the Supreme Court of the United States; but the decision of it was deferred until after the election. Still, before the election, Senator Trumbull, on the floor of the Senate, requested the leading advocate of the Nebraska Bill to state his opinion whether the people of a Territory can constitutionally exclude slavery from their limits; and the latter answers: "That is a question for the Supreme Court."

Abraham Lincoln, photograph by Mathew Brady, 1864.

The election came. Mr. Buchanan was elected, and the indorsement, such as it was, secured. That was the second point gained. . . . The Presidential inauguration came, and still no decision of the court; but the incoming President, in his inaugural address, fervently exhorted the people to abide by the forthcoming decision, whatever it might be. Then, in a few days, came the decision.

The reputed author of the Nebraska Bill finds an early occasion to make a speech at this capital indorsing the Dred Scott decision, and vehemently denouncing all opposition to it. The new President, too, seizes the early occasion of the Silliman letter to indorse and strongly construe that decision, and to express his astonishment that any different view had ever been entertained!

At length a squabble springs up between the President and the author of the Nebraska Bill, on the mere question of fact, whether the Lecompton Constitution was or was not in any just sense made by the people of Kansas; and in that quarrel the latter declares that all he wants is a fair vote for the people, and that he cares not whether slavery be voted down or voted up. I do not understand his declaration, that he cares not whether slavery be voted down or voted up, to be intended by him other than as an apt definition of the policy he would impress upon the public mind. . . . That principle is the only shred left of his original Nebraska doctrine. Under the Dred Scott decision "squatter sovereignty" squatted out of existence, tumbled down like temporary scaffolding; like the mould at the foundry, served through one blast, and fell back into loose sand; helped to carry an election, and then was kicked to the winds. His late joint struggle with the Republicans, against the Lecompton Constitution, involves nothing of the original Nebraska doctrine. That struggle was made on a point—the right of a people to make their own constitution—upon which he and the Republicans have never differed.

The several points of the Dred Scott decision, in connection with Senator Douglas's "care not" policy, constitute the piece of machinery, in its present state of advancement. This was the third point gained. The working points of that machinery are:

Firstly, That no negro slave, imported as such from Africa, and no descendant of such slave, can ever be a citizen of any State, in the sense of that term as used in the Constitution of the United States. This point is made in order to deprive the negro, in every possible event, of the benefit of that provision of the United States Constitution which declares that "The citizens of each State shall be entitled to all privileges and immunities of citizens in the several States."

Secondly, That, "subject to the Constitution of the United States," neither Congress nor a Territorial Legislature can exclude slavery from any United States Territory. This point is made in order that individual men may fill up the Territories with slaves, without danger of losing them as property, and thus to enhance the chances of permanency to the institution through all the future.

Thirdly, That whether the holding a negro in actual slavery in a free State makes him free, as against the holder, the United States courts will not decide, but will leave to be decided by the courts of any slave State the negro may be forced into by the master. This point is made, not to be pressed immediately; but, if acquiesced in for a while, and apparently indorsed by the people at an election, then to sustain the logical conclusion that what Dred Scott's master might lawfully do with Dred Scott, in the free State of Illinois, every other master may lawfully do with any other one, or one thousand slaves, in Illinois, or in any other free State.

Auxiliary to all this, and working hand in hand with it, the Nebraska doctrine, or what is left of it, is to educate and mould public opinion, at least Northern public opinion, not to care whether slavery is voted down or voted up. This shows exactly where we now are; and partially, also, whither we are tending. . . .

Why was the amendment, expressly declaring the right of the people, voted down? Plainly enough now,—the adopting of it would have spoiled the niche for the Dred Scott decision. Why was the court decision held up? Why even a Senator's individual opinion withheld, till after the Presidential election? Plainly enough now,—the speaking out then would have damaged the "perfectly free" argument upon which the election was to be carried. Why was the outgoing President's felicitation on the indorsement? Why the delay of a reargument? Why the incoming President's advance exhortation in favor of the decision? These things look like the cautious patting and petting of a spirited horse preparatory to mounting him, when it is dreaded that he may give the rider a fall. And why the hasty after-indorsement of the decision by the President and others?

We cannot absolutely know that all these exact adaptations are the result of preconcert. But when we see a lot of framed timbers, different portions of which we know have been gotten out at different times and places and by different workmen,—Stephen, Franklin, Roger, and James, for instance,—and when we see these timbers joined together, and see they exactly make the frame of a house or a mill, all the tenons and mortises exactly fitting, and all the lengths and proportions of the different pieces exactly adapted to their respective places, and not a piece too many or too few,—not omitting even scaffolding,—or, if a single piece be lacking, we see the place in the frame exactly fitted and prepared yet to bring such piece in,—in such a case, we find it impossible not to believe that Stephen and Franklin and Roger and James all understood one another from the beginning, and all worked upon a common plan or draft drawn up before the first blow was struck. . . .

Address to the Virginia Court

John Brown   *November 2, 1859*

In the late 1840s John Brown, long a disciple of William Lloyd Garrison, became convinced that slavery could only be abolished through violent action. In 1855 he and his five sons set out for Kansas with a wagon load of guns and ammunition. For the next three years he played a leading role in the war for control of "Bleeding Kansas."

In 1858 Brown conceived the idea of forming a provisional government of freed slaves in the mountains of western Virginia and Maryland. On October 16, 1859, Brown led a raiding party into Harper's Ferry, taking the arsenal and sixty hostages. For a day and a night, Brown's army held out, but finally succumbed to an assault of United States Marines commanded by Colonel Robert E. Lee. Brown was arrested and tried for murder, insurrection and treason.

Brown's trial became a focal point of the slavery controversy. Northern editorialists lionized him; southerners saw him as a dangerous advocate of violence and the man who had attempted to arm slaves. The high moral tone of his final statement before the court immortalized him as a martyr for the abolitionist cause. Though he failed to provoke the slave insurrection he had hoped for, Brown's raid and execution were instrumental in increasing hostility between North and South.

I have, may it please the Court, a few words to say.

In the first place, I deny every thing but what I have already admitted, of a design on my part to free Slaves. I intended, certainly, to have made a clean thing of that matter, as I did last winter, when I went into Missouri, and there took Slaves, without the snapping of a gun on either side, moving them through the country, and finally leaving them in Canada. I desired to have done the same thing again on a much larger scale. That was all I intended. I never did intend murder, or treason, or the destruction of property, or to excite or incite Slaves to rebellion, or to make insurrection.

I have another objection, and that is, that it is unjust that I should suffer such a penalty. Had I interfered in the manner, and which I admit has been fairly proved,—for I admire the truthfulness and candor of the greater portion of the witnesses who have testified in this case,—had I so interfered in behalf of the Rich, the Powerful, the Intelligent, the so-called Great, or in behalf of any of their friends, either father, mother, brother, sister, wife, or children, or any of that class, and suffered and sacrificed what I have in this interference, it would have been all right. Every man in this Court would have deemed it an act worthy a reward, rather than a punishment.

This Court acknowledges too, as I suppose, the validity of the Law of God. I saw a book kissed, which I suppose to be the Bible, or at least the New Testament, which teaches me that, "All things whatsoever I would that men should do to me, I should do even so to them." It teaches me further, to "Remember them that are in bonds, as bound with them." I endeavored to act up to that instruction. I say I am yet too young to understand that God is any respecter of persons. I believe that to have interfered as I have done, as I have always freely admitted I have done, in behalf of his despised poor, I have done no wrong, but right.

Now, if it is deemed necessary that I should forfeit my life, for the furtherance of the ends of justice, and mingle my blood further with the blood of my children, and with the blood of millions in this slave country, whose rights are disregarded by wicked, cruel, and unjust enactments,—I say, let it be done.

Let me say one word further: I feel entirely satisfied with the treatment I have received on my trial. Considering all the circumstances, it has been more generous than I expected; but I feel no consciousness of guilt. I have stated from the first what was my intention, and what was not. I never had any design against the liberty of any person, nor any disposition to commit treason, or excite slaves to rebel, or make any general insurrection. I never encouraged any man to do so, but always discouraged any idea of that kind.

Let me say something, also, in regard to the statements made by some of those who were connected with me. I hear that it has been stated by some of them, that I have induced them to join me; but the contrary is true. I do not say this to injure them, but as regarding their weakness. Not one but joined me of his own accord, and the greater part at their own expense. A number of them I never saw and never had a word of conversation with, till the day they came to me, and that was for the purpose I have stated. Now I have done.

South Carolina Ordinance and Declaration of Causes of Secession

December 20–24, 1860

Abraham Lincoln's election as the Republican presidential candidate in 1860 was beyond the tolerance of radical southerners. South Carolina, ever the champion of states' rights, was the first to secede from the Union. As soon as Lincoln's election had been confirmed in the electoral college, a state convention was convened, unanimously adopting an ordinance of secession on December 20, 1860. A few days later, the convention passed a declaration of the causes justifying secession. Within weeks, six other states followed South Carolina out of the Union. In early February 1861, representatives met in Montgomery, Alabama, to form the Confederate States of America.

South Carolina Ordinance of Secession

December 20, 1860

AN Ordinance to Dissolve the Union between the State of South Carolina and other States united with her under the compact entitled the Constitution of the United States of America:

We, the people of the State of South Carolina, in Convention assembled, do declare and ordain, and it is hereby declared and ordained, that the ordinance adopted by us in Convention, on the 23d day of May, in the year of our Lord 1788, whereby the Constitution of the United States of America was ratified, and also all Acts and parts of Acts of the General Assembly of this State ratifying the amendments of the said Constitution, are hereby repealed, and that the union now subsisting between South Carolina and other States under the name of the United States of America is hereby dissolved.

South Carolina Declaration of Causes of Secession

December 24, 1860

The people of the State of South Carolina in Convention assembled, on the 2d day of April, A.D. 1852, declared that the frequent violations of the Constitution of the United States by the Federal Government, and its encroachments upon the reserved rights of the States, fully justified this State in their withdrawal from the Federal Union; but in deference to the opinions and wishes of the other Slaveholding States, she forbore at that time to exercise this right. Since that time these encroachments have continued to increase, and further forbearance ceases to be a virtue.

And now the State of South Carolina having resumed her separate and equal place among nations, deems it due to herself, to the remaining United States of America, and to the nations of the world, that she should declare the immediate causes which have led to this act.

In 1787, Deputies were appointed by the States to revise the articles of Confederation; and on 17th September, 1787, these Deputies recommended, for the adoption of the States, the Articles of Union, known as the Constitution of the United States.

... Thus was established by compact between the States, a Government with defined objects and powers, limited to the express words of the grant. . . . We hold that the Government thus established is subject to the two great principles asserted in the Declaration of Independence; and we hold further, that the mode of its formation subjects it to a third fundamental principle, namely, the law of compact. We maintain that in every compact between two or more parties, the obligation is mutual; that the failure of one of the contracting parties to perform a material part of the agreement, entirely releases the obligation of the other; and that, where no arbiter is provided, each party is remitted to his own judgment to determine the fact of failure, with all its consequences.

In the present case, that fact is established with certainty. We assert that fourteen of the States have deliberately refused for years past to fulfill their constitutional obligations, and we refer to their own statutes for the proof.

The Constitution of the United States, in its fourth Article, provides as follows:

"No person held to service or labor in one State under the laws thereof, escaping into another, shall, in consequence of any law or regulation therein, be discharged from such service or labor, but shall be delivered up, on claim of the party to whom such service or labor may be due."

This stipulation was so material to the compact that without it that compact would not have been made. The greater number of the contracting parties held slaves, and they had previously evinced their estimate of the value of such a stipulation by making it a condition in the Ordinance for the government of the territory ceded by Virginia, which obligations, and the laws of the General Government, have ceased to effect the objects of the Constitution. The States of Maine, New Hampshire, Vermont, Massachusetts, Connecticut, Rhode Island, New York, Pennsylvania, Illinois, Indiana, Michigan, Wisconsin and Iowa, have enacted laws which either nullify the acts of Congress, or render useless any attempt to execute them. In many of these States the fugitive is discharged from the service of labor claimed, and in none of them has the State Government complied with the stipulation made in the Constitution. The State of New Jersey, at an early day, passed a law in conformity with her constitutional obligation; but the current of Anti-Slavery feeling has led her more recently to enact laws which render inoperative the remedies provided by her own laws and by the laws of Congress. In the State of New York even the right of transit for a slave has been denied by her tribunals; and the States of Ohio and Iowa have refused to surrender to justice fugitives charged with murder, and with inciting servile insurrection in the State of Virginia. Thus the constitutional compact has been deliberately broken and disregarded by the non-slaveholding States; and the consequence follows that South Carolina is released from her obligation. . . .

We affirm that these ends for which this Government was instituted have been defeated, and the Government itself has been destructive of them by the action of the non-slaveholding States. Those States have assumed the right of deciding upon the propriety of our domestic institutions; and have denied the rights of property established in fifteen of the States and recognized by the Constitution; they have denounced as sinful the institution of Slavery; they have permitted the open establishment among them of societies, whose avowed object is to disturb the peace of and eloin the property of the citizens of other States. They have encouraged and assisted thousands of our slaves to leave their homes; and those who remain, have been incited by emissaries, books, and pictures, to servile insurrection.

For twenty-five years this agitation has been steadily increasing, until it has now secured to its aid the power of the common Government. Observing the forms of the Constitution, a sectional party has found within that article establishing the Executive Department, the means of subverting the Constitution itself. A geographical line has been drawn across the Union, and all the States north of that line have united in the election of a man to the high office of President of the United States whose opinions and purposes are hostile to Slavery. He is to be intrusted with the administration of the common Government, because he has declared that "Government cannot endure permanently half slave, half free," and that the public mind must rest in the belief that Slavery is in the course of ultimate extinction.

This sectional combination for the subversion of the Constitution has been aided, in some of the States, by elevating to citizenship persons who, by the supreme law of the land, are incapable of becoming citizens; and their votes have been used to inaugurate a new policy, hostile to the South, and destructive of its peace and safety.

On the 4th of March next this party will take possession of the Government. It has announced that the South shall be excluded from the common territory, that the Judicial tribunal shall be made sectional, and that a war must be waged against Slavery until it shall cease throughout the United States.

The guarantees of the Constitution will then no longer exist; the equal rights of the States will be lost. The Slaveholding States will no longer have the power of self-government, or self-protection, and the Federal Government will have become their enemy.

Sectional interest and animosity will deepen the irritation; and all hope of remedy is rendered vain, by the fact that the public opinion at the North has invested a great political error with the sanctions of a more erroneous religious belief.

We, therefore, the people of South Carolina, by our delegates in Convention assembled, appealing to the Supreme Judge of the world for the rectitude of our intentions, have solemnly declared that the Union heretofore existing between this State and the other States of North America is dissolved, and that the State of South Carolina has resumed her position among the nations of the world, as a separate and independent state, with full power to levy war, conclude peace, contract alliances, establish commerce, and to do all other acts and things which independent States may of right do.

FIRST INAUGURAL ADDRESS

Abraham Lincoln   *March 4, 1861*

Dedicated to maintaining the Union, Abraham Lincoln was also determined to avoid open conflict if possible. After his election he tried to reassure southerners that he would not interfere with existing laws or institutions, and that change could occur only through due process with their participation and consent. He hoped conciliation would coax dissenters back into the Union.

On the other hand, he clearly believed that the Union could not be dissolved. The Springfield lawyer was prepared to present several arguments against the legality or viability of secession. Beyond this, Lincoln could not accept separation as the solution to the crisis: the majority and minority could only resolve their differences by working together; otherwise, the majority would be forced to impose its will.

FELLOW Citizens of the United States:

—In compliance with a custom as old as the Government itself, I appear before you to address you briefly, and to take in your presence the oath prescribed by the Constitution of the United States to be taken by the President "before he enters on the execution of his office." . . .

Apprehension seems to exist among the people of the Southern States that by the accession of a Republican administration their property and their peace and personal security are to be endangered. There has never been any reasonable cause for such apprehension. Indeed, the most ample evidence to the contrary has all the while existed and been open to their inspection. It is found in nearly all the published speeches of him who now addresses you. I do but quote from one of those speeches when I declare that "I have no purpose, directly or indirectly, to interfere with the institution of slavery in the States where it exists. I believe I have no lawful right to do so, and I have no inclination to do so." . . .

I now reiterate these sentiments; and, in doing so, I only press upon the public attention the most conclusive evidence of which the case is susceptible, that the property, peace and security of no section are to be in any wise endangered by the now incoming administration. I add, too, that all the protection which, consistently with the Constitution and the laws, can be given, will be cheerfully given to all the States when lawfully demanded, for whatever cause—as cheerfully to one section as to another. . . .

I take the official oath to-day with no mental reservations, and with no purpose to construe the Constitution or laws by any hypercritical rules. And, while I do not choose now to specify particular acts of Congress as proper to be enforced, I do suggest that it will be much safer for all, both in official and private stations, to conform to and abide by all those acts which stand unrepealed, than to violate any of them, trusting to find impunity in having them held to be unconstitutional. . . .

A disruption of the Federal Union, heretofore only menaced, is now formidably attempted.

I hold that, in contemplation of universal law and of the Constitution, the Union of these States is perpetual. Perpetuity is implied, if not expressed, in the fundamental law of all national governments. It is safe to assert that no government proper ever had a provision in its organic law for its own termination. Continue to execute all the express provisions of our national Constitution, and the Union will endure forever—it being impossible to destroy it except by some action not provided for in the instrument itself.

Again, if the United States be not a government proper, but an association of States in the nature of contract merely, can it as a contract be peaceably unmade by less than all the parties who made it? One party to a contract may violate it—break it, so to speak; but does it not require all to lawfully rescind it?

Descending from these general principles, we find the proposition that in legal contemplation the Union is perpetual confirmed by the history of the Union itself. The Union is much older than the Constitution. It was formed, in fact, by the Articles of Association in 1774. It was matured and continued by the Declaration of Independence in 1776. It was further matured, and the faith of all the then thirteen States expressly plighted and engaged that it should be perpetual, by the Articles of Confederation in 1778. And, finally, in 1787 one of the declared objects for ordaining and establishing the Constitution was "to form a more perfect Union."

But if the destruction of the Union by one or by a part only of the States be lawfully possible, the Union is less perfect than before the Constitution, having lost the vital element of perpetuity.

It follows from these views that no State upon its own mere motion can lawfully get out of the Union; that resolves and ordinances to that effect are legally void; and that acts of violence, within any State or States, against the authority of the United States, are insurrectionary or revolutionary, according to circumstances.

I therefore consider that, in view of the Constitution and the laws, the Union is unbroken; and to the extent of my ability I shall take care, as the Constitution itself expressly enjoins upon me, that the laws of the Union be faithfully executed in all the States. Doing this I deem to be only a simple duty on my part; and I shall perform it so far as practicable, unless my rightful masters, the American people, shall withhold the requisite means, or in some authoritative manner direct the contrary. I trust this will not be regarded as a menace, but only as the declared purpose of the Union that it will constitutionally defend and maintain itself.

In doing this there needs to be no bloodshed or violence; and there shall be none, unless it be forced upon the national authority. The power confided to me will be used to hold, occupy, and possess the property and places belonging to the Government, and to collect the duties and imposts; but beyond what may be necessary for these objects, there will be no invasion, no using of force against or among the people anywhere. Where hostility to the United States, in any interior locality, shall be so great and universal as to prevent competent resident citizens from holding the Federal offices, there will be no attempt to force obnoxious strangers among the people for that object. While the strict legal right may exist in the government to enforce the exercise of these offices, the attempt to do so would be so irritating, and so nearly impracticable withal, that I deem it better to forego for the time the uses of such offices.

The mails, unless repelled, will continue to be furnished in all parts of the Union. So far as possible, the people everywhere shall have that sense of perfect security which is most favorable to calm thought and reflection. The course here indicated will be followed unless current events and experience shall show a modification or change to be proper, and in every case and exigency my best discretion will be exercised according to circumstances actually existing, and with a view and a hope of a peaceful solution of the national troubles and the restoration of fraternal sympathies and affections.

That there are persons in one section or another who seek to destroy the

Union at all events, and are glad of any pretext to do it, I will neither affirm nor deny; but if there be such, I need address no word to them. To those, however, who really love the Union may I not speak?

Before entering upon so grave a matter as the destruction of our national fabric, with all its benefits, its memories, and its hopes, would it not be wise to ascertain precisely why we do it? Will you hazard so desperate a step while there is any possibility that any portion of the ills you fly from have no real existence? Will you, while the certain ills you fly to are greater than all the real ones you fly from—will you risk the commission of so fearful a mistake?

All profess to be content in the Union if all constitutional rights can be maintained. Is it true, then, that any right, plainly written in the Constitution, has been denied? I think not. Happily the human mind is so constituted that no party can reach to the audacity of doing this. Think, if you can, of a single instance in which a plainly written provision of the Constitution has ever been denied. If by the mere force of numbers a majority should deprive a minority of any clearly written constitutional right, it might, in a moral point of view, justify revolution—certainly would if such a right were a vital one. But such is not our case. All the vital rights of minorities and of individuals are so plainly assured to them by affirmations and negations, guaranties and prohibitions, in the Constitution, that controversies never arise concerning them. But no organic law can ever be framed with a provision specifically applicable to every question which may occur in practical administration. No foresight can anticipate, nor any document of reasonable length contain, express provisions for all possible questions. Shall fugitives from labor be surrendered by national or by State authority? The Constitution does not expressly say. May Congress prohibit slavery in the Territories? The Constitution does not expressly say. Must Congress protect slavery in the Territories? The Constitution does not expressly say.

From questions of this class spring all our constitutional controversies, and we divide upon them into majorities and minorities. If the minority will not acquiesce, the majority must, or the Government must cease. There is no other alternative; for continuing the Government is acquiescence on one side or the other.

If a minority in such a case will secede rather than acquiesce, they make a precedent which in turn will divide and ruin them; for a minority of their own will secede from them whenever a majority refuses to be controlled by such minority. For instance, why may not any portion of a new confederacy a year or two hence arbitrarily secede again, precisely as portions of the present Union now claim to secede from it? All who cherish disunion sentiments are now being educated to the exact temper of doing this.

Is there such perfect identity of interests among the States to compose a new Union as to produce harmony only, and prevent renewed secession?

Plainly, the central idea of secession is the essence of anarchy. A majority held in restraint by constitutional checks and limitations, and always changing easily with deliberate changes of popular opinions and sentiments, is the only true sovereign of a free people. Whoever rejects it does, of necessity, fly to anarchy or to despotism. Unanimity is impossible; the rule of a minority, as a permanent arrangement, is wholly inadmissible; so that, rejecting the majority principle, anarchy or despotism in some form is all that is left.

I do not forget the position assumed by some, that constitutional questions are to be decided by the Supreme Court; nor do I deny that such decisions must be binding, in any case, upon the parties to a suit, as to the object of that suit, while they are also entitled to a very high respect and consideration in all parallel cases by all other departments of the government. And, while it is obviously possible that such decision may be erroneous in any given case, still the evil effect following it, being limited to that particular case, with the chance that it may be overruled and never become a precedent for other cases, can better be borne than could the evils of a different practice. At the same time, the candid citizen must confess that if the policy of the government, upon vital questions affecting the whole people, is to be irrevocably fixed by decisions of the Supreme Court, the instant they are made, in ordinary litigation between parties in personal actions, the people will have ceased to be their own rulers, having to that extent practically resigned the government into the hands of that eminent tribunal. Nor is there in this view any assault upon the court or the judges. It is a duty from which they may not shrink to decide cases properly brought before them, and it is no fault of theirs if others seek to turn their decisions to political purposes.

One section of our country believes slavery is right, and ought to be extended, while the other believes it is wrong, and ought not to be extended. This is the only substantial dispute. The fugitive slave clause of the Constitution and the law for the suppression of the foreign slave trade are each as well enforced, perhaps, as any law can ever be in a community where the moral sense of the people imperfectly supports the law itself. The great body of the people abide by the dry legal obligation in both cases, and a few break over in each. This, I think, cannot be perfectly cured; and it would be worse in both cases after the separation of the sections than before. The foreign slave trade, now imperfectly suppressed, would be ultimately revived, without restriction, in one section, while fugitive slaves, now only partially surrendered, would not be surrendered at all by the other.

Physically speaking, we cannot separate. We cannot remove our respective sections from each other, nor build an impassable wall between them.

A husband and wife may be divorced and go out of the presence and beyond the reach of each other; but the different parts of our country cannot do this. They cannot but remain face to face, and intercourse, either amicable or hostile, must continue between them. Is it possible, then, to make that intercourse more advantageous or more satisfactory after separation than before? Can aliens make treaties easier than friends can make laws? Can treaties be more faithfully enforced between aliens than laws can among friends? Suppose you go to war, you cannot fight always; and when, after much loss on both sides, and no gain on either, you cease fighting, the identical old questions as to terms of intercourse are again upon you.

This country, with its institutions, belongs to the people who inhabit it. Whenever they shall grow weary of the existing government, they can exercise their constitutional right of amending it, or their revolutionary right to dismember or overthrow it. I cannot be ignorant of the fact that many worthy and patriotic citizens are desirous of having the national Constitution amended. While I make no recommendation of amendments, I fully recognize the rightful authority of the people over the whole subject, to be exercised in either of the modes prescribed in the instrument itself, and I should, under existing circumstances, favor rather than oppose a fair opportunity being afforded the people to act upon it. I will venture to add that to me the convention mode seems preferable, in that it allows amendments to originate with the people themselves, instead of only permitting them to take or reject propositions originated by others not especially chosen for the purpose, and which might not be precisely such as they would wish to either accept or refuse. I understand a proposed amendment to the Constitution—which amendment, however, I have not seen—has passed Congress, to the effect that the Federal Government shall never interfere with the domestic institutions of the States, including that of persons held to service. To avoid misconstruction of what I have said, I depart from my purpose not to speak of particular amendments so far as to say that, holding such a provision to now be implied constitutional law, I have no objection to its being made express and irrevocable. . . .

Why should there not be a patient confidence in the ultimate justice of the people? Is there any better or equal hope in the world? In our present differences is either party without faith of being in the right? If the Almighty Ruler of nations, with his eternal truth and justice, be on your side of the North, or on yours of the South, that truth and that justice will surely prevail by the judgment of this great tribunal of the American people.

By the frame of the government under which we live, this same people have wisely given their public servants but little power for mischief; and have, with equal wisdom, provided for the return of that little to their own hands at very short intervals. While the people retain their virtue and vigilance, no administration, by any extreme of wickedness or folly, can very seriously injure the government in the short space of four years.

My countrymen, one and all, think calmly and well upon this whole subject. Nothing valuable can be lost by taking time. If there be an object to hurry any of you in hot haste to a step which you would never take deliberately, that object will be frustrated by taking time; but no good object can be frustrated by it. Such of you as are now dissatisfied still have the old Constitution unimpaired, and, on the sensitive point, the laws of your own framing under it; while the new administration will have no immediate power, if it would, to change either. If it were admitted that you who are dissatisfied hold the right side in the dispute, there still is no single good reason for precipitate action. Intelligence, patriotism, Christianity, and a firm reliance on Him who has never yet forsaken this favored land, are still competent to adjust in the best way all our present difficulty.

In your hands, my dissatisfied fellow countrymen, and not in mine, is the momentous issue of civil war. The government will not assail you. You can have no conflict without being yourselves the aggressors. You have no oath registered in heaven to destroy the government, while I shall have the most solemn one to "preserve, protect, and defend" it.

I am loath to close. We are not enemies, but friends. We must not be enemies. Though passion may have strained, it must not break, our bonds of affection. The mystic chords of memory, stretching from every battle-field and patriot grave to every living heart and hearthstone all over this broad land, will yet swell the chorus of the Union when again touched, as surely they will be, by the better angels of our nature.

THE BATTLE HYMN OF THE REPUBLIC

Julia Ward Howe   *December 1861*

――――――――――

John Brown's execution for treason in 1859 galvanized abolitionist determination. After the outbreak of war, one of the most popular marching songs of the Union army commemorated his martyrdom:

     John Brown's body lies a-mouldering in the grave,
       His soul is marching on.
Many variations of this song, sung to the tune of an old

southern camp meeting hymn, appeared in the course of the war. Certainly the most famous was Julia Ward Howe's "Battle Hymn of the Republic," inspired when Howe witnessed a battle in December 1861. The poem was published in the Atlantic Monthly *in February 1862.*

———————————

Mine eyes have seen the glory of the coming of the Lord:
He is trampling out the vintage where the grapes of wrath are stored;
He hath loosed the fateful lightning of his terrible swift sword:
     His truth is marching on.

I have seen Him in the watch fires of a hundred circling camps;
They have builded Him an altar in the evening dews and damps;
I can read His righteous sentence by the dim and flaring lamps.
     His day is marching on.

I have read a fiery gospel writ in burnished rows of steel:
"As ye deal with my contemners, so with you my grace shall deal;
Let the Hero, born of woman, crush the serpent with his heel,
     Since God is marching on."

He has sounded forth the trumpet that shall never call retreat;
He is sifting out the hearts of men before his judgment seat:
Oh! be swift, my soul, to answer Him! be jubilant, my feet!
     Our God is marching on.

In the beauty of the lilies Christ was born across the sea,
With a glory in His bosom that transfigures you and me:
As He died to make men holy, let us die to make men free,
     While God is marching on.

THE HOMESTEAD ACT

May 20, 1862

Sales of public lands in the early years of the republic were intended primarily to help reduce the national debt, resulting in most lands being sold in large blocks to speculators. By 1835, though, the debt had been retired and pressure grew to provide lands freely from the public domain to hard-pressed tenant farmers and urban laborers. The Republican Party adopted the "homestead" proposal in 1856, tying it to a prohibition on slavery in the territories ("Free Men, Free Soil"). The Republican victory in 1860, and the consequent secession of the southern states, guaranteed a strong congressional majority favoring free farms. The Homestead Act was passed by the thirty-seventh Congress on May 20, 1862.

The act achieved only limited results, since little easily cultivated land remained available, and many farmers still had difficulty raising capital. By 1890, only a third of the homesteaders had actually obtained deeds. Nonetheless, the act did contribute to the development of the last agricultural frontiers in the Dakotas, Oklahoma and other western regions.

AN act to secure homesteads to actual settlers on the public domain.

Be it enacted, That any person who is the head of a family, or who has arrived at the age of twenty-one years, and is a citizen of the United States, or who shall have filed his declaration of intention to become such, as required by the naturalization laws of the United States, and who has never borne arms against the United States Government or given aid and comfort to its enemies, shall, from and after the first of January, eighteen hundred and sixty-three, be entitled to enter one quarter-section or a less quantity of unappropriated public lands, upon which said person may have filed a pre-emption claim, or which may, at the time the application is made, be subject to pre-emption at one dollar and twenty-five cents, or less, per acre; or eighty acres or less of such unappropriated lands, at two dollars and fifty cents per acre, to be located in a body, in conformity to the legal subdivisions of the public lands, and after the same shall have been surveyed: Provided, That any person owning or residing on land may, under the provisions of this act, enter other land lying contiguous to his or her said land, which shall not, with the land so already owned and occupied, exceed in the aggregate one hundred and sixty acres.

SEC. 2. That the person applying for the benefit of this act shall, upon application to the register of the land office in which he or she is about to make such entry, make affidavit before the said register or receiver that he or she is the head of a family, or is twenty-one or more years of age, or shall have performed service in the Army or Navy of the United States, and that he has never borne arms against the Government of the United States or given aid and comfort to its enemies, and that such application is made for his or her exclusive use and benefit, and that said entry is made for the purpose of actual settlement and cultivation, and not, either directly or indirectly, for the use or benefit of any other person or persons whomsoever; and upon filing the said affidavit with the register or receiver, and on payment of ten dollars, he or she shall thereupon be permitted to enter the quantity of land specified: Provided, however, That no certificate shall be given or patent issued therefor until the expiration of five years from the date of such entry; and if, at the expiration of such time, or at any time within two years thereafter, the person making such entry—or if he be dead, his widow; or in case of her death, his heirs or devisee; or in case of a widow making such entry, her heirs or devisee, in case of her death—shall prove by two credible witnesses that he, she, or they have resided upon or cultivated the same for the term of five years immediately succeeding the time of filing the affidavit aforesaid, and shall make affidavit that no part of said land has been alienated, and that he has borne true allegiance to the Government of the United States; then, in such case, he, she, or they, if at that time a citizen of the United States, shall be entitled to a patent, as in other cases provided for by law: And provided, further, That in case of the death of both father and mother, leaving an infant child or children under twenty-one years of age, the right and fee shall insure to the benefit of said infant child or children; and the executor, administrator, or guardian may, at any time within two years after the death of the surviving parent, and in accordance with the laws of the State in which such children for the time being have their domicile, sell said land for the benefit of said infants, but for no other purpose; and the purchaser shall acquire the absolute title by the purchase, and be entitled to a patent from the United States, on payment of the office fees and sum of money herein specified. . . .

THE MORRILL ACT

July 2, 1862

The mechanic arts movement began with the founding of the Franklin Institute in Philadelphia in 1824. The object of creating a skilled labor class educated in the arts and sciences remained only partially achievable through privately funded institutions, however. The great leap forward in mechanical and agricultural education came only with passage of the Morrill Act.

Justin Morrill of Vermont, author of the act, served forty-three years in the House of Representatives and Senate. He was a fiscal conservative, and was well known for his Tariff of 1861. But his most important legislative legacy was the Morrill Act of 1862, providing grants of federal land to state colleges. Today the "land grant" universities comprise some thirteen million acres, and include some of the leading educational institutions in the nation.

AN Act donating Public Lands to the several States and Territories which may provide Colleges for the Benefit of Agriculture and the Mechanic Arts.

Be it enacted by the Senate and House of Representatives of the United States of America in Congress assembled, That there be granted to the several States, for the purpose hereinafter mentioned, an amount of public land, to be apportioned to each State a quantity equal to thirty thousand acres for each senator and representative in Congress to which the States are respectively entitled by the apportionment under the census of eighteen hundred and sixty: Provided, That no mineral lands shall be selected or purchased under the provisions of this act.

SEC. 2. And be it further enacted, That the land aforesaid, after being surveyed, shall be apportioned to the several States in sections or subdivisions of sections, not less than one quarter of a section; and whenever there are public lands in a State subject to sale at private entry at one dollar and twenty-five cents per acre, the quantity to which said State shall be entitled shall be selected from such lands within the limits of such State, and the Secretary of the Interior is hereby directed to issue to each of the States in which there is not the quantity of public lands subject to sale at private entry at one dollar and twenty-five cents per acre, to which said State may be entitled under the provisions of this act, land scrip to the amount in acres for the deficiency of its distributive share: said scrip to be sold by said States and the proceeds thereof applied to the uses and purposes prescribed in this act, and for no other use or purpose whatsoever. . . .

SEC. 4. And be it further enacted, That all moneys derived from the sale of the lands aforesaid by the States to which the lands are apportioned, and from the sale of land scrip hereinbefore provided for, shall be invested in stocks of the United States, or of the States, or some other safe stocks, yielding not less than five per centum upon the par value of said stocks; and that the moneys so invested shall constitute a perpetual fund, the capital of which shall remain forever undiminished, (except so far as may be provided in section fifth of this act,) and the interest of which shall be inviolably appropriated, by each State which may take and claim the benefit of this act, to the endowment, support, and maintenance of at least one college where the leading object shall be, without excluding other scientific and classical studies, and including military tactics, to teach such branches of learning as are related to agriculture and mechanic arts, in such manner as the legislatures of the State may respectively prescribe, in order to promote the liberal and practical education of the industrial classes in the several pursuits and professions in life. . . .

SEC. 6. No State while in a condition of rebellion or insurrection against the government of the United States shall be entitled to the benefit of this Act. . . .

The Emancipation Proclamation

Abraham Lincoln   *January 1, 1863*

---

*Having been elected on a platform pledging nonin-
terference with slavery, Abraham Lincoln was reluctant at first
to adopt national abolitionist policies. Above all, his primary
concern at the beginning of the war was to keep the border
states in the Union.*

*But two summers of lackluster campaigning by the Army
of the Potomac, producing only a series of humiliating defeats
or standoffs, had instilled a grim determination to see the war*

through to its conclusion. As it became apparent that no easy outcome was in sight, Lincoln could no longer avoid final settlement of the slavery issue. In September 1862, the Union army finally delivered a victory at Antietam. Lincoln took the opportunity to announce that, as of January 1, 1863, all slaves in the seceding states would be emancipated. Since the Emancipation Proclamation applied only to territories outside Union control, few slaves were directly affected. Its importance was largely symbolic and did help to gain support abroad for the Union cause.

WHEREAS on the 22d day of September, A.D. 1862, a proclamation was issued by the President of the United States, containing, among other things, the following, to wit:

"That on the 1st day of January, A.D. 1863, all persons held as slaves within any State or designated part of a State the people whereof shall then be in rebellion against the United States shall be then, thenceforward, and forever free; and the executive government of the United States, including the military and naval authority thereof, will recognize and maintain the freedom of such persons and will do no act or acts to repress such persons, or any of them, in any efforts they may make for their actual freedom.

"That the executive will on the 1st day of January aforesaid, by proclamation, designate the States and parts of States, if any, in which the people thereof, respectively, shall then be in rebellion against the United States; and the fact that any State or the people thereof shall on that day be in good faith represented in the Congress of the United States by members chosen thereto at elections wherein a majority of the qualified voters of such States shall have participated shall, in the absence of strong countervailing testimony, be deemed conclusive evidence that such State and the people thereof are not then in rebellion against the United States."

Now, therefore, I, Abraham Lincoln, President of the United States, by virtue of the power in me vested as Commander-in-Chief of the Army and Navy of the United States in time of actual armed rebellion against the authority and government of the United States, and as a fit and necessary war measure for suppressing said rebellion, do, on this 1st day of January, A.D. 1863, and in accordance with my purpose so to do, publicly proclaimed for the full period of one hundred days from the first day above mentioned, order and designate as the States and parts of States wherein the people thereof, respectively, are this day in rebellion against the United States the following, to wit:

Arkansas, Texas, Louisiana (except the parishes of St. Bernard, Plaquemines, Jefferson, St. John, St. Charles, St. James, Ascension, Assumption, Terrebonne, Lafourche, St. Mary, St. Martin, and Orleans, including the city of New Orleans), Mississippi, Alabama, Florida, Georgia, South Carolina, North Carolina, and Virginia (except the forty-eight counties designated as West Virginia, and also the counties of Berkeley, Accomac, Northampton, Elizabeth City, York, Princess Anne, and Norfolk, including the cities of Norfolk and Portsmouth), and which excepted parts are for the present left precisely as if this proclamation were not issued.

And by virtue of the power and for the purpose aforesaid, I do order and declare that all persons held as slaves within said designated States and parts of States are, and henceforward shall be, free; and that the Executive Government of the United States, including the military and naval authorities thereof, will recognize and maintain the freedom of said persons.

And I hereby enjoin upon the people so declared to be free to abstain from all violence, unless in necessary self-defense; and I recommend to them that, in all cases when allowed, they labor faithfully for reasonable wages.

And I further declare and make known that such persons of suitable condition will be received into the armed service of the United States to garrison forts, positions, stations, and other places, and to man vessels of all sorts in said service.

And upon this act, sincerely believed to be an act of justice, warranted by the Constitution upon military necessity, I invoke the considerate judgment of mankind and the gracious favor of Almighty God.

ADDRESS AT GETTYSBURG

Abraham Lincoln   *November 19, 1863*

On July 4, 1863, the Army of the Potomac watched as Robert E. Lee's Army of Northern Virginia retreated from the battlefield at Gettysburg, Pennsylvania. Three days of hard fighting had given the Union one of the greatest victories of the war. When, a few days later, news came of the fall of Vicksburg, Mississippi, Abraham Lincoln must have thought that finally things seemed to be going right.

A time for reflection had come. Called upon to deliver

remarks dedicating a cemetery at Gettysburg, Lincoln took the occasion to express his personal sorrow at the human costs of war and to revive faith in democracy and the Union.

———————————

FOUR score and seven years ago our fathers brought forth on this continent, a new nation, conceived in liberty, and dedicated to the proposition that all men are created equal.

Now we are engaged in a great civil war, testing whether that nation or any nation so conceived and so dedicated, can long endure. We are met on a great battle-field of that war. We have come to dedicate a portion of that field, as a final resting place for those who here gave their lives that that nation might live. It is altogether fitting and proper that we should do this.

But, in a larger sense, we can not dedicate—we can not consecrate—we can not hallow—this ground. The brave men, living and dead, who struggled here, have consecrated it, far above our poor power to add or detract. The world will little note, nor long remember what we say here, but it can never forget what they did here. It is for us the living, rather, to be dedicated here to the unfinished work which they who fought here have thus far so nobly advanced. It is rather for us to be here dedicated to the great task remaining before us—that from these honored dead we take increased devotion to that cause for which they gave the last full measure of devotion—that we here highly resolve that these dead shall not have died in vain—that this nation, under God, shall have a new birth of freedom—and that government of the people, by the people, for the people, shall not perish from the earth.

Wounded Soldier, date unknown, from the records of the Office of the Chief Signal Officer, photograph by Mathew Brady.

Second Inaugural Address

Abraham Lincoln   *March 4, 1865*

---

*With victory imminent, President Abraham Lincoln used
his second inaugural to set the tone for reconciliation and
restoration of the nation. A freethinker, Lincoln never joined a
church, yet his faith is evident in his message. There is also some
sense of Lincoln's conviction that he was an instrument of
Providence. Above all, his belief in the need for leniency was
never better expressed than in the final paragraph of this speech.*

FELLOW-Countrymen:—At this second appearing to take the oath of the
presidential office there is less occasion for an extended address than there was
at the first. Then a statement somewhat in detail of a course to be pursued seemed
fitting and proper. Now, at the expiration of four years, during which public
declarations have been constantly called forth on every point and phase of the
great contest which still absorbs the attention and engrosses the energies of the
nation, little that is new could be presented. The progress of our arms, upon
which all else chiefly depends, is as well known to the public as to myself, and
it is, I trust, reasonably satisfactory and encouraging to all. With high hope for
the future, no prediction in regard to it is ventured.

On the occasion corresponding to this four years ago all thoughts were
anxiously directed to an impending civil war. All dreaded it, all sought to avert
it. While the inaugural address was being delivered from this place, devoted
altogether to saving the Union without war, insurgent agents were in the city
seeking to destroy it without war—seeking to dissolve the Union and divide
effects by negotiation. Both parties deprecated war, but one of them would make
war rather than let the nation survive, and the other would accept war rather than
let it perish, and the war came.

One eighth of the whole population was colored slaves, not distributed
generally over the Union, but localized in the southern part of it. These slaves
constituted a peculiar and powerful interest. All knew that this interest was
somehow the cause of the war. To strengthen, perpetuate, and extend this
interest was the object for which the insurgents would rend the Union even by
war, while the Government claimed no right to do more than to restrict the
territorial enlargement of it. Neither party expected for the war the magnitude

or the duration which it has already attained. Neither anticipated that the cause of the conflict might cease with or even before the conflict itself should cease. Each looked for an easier triumph, and a result less fundamental and astounding. Both read the same Bible and pray to the same God, and each invokes His aid against the other. It may seem strange that any men should dare to ask a just God's assistance in wringing their bread from the sweat of other men's faces, but let us judge not that we be not judged. The prayers of both could not be answered. That of neither has been answered fully. The Almighty has His own purposes. "Woe unto the world because of offenses; for it must needs be that offenses come, but woe to that man by whom the offense cometh." If we shall suppose that American slavery is one of those offenses which, in the providence of God, must needs come, but which, having continued through His appointed time, He now wills to remove, and that He gives to both North and South this terrible war as the woe due to those by whom the offense came, shall we discern therein any departure from those divine attributes which the believers in a living God always ascribe to Him? Fondly do we hope, fervently do we pray, that this mighty scourge of war may speedily pass away. Yet, if God wills that it continue until all the wealth piled by the bondsman's two hundred and fifty years of unrequited toil shall be sunk, and until every drop of blood drawn with the lash shall be paid by another drawn with the sword, as was said three thousand years ago, so still it must be said, "The judgments of the Lord are true and righteous altogether."

With malice towards none, with charity for all, with firmness in the right as God gives us to see the right, let us strive on to finish the work we are in, to bind up the nation's wounds, to care for him who shall have borne the battle and for his widow and his orphan, to do all which may achieve and cherish a just and lasting peace among ourselves and with all nations.

FAREWELL TO HIS ARMY

Robert E. Lee   *April 10, 1865*

> *Following the fall of the Confederate capital at Richmond, Virginia, April 2, 1865, Robert E. Lee led his army west, hoping to link up with General Joseph E. Johnston and establish a new base. After only a few days, he found himself boxed in and cut off from any supplies. He wrote General Ulysses Grant, asking for terms of surrender, and the two met at Appomattox*

Courthouse, Virginia, on April 9, 1865. The following day he said goodbye to his troops, expressing his gratitude and high regard for their valor.

———————

HEADQUARTERS, Army of Northern Virginia,
After four years of arduous service, marked by unsurpassed courage and fortitude, the Army of Northern Virginia has been compelled to yield to overwhelming numbers and resources. I need not tell the survivors of so many hard-fought battles, who have remained steadfast to the last, that I have consented to this result from no distrust of them; but, feeling that valour and devotion could accomplish nothing that could compensate for the loss that would have attended the continuation of the contest, I have determined to avoid the useless sacrifice of those whose past services have endeared them to their countrymen. By the terms of the agreement, officers and men can return to their homes and remain there until exchanged. You will take with you the satisfaction that proceeds from the consciousness of duty faithfully performed; and I earnestly pray that a merciful God will extend to you His blessing and protection. With an increasing admiration of your constancy and devotion to your country, and a grateful remembrance of your kind and generous consideration of myself, I bid you an affectionate farewell.

AMENDMENT XIII: SLAVERY ABOLISHED

December 18, 1865

———————

Proposed by Congress January 31, 1865, this amendment's ratification was completed December 18, 1865. The Emancipation Proclamation had been intended primarily as a temporary exercise of presidential war powers. Abraham Lincoln himself doubted its constitutionality and recognized the need for a more permanent measure. At the 1864 Republican convention, he urged the inclusion of a plank supporting a constitutional amendment abolishing slavery. The sweeping Republican victory that fall provided a mandate for the amendment, which Lincoln pushed through the lame duck Congress by the end of the year. Though he did not live to see its final ratification, Lincoln's sponsorship of the Thirteenth Amendment cemented his reputation as the "Great Emancipator."

SEC. 1. Neither slavery nor involuntary servitude, except as a punishment for crime whereof the party shall have been duly convicted, shall exist within the United States, or any place subject to their jurisdiction.

SEC. 2. Congress shall have power to enforce this article by appropriate legislation.

THE IMPEACHMENT AND TRIAL OF PRESIDENT ANDREW JOHNSON

March 2–May 26, 1868

The Civil War was fought to preserve the Union and to end slavery. But radical Republicans feared that abolition alone would be insufficient, that the restructuring of southern society in order to guarantee former slaves' rights would be required to assure complete victory.

Had Abraham Lincoln survived his second term, his prestige and pragmatic approach might have been sufficient to moderate radical reconstruction. After Lincoln's assassination, Vice President Andrew Johnson attempted to continue his program. Where a northern Republican might have succeeded, though, a southern Democrat was bound to fail since radicals suspected Johnson's loyalties and motives.

Johnson repeatedly vetoed radical civil rights bills and reconstruction programs, and campaigned vigorously in the 1866 elections, denouncing Republican congressional leadership. In 1867, Congress acted to limit presidential power through the Tenure of Office Act. When Johnson continued to block enforcement of reconstruction legislation, the radicals finally decided to remove him from office, but failed by a single vote.

ARTICLES exhibited by the House of Representatives of the United States, in the name of themselves and all the people of the United States, against Andrew Johnson, President of the United States, in maintenance and support of their impeachment against him for high crimes and misdemeanors in office.

ARTICLE I. That said Andrew Johnson, President of the United States, on the 21st day of February, A.D. 1868, at Washington, in the district of Columbia, unmindful of the high duties of his office, of his oath of office, and of the requirement of the Constitution that he should take care that the laws be faithfully executed, did unlawfully and in violation of the Constitution and laws of the United States issue an order in writing for the removal of Edwin M. Stanton from the office of Secretary for the Department of War, said Edwin M. Stanton having been theretofore duly appointed and commissioned, by and with the advice and consent of the Senate of the United States, as such Secretary; and said Andrew Johnson, President of the United States, on the 12th day of August, A.D. 1867, and during the recess of said Senate, having suspended by his order Edwin M. Stanton from said office, and within twenty days after the first day of the next meeting of said Senate—that is to say, on the 12th day of December, in the year last aforesaid—having reported to said Senate such suspension, with the evidence and reasons for his action in the case and the name of the person designated to perform the duties of such office temporarily until the next meeting of the Senate; and said Senate thereafterwards, on the 13th day of January, A.D. 1868, having duly considered the evidence and reasons reported by said Andrew Johnson for said suspension, and having refused to concur in said suspension, whereby and by force of the provisions of an act entitled "An Act regulating the tenure of certain civil offices," passed March 2, 1867, said Edwin M. Stanton did forthwith resume the functions of his office, whereof the said Andrew Johnson had then and there due notice; and said Edwin M. Stanton, by reason of the premises, on said 21st day of February, being lawfully entitled to hold said office of Secretary for the Department of War; which said order for the removal of said Edwin M. Stanton is in substance as follows; that is to say:

Executive Mansion,
Washington, D.C., February 21, 1868.

HON. EDWIN M. STANTON,
Washington, D.C.

SIR: By virtue of the power and authority vested in me as President by the Constitution and laws of the United States, you are hereby removed from office as Secretary for the Department of War, and your functions as such will terminate upon the receipt of this communication.

You will transfer to Brevet Major-General Lorenzo Thomas, Adjutant-General of the Army, who has this day been authorized and empowered to act as Secretary of War *ad interim*, all records, books, papers, and other public property now in your custody and charge.

Respectfully, yours,

ANDREW JOHNSON.

which order was unlawfully issued with intent then and there to violate the act entitled "An act regulating the tenure of certain civil offices," passed March 2, 1867 . . . whereby said Andrew Johnson, President of the United States, did then and there commit and was guilty of a high misdemeanor in office.

ART. II. That on said 21st day of February, A.D. 1868, at Washington, in the District of Columbia, said Andrew Johnson, President of the United States, . . . did, with intent to violate the Constitution of the United States and the act aforesaid, issue and deliver to one Lorenzo Thomas a letter of authority in substance as follows; that is to say:

Executive Mansion

Washington, D.C., February 21, 1868.

Brevet Major-General LORENZO THOMAS,

Adjutant-General United States Army,

Washington, D.C.

SIR: The Hon. Edwin M. Stanton having been this day removed from office as Secretary for the Department of War, you are hereby authorized and empowered to act as Secretary of War *ad interim*, and will immediately enter upon the discharge of the duties pertaining to that office.

Mr. Stanton has been instructed to transfer to you all the records, books, papers, and other public property now in his custody and charge.

Respectfully, yours,

ANDREW JOHNSON.

then and there being no vacancy in said office of Secretary for the Department of War; whereby said Andrew Johnson, President of the United States, did then and there commit and was guilty of a high misdemeanor in office.

ART. III. That said Andrew Johnson, President of the United States, on the 21st day of February, A.D. 1868, at Washington, in the District of Columbia, did commit and was guilty of a high misdemeanor in office in this, that without authority of law, while the Senate of the United States was then and there in session, he did appoint one Lorenzo Thomas to be Secretary for the Department of War *ad interim*, without the advice and consent of the Senate, and with intent to violate the Constitution of the United States, . . .

ART. IV. That said Andrew Johnson, President of the United States, . . . did unlawfully conspire with one Lorenzo Thomas, and with other persons to the House of Representatives unknown . . .

[Articles IV-IX specify in detail the nature of President Johnson's alleged conspiracy and crimes.]

March 3, 1868.

The following additional articles of impeachment were agreed to, *viz:*

ART. X. That said Andrew Johnson, President of the United States, unmindful of the high duties of his office and the dignity and proprieties thereof, and of the harmony and courtesies which ought to exist and be maintained between the executive and legislative branches of the Government of the United States, . . . did attempt to bring into disgrace, ridicule, hatred, contempt, and reproach the Congress of the United States and the several branches thereof, to impair and destroy the regard and respect of all the good people of the United States for the Congress and legislative power thereof (which all officers of the Government ought inviolably to preserve and maintain), and to excite the odium and resentment of all the good people of the United States against Congress and the laws by it duly and constitutionally enacted; and, in pursuance of his said design and intent, openly and publicly, and before diverse assemblages of the citizens of the United States, . . . did, on the 18th day of August, A.D. 1868, and on divers other days and times, . . . make and deliver with a loud voice certain intemperate, inflammatory, and scandalous harangues, and did therein utter loud threats and bitter menaces, as well against Congress as the laws of the United States, duly enacted thereby, amid the cries, jeers, and laughter of the multitudes then assembled and in hearing. . . [The bulk of Article X concerns specifications of occasions where President Johnson slandered Congress.]

ART. XI. That said Andrew Johnson, President of the United States, . . . did on the 18th day of August, A.D. 1866, at the city of Washington, in the District of Columbia, by public speech, declare and affirm in substance that the Thirty-ninth Congress of the United States was not a Congress of the United States authorized by the Constitution to exercise legislative power under the same, but, on the contrary, was a Congress of only part of the States; thereby denying and intending to deny that the legislation of said Congress was valid or obligatory upon him the said Andrew Johnson, except in so far as he saw fit to approve the same . . . in pursuance of said declaration the said Andrew Johnson, President of the United States, . . . on the 21st day of February, A.D. 1868, at the city of Washington, in the District of Columbia, did unlawfully, and in disregard of the requirement of the Constitution that he should take care that the laws be faithfully executed, attempt to prevent the execution of an act entitled "An act regulating the tenure of certain civil offices," passed March 2, 1867, by unlawfully devising and contriving, and attempting to devise and contrive, means by which he should prevent Edwin M. Stanton from forthwith resuming the functions of the office of Secretary for the Department of War, notwithstanding the refusal of the Senate to concur in the suspension theretofore by said Andrew Johnson of said Edwin M. Stanton from said office of Secretary for the Department of War, and also by further unlawfully devising and contriving, and attempting to devise and contrive, means then and there to prevent the execution of an act entitled "An act making appropriations for the support of the Army for the fiscal year ending June 30, 1868, and for other purposes," approved March 2, 1867, and also to prevent the execution of an act entitled "An act to provide for the more efficient government of the rebel States," passed March 2, 1867, whereby the said Andrew Johnson, President of the United States, did then, to wit, on the 21st day of February, A.D. 1868, at the city of Washington, commit and was guilty of a high misdemeanor in office.

Saturday, May 16, 1868.
The United States vs. Andrew Johnson, President.
The Chief Justice stated that, in pursuance of the order of the Senate, he would first proceed to take the judgment of the Senate on the eleventh article. The roll of the Senate was called, with the following result: . . .
The Chief Justice announced that upon this article thirty-five Senators had voted "guilty" and nineteen Senators "not guilty," and declared that two-thirds of the Senators present not having pronounced him guilty, Andrew Johnson, President of the United States, stood acquitted of the charges contained in the eleventh article of impeachment.

Tuesday, May 26, 1868.
The United States vs. Andrew Johnson, President.
The Senate ordered that the vote be taken upon the second article of impeachment. The roll of the Senate was called, with the following result: . . .
The Chief Justice announced that upon this article thirty-five Senators had voted "guilty" and nineteen Senators had voted "not guilty," and declared that two-thirds of the Senators present not having pronounced him guilty, Andrew Johnson, President of the United States, stood acquitted of the charges contained in the second article of impeachment.
The Senate ordered that the vote be taken upon the third article of impeachment. The roll of the Senate was called, with the following result : . . .
The Chief Justice announced that upon this article thirty-five Senators had

voted "guilty" and nineteen Senators had voted "not guilty," and declared that two-thirds of the Senators present not having pronounced him guilty, Andrew Johnson, President of the United States, stood acquitted of the charges contained in the third article.

No objection being made, the secretary, by direction of the Chief Justice, entered the judgment of the Senate upon the second, third, and eleventh articles, as follows:

The Senate having tried Andrew Johnson, President of the United States, upon articles of impeachment exhibited against him by the House of Representatives, and two-thirds of the Senators present not having found him guilty of the charges contained in the second, third, and eleventh articles of impeachment, it is therefore

Ordered and adjudged, That the said Andrew Johnson, President of the United States, be, and he is, acquitted of the charges in said articles made and set forth.

A motion "that the Senate sitting for the trial of the President upon articles of impeachment do now adjourn without delay" was adopted by a vote of 34 yeas to 16 nays. . . .

The Chief Justice declared the Senate sitting as a court of impeachment for the trial of Andrew Johnson, President of the United States, upon articles of impeachment exhibited against him by the House of Representatives, adjourned without delay.

AMENDMENT XIV: CITIZENSHIP RIGHTS NOT TO BE ABRIDGED

July 28, 1868

Proposed by Congress June 13, 1866, this amendment's ratification was completed July 28, 1868. The Civil Rights Act, passed over Andrew Johnson's veto on April 9, 1866, formally conferred citizenship on emancipated slaves. Extensive doubt as to the constitutionality of the act arose, though, especially considering the implications of the Dred Scott decision. In 1866, a joint committee of Congress formulated a constitutional amendment incorporating the act's provisions. At first rejected by southern legislatures, ratification of the amendment was made a precondition for readmission to the Union, thus assuring its adoption. The Fourteenth Amendment, for the first time, defined citizenship and guaranteed federal protection for citizen's rights against the powers of the states.

SEC. 1. All persons born or naturalized in the United States, and subject to the jurisdiction thereof, are citizens of the United States and of the State wherein they reside. No State shall make or enforce any law which shall abridge the privileges or immunities of citizens of the United States; nor shall any State deprive any person of life, liberty, or property, without due process of law; nor deny to any person within its jurisdiction the equal protection of the laws.

SEC. 2. Representatives shall be apportioned among the several States according to their respective numbers, counting the whole number of persons in each State, excluding Indians not taxed. But when the right to vote at any election for the choice of electors for President and Vice President of the United States, Representatives in Congress, the Executive and Judicial officers of a State, or the members of the Legislature thereof, is denied to any of the male inhabitants of such State, being twenty-one years of age, and citizens of the United States, or in any way abridged, except for participation in rebellion, or other crime, the basis of representation therein shall be reduced in the proportion which the number of such male citizens shall bear to the whole number of male citizens twenty-one years of age in such State.

SEC. 3. No person shall be a Senator or Representative in Congress, or elector of President and Vice President, or hold any office, civil or military, under the United States, or under any State, who, having previously taken an oath, as a member of Congress, or as an officer of the United States, or as a member of any State legislature, or as an executive or judicial officer of any State, to support the Constitution of the United States, shall have engaged in insurrection or rebellion against the same, or given aid or comfort to the enemies thereof. But Congress may be a vote of two-thirds of each House, remove such disability.

SEC. 4. The validity of the public debt of the United States, authorized by law, including debts incurred for payment of pensions and bounties for services in suppressing insurrection or rebellion, shall not be questioned. But neither the United States nor any State shall assume or pay any debt or obligation incurred in aid of insurrection or rebellion against the United States, or any claim for the loss or emancipation of any slave; but all such debts, obligations and claims, shall be held illegal and void.

SEC. 5. The Congress shall have power to enforce, by appropriate legislation, the provisions of this article.

AMENDMENT XV: RACE NO BAR TO VOTING RIGHTS

March 30, 1870

Proposed by Congress February 26, 1869, this amendment's ratification was completed March 30, 1870. The Fourteenth Amendment implied, but did not guarantee, black suffrage. A landslide Republican victory in the 1868 election gave the radicals a mandate to add the finishing touch to reconstruction. Some radicals would have liked to have gone further with the Fifteenth Amendment's provisions, forbidding the use of property or literacy qualifications. This was denied, though, since many northern and western states wanted to preserve these tactics to exclude immigrants.

SEC. 1. The right of citizens of the United States to vote shall not be denied or abridged by the United States or by any State on account of race, color, or previous condition of servitude—

SEC. 2. The congress shall have power to enforce this article by appropriate legislation—

VII

AMERICA
COMES OF AGE

ON WOMAN'S RIGHT TO SUFFRAGE

Susan B. Anthony   *1873*

---

*For a generation, the women's rights campaign had
paralleled the abolition campaign. Logically, the granting of
black citizenship implied full citizenship for women, too. The
most radical feminist leaders, in fact, refused to support passage
of the Fifteenth Amendment unless it was accompanied by a
sixteenth amendment enfranchising women.*

*One of the women's rights advocates was Susan B.
Anthony, born February 15, 1820, in Adams, Massachusetts.
She was the daughter of a Quaker abolitionist and, from the
1840s, active in the women's, abolition and temperance
movements. In 1872 she led a group of women to the polls in
Rochester, New York, and was arrested. At her trial the following year, she made this definitive statement on women's right to
vote. Eventually convicted, she refused to pay her fine. Anthony
continued her crusade, collaborating with Elizabeth Cady
Stanton, Matilda Joslyn Gage and Ida Harper on four volumes*

of the History of Woman Suffrage, *and helping to organize the*
National Woman Suffrage Association.

———————————

FRIENDS and Fellow Citizens:—I stand before you to-night under indictment for the alleged crime of having voted at the last presidential election, without having a lawful right to vote. It shall be my work this evening to prove to you that in thus voting, I not only committed no crime, but, instead, simply exercised my citizen's rights, guaranteed to me and all United States citizens by the National Constitution, beyond the power of any State to deny.

The preamble of the Federal Constitution says:

"We, the people of the United States, in order to form a more perfect union, establish justice, insure domestic tranquility, provide for the common defense, promote the general welfare, and secure the blessings of liberty to ourselves and our posterity, do ordain and establish this Constitution for the United States of America."

It was we, the people; not we, the white male citizens; nor yet we, the male citizens; but we, the whole people, who formed the Union. And we formed it, not to give the blessings of liberty, but to secure them; not to the half of ourselves and the half of our posterity, but to the whole people—women as well as men. And it is a downright mockery to talk to women of their enjoyment of the blessings of liberty while they are denied the use of the only means of securing them provided by this democratic-republican government—the ballot.

For any State to make sex a qualification that must ever result in the disfranchisement of one entire half of the people is to pass a bill of attainder, or an *ex post facto* law, and is therefore a violation of the supreme law of the land. By it the blessings of liberty are for ever withheld from women and their female posterity. To them this government has no just powers derived from the consent of the governed. To them this government is not a democracy. It is not a republic. It is an odious aristocracy; a hateful oligarchy of sex: the most hateful aristocracy ever established on the face of the globe; an oligarchy of wealth, where the rich govern the poor. An oligarchy of learning, where the educated govern the ignorant, or even an oligarchy of race, where the Saxon rules the African, might be endured; but this oligarchy of sex, which makes father, brothers, husband, sons, the oligarchs over the mother and sisters, the wife and daughters of every household—which ordains all men sovereigns, all women subjects, carries dissension, discord and rebellion into every home of the nation.

Webster, Worcester and Bouvier all define a citizen to be a person in the United States, entitled to vote and hold office.

The only question left to be settled now is: Are women persons? And I hardly believe any of our opponents will have the hardihood to say they are not. Being persons, then, women are citizens; and no State has a right to make any law, or to enforce any old law, that shall abridge their privileges or immunities. Hence, every discrimination against women in the constitutions and laws of the several States is to-day null and void, precisely as is every one against negroes.

REPORT ON THE LANDS
OF THE ARID REGION

John Wesley Powell   *1878*

John Wesley Powell was born in rural New York on March 24, 1834. He served in the United States Army during the Civil War, losing his right arm at Shiloh. Resigning his commission in 1865, he taught geology for a time in Illinois. From 1871 to 1879, he directed government surveys of public lands in the West, leading a series of expeditions to the Rocky Mountains and Great Basin. During the same period, he published three major works: Exploration of the Colorado River and Its Tributaries *(1875),* An Introduction to the Study of Indian Languages *(1877) and* Report on the Lands of the Arid Region of the United States *(1878).*

The report for the first time analyzed the role of water in developing the West, and is a landmark statement regarding the importance of conservation and free access to resources. From 1881 to 1892, Powell directed the United States Geological Survey, working to map water resources and expand agricultural projects.

. . . IF the whole of the Arid Region was yet unsettled, it might be wise for the Government to undertake the parceling of the lands and to employ skilled engineers to do the work, whose duties could be performed in advance of settlement. . . . Many of the lands surveyed along the minor streams have been entered, and the titles to these lands are in the hands of actual settlers. Many pasturage farms, or ranches, as they are called locally, have been established throughout the country. These remarks are true of every state and territory in the Arid Region. In the main these ranches or pasturage farms are on Government land, and the settlers are squatters, and some are not expecting to make permanent homes. . . . It is now too late for the Government to parcel the pasturage lands in advance of the wants of settlers in the most available way, so as to closely group residences and give water privileges to the several farms. Many of the farmers are actually on the ground, and are clamoring for some means by which they can obtain titles to pasturage farms of an extent adequate to their wants, and the tens of thousands of individual interests would make the problem a difficult one for the officers of the Government to solve. A system less arbitrary than that of the rectangular surveys now in vogue, and requiring unbiased judgment, overlooking the interests of single individuals and considering only the interests of the greatest number, would meet with local opposition. . . .

Under these circumstances it is believed that it is best to permit the people to divide their lands for themselves—not in a way by which each man may take what he pleases for himself, but by providing methods by which these settlers may organize and mutually protect each other from the rapacity of individuals. The lands, as lands, are of but slight value, as they cannot be used for ordinary agricultural purposes, i.e., the cultivation of crops; but their value consists in the scant grasses which they spontaneously produce, and these values can be made available only by the use of the waters necessary for the subsistence of stock, and that necessary for the small amount of irrigable land which should be attached to the several pasturage farms. Thus, practically, all values inherent in the water, and an equitable division of the waters can be made only by a wise system of parcelling the lands; and the people in organized bodies can well be trusted with this right, while individuals could not thus be trusted. These considerations have led to the plan suggested in the bill submitted for the organization of pasturage districts.

In like manner, in the bill designed for the purpose of suggesting a plan for the organization of irrigation districts, the same principle is involved, *viz*, that of permitting the settlers themselves to subdivide the lands into such tracts as they may desire.

The lands along the streams are not valuable for agricultural purposes in continuous bodies or squares, but only in irrigable tracts governed by the levels of the meandering canals which carry the water for irrigation, and it would be greatly to the advantage of every such district if the lands could be divided into parcels, governed solely by the conditions under which the water could be distributed over them; and such parcelling cannot be done prior to the occupancy of the lands, but can only be made *pari passu* with the adoption of a system of canals; and the people settling on these lands should be allowed the privilege of dividing the lands into such tracts as may be most available for such purposes, and they should not be hampered with the present arbitrary system of dividing tracts into rectangular tracts. . . .

The title to no tract of land should be conveyed from the Government to the individual until the proper survey of the same is made and the plat prepared for record. With this precaution, which the Government already invariably takes in disposing of its lands, no fear of uncertainty of identification need be entertained. . . .

. . . The general subject of water rights is one of great importance. In many places in the Arid Region irrigation companies are organized who obtain vested rights in the waters they control, and consequently the rights to such waters do not inhere in any particular tracts of land.

When the area to which it is possible to take the water of any given stream is much greater than the stream is competent to serve, if the land titles and water rights are severed, the owner of any tract of land is at the mercy of the owner of the water right. In general the lands greatly exceed the capacities of the streams. Thus the lands have no value without water. If the water rights fall into the hands of irrigating companies and the lands into the hands of individual farmers, the farmers then will be dependent upon the stock companies, and eventually the monopoly of water rights will be an intolerable burden to the people.

The magnitude of the interests involved must not be overlooked. All the present and future agriculture of more than four-tenths of the area of the United States is dependent upon irrigation, and practically all values for agricultural industries inhere, not in the lands, but in the water. Monopoly of land need not be feared. The question for legislators to solve is to devise some practical means by which water rights may be distributed among individual farmers and water monopolies prevented. . . .

The pioneer is fully engaged in the present with its hopes of immediate remuneration for labor. The present development of the country fully occupies him. For this reason every effort put forth to increase the area of the agricultural land by irrigation is welcomed. Every man who turns his attention to this department of industry is considered a public benefactor. But if in the eagerness for present development a land and water system shall grow up in which the practical control of agriculture shall fall into the hands of water companies, evils will result therefrom that generations may not be able to correct, and the very men who are now lauded as benefactors to the country will, in the ungovernable reaction which is sure to come, be denounced as oppressors of the people.

The right to use water should inhere in the land to be irrigated, and water rights should go with land titles.

Those unacquainted with the industrial institutions of the far west, involving the use of lands and waters, may without careful thought suppose that the long recognized principles of the common law are sufficient to prevent the severance of land and water rights; but other practices are obtaining which have, or eventually will have, all the force of common law because the necessities of the country require the change, and these practices are obtaining the color of right from state and territorial legislation, and to some extent by national legislation. In all that country the natural channels of the streams cannot be made to govern water rights without great injury to its agricultural and mining industries. For the great purposes of irrigation and hydraulic mining the water has no value in its natural channel. In general the water cannot be used for irrigation on the lands immediately contiguous to the streams—i.e., the flood plains or bottom valleys. . . . The waters must be taken to a greater or less extent on the bench lands to be used in irrigation. All the waters of all the arid lands will eventually be taken from their natural channels, and they can be utilized only to the extent to which they are thus removed, and water rights must of necessity be severed from the natural channels. There is another important factor to be considered. The water when used in irrigation is absorbed by the soil and reëvaporated to the heavens. It cannot be taken from its natural channel, used, and returned. Again, the water cannot in general be properly utilized in irrigation by requiring it to be taken from its natural channel within the limits ordinarily included in a single ownership. In order to conduct the water on the higher bench lands where it is to be used in irrigation, it is necessary to go up the stream until a level is reached from which the waters will flow to the lands to be redeemed. The exceptions to this are so small that the statement scarcely needs qualification. Thus, to use the water it must be diverted from its natural course often miles or scores of miles from where it is to be used.

The ancient principles of common law applying to the use of natural streams, so wise and equitable in a humid region, would, if applied to the Arid Region, practically prohibit the growth of its most important industries. Thus it is that a custom is springing up in the Arid Region which may or may not have color of authority in statutory or common law; on this I do not wish to express an opinion; but certain it is that water rights are practically being severed from the natural channels of the streams; and this must be done. In the change, it is to be feared that water rights will in many cases be separated from all land rights as the system is now forming. If this fear is not groundless, to the extent that such a separation is secured, water will become a property independent of the land, and this property will be gradually absorbed by a few. Monopolies of water will be secured, and the whole agriculture of the country will be tributary thereto— a condition of affairs which an American citizen having in view the interests of the largest number of the people cannot contemplate with favor.

Practically, in that country the right to water is acquired by priority of utilization, and this is as it should be from the necessities of the country. But two important qualifications are needed. The user right should attach to the land where used, not to the individual or company constructing the canals by which it is used; the priority of usage should secure the right. But this needs some slight modification. A farmer settling on a small tract, to be redeemed by irrigation, should be given a reasonable length of time in which to secure his water right by utilization, that he may secure it by his own labor, either directly by constructing the waterways himself, or indirectly by coöperating with his neighbours in constructing systems of waterways. Without this provision there is little inducement for poor men to commence farming operations, and men of ready capital only will engage in such enterprises. . . .

If there be any doubt of the ultimate legality of the practices of the people in the arid country relating to water and land rights, all such doubts should be speedily quieted through the enactment of appropriate laws by the national legislature. Perhaps an amplification by the courts of what has been designated as the natural right to the use of water may be made to cover the practices now obtaining; but it hardly seems wise to imperil interests so great by intrusting them to the possibility of some future court made law.

NARRATIVE

Chief Joseph   *April 1879*

> *By the late 1870s, nearly all the Native American population had been restricted to reservations. Only a few bands remained free: Sitting Bull's Lakota in Canada, Geronimo's Apache in Mexico, and, in the mountains of northeastern Oregon, a single band of the Nez Percé. In May 1877 all nontreaty Nez Percé were given an ultimatum to move to the Lapwai Reservation in Idaho. At first, In-mut-too-yah-lat-lat, called Chief Joseph by the whites, agreed. But, hearing that some of his young men had killed a few white squatters, he decided to escape north.*
>
> *In a brilliant series of rearguard holding actions, 250 Nez Percé warriors managed to protect the band's retreat*

against four United States Army columns. After fleeing 1,600 miles across Oregon, Washington, Idaho and Montana, the band was finally cornered only forty miles from the Canadian border. On October 5, 1877, Joseph surrendered to General Miles. In 1879, Chief Joseph traveled to Washington, D.C., to state the Indians' case before President Hayes, several congressmen and other government officials. His account recording his dealings with the government was published in the North American Review *in April 1879. Contrary to government promises, the Wallamwatkin band were sent to a barren reservation in the Indian Territory and were not allowed to return to the mountains of eastern Washington until 1885.*

———————————

MY friends, I have been asked to show you my heart. I am glad to have a chance to do so. I want the white people to understand my people. Some of you think an Indian is like a wild animal. This is a mistake. I will tell you all about our people, and then you can judge whether an Indian is a man or not. I believe much trouble and blood would be saved if we opened our hearts more. I will tell you in my way how the Indian sees things. The white man has more words to tell you how they look to him, but it does not require many words to speak the truth. What I have to say will come from my heart, and I will speak with a straight tongue. Ah-cum-kin-i-ma-me-hut [the Great Spirit] is looking at me, and will hear me.

My name is In-mut-too-yah-lat-lat [Thunder traveling over the mountains]. I am chief of the Wal-lam-wat-kin band of Chute-pa-lu, or Nez Percés. I was born in eastern Oregon, thirty-eight winters ago. My father was chief before me. When a young man, he was called Joseph by Mr. Spaulding, a missionary. He died a few years ago. There was no stain on his hands of the blood of a white man. He left a good name on the earth. He advised me well for my people.

Our fathers gave us many laws, which they had learned from their fathers. These laws were good. They told us to treat all men as they treated us; that we should never be the first to break a bargain; that it was a disgrace to tell a lie; that we should speak only the truth; that it was a shame for one man to take from another his wife, or his property without paying for it. We were taught to believe that the Great Spirit sees and hears everything, and that he never forgets; that hereafter he will give every man a spirit-home according to his deserts: if he has been a good man, he will have a good home; if he has been a bad man, he will have a bad home. This I believe, and all my people believe the same. . . .

The first white men of your people who came to our country were named

Lewis and Clarke. They also brought many things that our people had never seen. They talked straight, and our people gave them a great feast, as a proof that their hearts were friendly. These men were very kind. They made presents to our chiefs and our people made presents to them. We had a great many horses, of which we gave them what they needed, and they gave us guns and tobacco in return. All the Nez Percés made friends with Lewis and Clarke, and agreed to let them pass through their country, and never to make war on white men. This promise the Nez Percés have never broken. No white man can accuse them of bad faith, and speak with a straight tongue. It has always been the pride of the Nez Percés that they were the friends of the white men. . . .

For a short time we lived quietly. But this could not last. White men had found gold in the mountains around the land of winding water. They stole a great many horses from us, and we could not get them back because we were Indians. The white men told lies for each other. They drove off a great many of our cattle. Some white men branded our young cattle so they could claim them. We had no friend who would plead our cause before the law councils. It seemed to me that some of the white men in Wallowa were doing these things on purpose to get up a war. They knew that we were not strong enough to fight them. I labored hard to avoid trouble and bloodshed. We gave up some of our country to the white men, thinking that then we could have peace. We were mistaken. The white man would not let us alone. We could have avenged our wrongs many times, but we did not. Whenever the Government has asked us to help them against other Indians, we have never refused. When the white men were few and we were strong we could have killed them all off, but the Nez Percés wished to live at peace. . . .

I could see no other way to avoid a war. We moved over to White Bird Creek, sixteen miles away, and there encamped, intending to collect our stock before leaving; but the soldiers attacked us, and the first battle was fought. . . .

I could not bear to see my wounded men and women suffer any longer; we had lost enough already. General Miles had promised that we might return to our own country with what stock we had left. I thought we could start again. I believed General Miles, or I never would have surrendered. I have heard that he has been censured for making the promise to return us to Lapwai. He could not have made any other terms with me at that time. I would have held him in check until my friends came to my assistance, and then neither of the generals nor their soldiers would have ever left Bear Paw Mountain alive.

On the fifth day I went to General Miles and gave up my gun, and said, "From where the sun now stands I will fight no more." My people needed rest— we wanted peace. . . .

At last I was granted permission to come to Washington and bring my friend Yellow Bull and our interpreter with me. I am glad we came. I have shaken hands with a great many friends, but there are some things I want to know which no one seems able to explain. I can not understand how the Government sends a man out to fight us, as it did General Miles, and then breaks his word. Such a Government has something wrong about it. I can not understand why so many chiefs are allowed to talk so many different ways, and promise so many different things. I have seen the Great Father Chief [the President], the next Great Chief [Secretary of the Interior], the Commissioner Chief [Hayt], the Law Chief [General Butler], and many other law chiefs [Congressmen], and they all say they are my friends, and that I shall have justice, but while all their mouths talk right I do not understand why nothing is done for my people. I have heard talk and talk, but nothing is done. Good words do not last long unless they amount to something. Words do not pay for my dead people. They do not pay for my country, now overrun by white men. They do not protect my father's grave. They do not pay for all my horses and cattle. Good words will not give me back my children. Good words will not make good the promise of your War Chief General Miles. Good words will not give my people good health and stop them from dying. Good words will not get my people a home where they can live in peace and take care of themselves. I am tired of talk that comes to nothing. It makes my heart sick when I remember all the good words and all the broken promises. There has been too much talking by men who had no right to talk. Too many misinterpretations have been made, too many misunderstandings have come up between the white men about the Indians. If the white man wants to live in peace with the Indian he can live in peace. There need be no trouble. Treat all men alike. Give them the same laws. Give them all an even chance to live and grow. All men were made by the same Great Spirit Chief. They are all brothers. The earth is the mother of all people, and all people should have equal rights upon it. You might as well expect the rivers to run backward as that any man who was born a free man should be contented when penned up and denied liberty to go where he pleases. If you tie a horse to a stake, do you expect he will grow fat? If you pen an Indian up on a small spot of earth, and compel him to stay there, he will not be contented, nor will he grow and prosper. I have asked some of the great white chiefs where they get their authority to say to the Indian that he shall stay in one place, while he sees white men going where they please. They can not tell me.

I only ask of the Government to be treated as all other men are treated. If I can not go to my own home, let me have a home in a country where my people will not die so fast. I would like to go to Bitter Root Valley. There my people would be healthy; where they are now they are dying. Three have died since I left my camp to come to Washington.

When I think of our condition my heart is heavy. I see men of my race treated as outlaws and driven from country to country, or shot down like animals.

I know that my race must change. We cannot hold our own with the white men as we are. We only ask an even chance to live as other men live. We ask to be recognized as men. We ask that the same law shall work alike on all men. If an Indian breaks the law, punish him by the law. If a white man breaks the law, punish him also.

Let me be a free man—free to travel, free to stop, free to work, free to trade where I choose, free to choose my own teachers, free to follow the religion of my fathers, free to talk and think and act for myself—and I will obey every law, or submit to the penalty.

Whenever the white man treats the Indian as they treat each other, then we shall have no more wars. We shall be all alike—brothers of one father and mother, with one sky above us and one country around us, and one government for all. Then the Great Spirit Chief who rules above will smile upon this land, and send rain to wash out the bloody spots made by brothers' hands from the face of the earth. For this time the Indian race are waiting and praying. I hope that no more groans of wounded men and women will ever go to the ear of the Great Spirit Chief above, and that all people may be one people.

In-mut-too-yah-lat-lat has spoken for his people.

THE NEW COLOSSUS

Emma Lazarus   *1883*

Following the Civil War, the French historian Edward Laboulaye suggested a gift to the United States, commemorating the friendship and shared ideals of the two nations. The Statue of Liberty, by Frederic-Auguste Bartholdi, with an internal framework designed by Gustave Eiffel, was completed in 1885 and shipped to New York. The pedestal was finished the following year and, on October 28, 1886, the statue was dedicated by President Grover Cleveland. Inscribed on a bronze plaque inside the base of the statue were lines from Emma Lazarus's sonnet, "The New Colossus," first published in 1883.

Not like the brazen giant of Greek fame,
With conquering limbs astride from land to land;
Here at our sea-washed, sunset gates shall stand
A mighty woman with a torch, whose flame
Is the imprisoned lightning, and her name
Mother of Exiles. From her beacon hand
Glows world-wide welcome; her mild eyes command
The air-bridged harbor that twin cities frame.

"Keep, ancient lands, your storied pomp!" cries she
With silent lips, "Give me your tired, your poor,
Your huddled masses yearning to breathe free,
The wretched refuse of your teeming shore.
Send these, the homeless, tempest-tost to me,
I lift my lamp beside the golden door!"

THE SHERMAN ANTI-TRUST ACT

July 2, 1890

The last three decades of the nineteenth century were a period of industrial revolution in the United States. The growth of American manufacturing was led by a few businessmen who established leadership in an industry and then attempted to create monopoly domination of the market. In 1882, John D. Rockefeller incorporated the Standard Oil Trust in Ohio. The trust was designed to control voting rights in competing corporations within a small group of "trustees," eliminating the risks, and benefits, of competition. By 1890, trusts had been established in half a dozen industries.

By this time, however, reform-minded journalists and politicians had determined to break up the trusts. Among these was Senator John Sherman of Ohio, younger brother of General William Tecumseh Sherman. Sherman was chairman of the Senate Finance Committee and author of the first legislative attempt to deter monopoly trade. Though weak and generally ineffective, the Anti-Trust Act did provide the groundwork for later legislation promoting a freer marketplace.

———————————

AN Act To protect trade and commerce against unlawful restraints and monopolies. . . .

Be it enacted

SEC. 1. Every contract, combination in the form of trust or otherwise, or conspiracy, in restraint of trade or commerce among the several States, or with foreign nations, is hereby declared to be illegal. Every person who shall make any such contract or engage in any such combination or conspiracy, shall be deemed guilty of a misdemeanor, and, on conviction thereof, shall be punished by fine not exceeding five thousand dollars, or by imprisonment not exceeding one year, or by both said punishments, in the discretion of the court.

SEC. 2. Every person who shall monopolize, or attempt to monopolize, or combine or conspire with any other person or persons, to monopolize any part of the trade or commerce among the several States, or with foreign nations, shall be deemed guilty of a misdemeanor, and, on conviction thereof, shall be punished by fine not exceeding five thousand dollars, or by imprisonment not exceeding one year, or by both said punishments, in the discretion of the court.

SEC. 3. Every contract, combination in form of trust or otherwise, or conspiracy, in restraint of trade or commerce in any Territory of the United States or of the District of Columbia, or in restraint of trade or commerce between any such Territory and another, or between any such Territory or Territories and any State or States or the District of Columbia, or with foreign nations, or between the District of Columbia and any State or States or foreign nations, is hereby declared illegal. Every person who shall make any such contract or engage in any such combination or conspiracy, shall be deemed guilty of a misdemeanor, and, on conviction thereof, shall be punished by fine not exceeding five thousand dollars, or by imprisonment not exceeding one year, or by both said punishments, in the discretion of the court.

SEC. 4. The several circuit courts of the United States are hereby invested with jurisdiction to prevent and restrain violations of this act; and it shall be the duty of the several district attorneys of the United States in their respective districts, under the direction of the Attorney-General, to institute proceedings in equity to prevent and restrain such violations. Such proceedings may be by way of petition setting forth the case and praying that such violation shall be enjoined or otherwise prohibited. When the parties complained of shall have been duly notified of such petition the courts shall proceed, as soon as may be, to the hearing and determination of the case; and pending such petition and before final decrees, the court may at any time make such temporary restraining order or prohibition as shall be deemed just in the premises.

SEC. 5. Whenever it shall appear to the court before which any proceeding under Section four of this act may be pending, that the ends of justice require that other parties should be brought before the court, the court may cause them to be summoned, whether they reside in the district in which the court is held or not; and subpoenas to that end may be served in any district by the marshal thereof.

SEC. 6. Any property owned under any contract or by any combination, or pursuant to any conspiracy (and being the subject thereof) mentioned in section one of this act, and being in the course of transportation from one State to another, or to a foreign country, shall be forfeited to the United States, and may be seized and condemned by like proceedings as those provided by law for the forfeiture, seizure, and condemnation of property imported into the United States contrary to law.

SEC. 7. Any person who shall be injured in his business or property by any other person or corporation by reason of anything forbidden or declared to be unlawful by this act, may sue therefor in any circuit court of the United States in the district in which the defendant resides or is found, without respect to the amount in controversy, and shall recover threefold the damages by him sustained, and the costs of suit, including a reasonable attorney's fee.

SEC. 8. That the word "person" or "persons," wherever used in this act shall be deemed to include corporations and associations existing under or authorized by the laws of either the United States, the laws of any of the Territories, the laws of any State, or the laws of any foreign country.

AMERICA THE BEAUTIFUL

Katharine Lee Bates   *1893*

Katharine Lee Bates was an author and educator born in Falmouth, Massachusetts, on August 12, 1859. She received a degree from Wellesley College and remained to teach English literature from 1885 to 1925. Inspired by the view from the summit of Pikes Peak during a summer visit to Colorado, she composed her famous poem, "America the Beautiful." She also

published several short stories and collections of children's
literature before her death in 1929.

O beautiful for spacious skies,
    For amber waves of grain,
For purple mountain majesties
    Above the fruited plain!
      America! America!
    God shed His grace on thee
And crown thy good with brotherhood
    From sea to shining sea!

O beautiful for pilgrim feet,
    Whose stern, impassioned stress
A thoroughfare for freedom beat
    Across the wilderness!
      America! America!
    God mend thine every flaw,
Confirm thy soul in self-control,
    Thy liberty in law!

O beautiful for heroes proved
    In liberating strife,
Who more than self their country loved,
    And mercy more than life!
      America! America!
    May God thy gold refine
Till all success be nobleness
    And every gain divine!

O beautiful for patriot dream
    That sees beyond the years
Thine alabaster cities gleam
    Undimmed by human tears!
      America! America!
    God shed His grace on thee
And crown thy good with brotherhood
    From sea to shining sea!

ATLANTA EXPOSITION SPEECH

Booker T. Washington   *1895*

    Despite the provisions of the Fourteenth and Fifteenth
Amendments, blacks remained semicitizens in the old Confed-
eracy. Literacy requirements, "grandfather" clauses and
property restrictions ensured an exclusively white franchise. In
addition, brutal extralegal measures, including lynchings,
helped keep blacks "in their place."
    Some black leaders, most notably Booker T. Washington,
felt that, under the circumstances, it was best to avoid conflict.
Washington urged accommodation and education in mechan-
ics and agriculture. He put this philosophy into practice after
becoming the first president of the Tuskegee Institute in 1881.

Through thrift and hard work, he thought blacks could earn the
respect of whites, and, in the long run, full citizenship. While
welcomed by many, Washington's advice was challenged by
some black intellectuals and led indirectly to the foundation of
the Niagara Movement by Washington's leading critic, W.E.B.
Du Bois. In the summer of 1895 Washington delivered his views
on black advancement to an integrated audience at the Atlanta
Exposition, a fair celebrating the recovery of the South from the
devastations of war and reconstruction.

———————

MR. President and Gentlemen of the Board of Directors and Citizens:

One-third of the population of the South is of the Negro race. No enterprise seeking the material, civil, or moral welfare of this section can disregard this element of our population and reach the highest success. I but convey to you, Mr. President and Directors, the sentiment of the masses of my race when I say that in no way have the value and manhood of the American Negro been more fittingly and generously recognized than by the managers of this magnificent exposition at every stage of its progress. It is a recognition that will do more to cement the friendship of the two races than any occurrence since the dawn of our freedom.

Not only this, but the opportunity here afforded will awaken among us a new era of industrial progress. Ignorant and inexperienced, it is not strange that in the first years of our new life we began at the top instead of at the bottom; that a seat in Congress or the state legislature was more sought than real estate or industrial skill; that the political convention or stump speaking had more attractions than starting a dairy farm or a truck garden.

A ship lost at sea for many days suddenly sighted a friendly vessel. From the mast of the unfortunate vessel was seen a signal, "Water, water; we die of thirst!" The answer from the friendly vessel at once came back, "Cast down your buckets where you are." A second time the signal, "Water, water; send us water!" ran up from the distressed vessel, and was answered, "Cast down your buckets where you are." A third and fourth signal for water was answered, "Cast down your buckets where you are." The captain of the distressed vessel, at last heeding the injunction, cast down his bucket, and it came up full of fresh, sparkling water from the mouth of the Amazon River. To those of my race who depend on bettering their condition in a foreign land or who underestimate the importance of cultivating friendly relations with the Southern white man, who is their next-door neighbor, I would say: "Cast down your bucket where you are"—cast it down in making friends in every manly way of the people of all races by whom we are surrounded.

To those of the white race who look to the incoming of those of foreign birth and strange tongue and habits for the prosperity of the South, were I permitted I would repeat what I say to my own race, "Cast down your bucket where you are." Cast it down among the eight millions of Negroes whose habits you know, whose fidelity and love you have tested in days when to have proved treacherous meant the ruin of your firesides. Cast down your bucket among these people who have, without strikes and labor wars, tilled your fields, cleared your forests, builded your railroads and cit-ies, and brought forth treasures from the bowels of the earth, and helped make possible this magnificent repre-sentation of the progress of the South. Casting down your bucket among my people, helping and encouraging them as you are doing on these grounds, and to education of head, hand, and heart, you will find that they will buy your surplus land, make blossom the waste places in your fields, and run your factories. While doing this, you can be sure in the future, as in the past, that you and your families will be sur-rounded by the most patient, faithful, law-abiding, and unresentful people

that the world has seen. As we have proved our loyalty to you in the past, in nursing your children, watching by the sickbed of your mothers and fathers, and often following them with tear-dimmed eyes to their graves, so in the future, in our humble way, we shall stand by you with a devotion that no foreigner can approach, ready to lay down our lives, if need be, in defense of yours, interlacing our industrial, commercial, civil, and religious life with yours in a way that shall make the interests of both races one. In all things that are purely social we can be as separate as the fingers, yet one as the hand in all things essential to mutual progress.

There is no defense or security for any of us except in the highest intelligence and development of all. If anywhere there are efforts tending to curtail the fullest growth of the Negro, let these efforts be turned into stimulating, encouraging, and making him the most useful and intelligent citizen. Effort or means so invested will pay a thousand per cent interest. These efforts will be twice blessed—"blessing him that gives and him that takes."

There is no escape through law of man or God from the inevitable:—

The laws of changeless justice bind
Oppressor with oppressed;
And close as sin and suffering joined
We march to fate abreast.

Nearly sixteen millions of hands will aid you in pulling the load upward, or they will pull against you the load downward. We shall constitute one-third and more of the ignorance and crime of the South, or one-third its intelligence and progress; we shall contribute one-third to the business and industrial prosperity of the South, or we shall prove a veritable body of death, stagnating, depressing, retarding every effort to advance the body politic.

Gentlemen of the Exposition, as we present to you our humble effort at an exhibition of our progress, you must not expect overmuch. Starting thirty years ago with ownership here and there in a few quilts and pumpkins and chickens (gathered from miscellaneous sources), remember the path that has led from these to the inventions and production of agricultural implements, buggies, steam-engines, newspapers, books, statuary, carving, paintings, the management of drugstores and banks, has not been trodden without contact with thorns and thistles. While we take pride in what we exhibit as a result of our independent efforts, we do not for a moment forget that our part in this exhibition would fall far short of your expectations but for the constant help that has come to our educational life, not only from the southern states, but especially from northern philanthropists, who have made their gifts a constant stream of blessing and encouragement.

The wisest among my race understand that the agitation of questions of social equality is the extremest folly, and that progress in the environment of all the privileges that will come to us must be the result of severe and constant struggle rather than of artificial forcing. No race that has anything to contribute to the markets of the world is long in any degree ostracized. It is important and right that all privileges of the law be ours, but it is vastly more important that we be prepared for the exercises of these privileges. The opportunity to earn a dollar in a factory just now is worth infinitely more than the opportunity to spend a dollar in an opera house.

In conclusion, may I repeat that nothing in thirty years has given us more hope and encouragement and drawn us so near to you of the white race, as this opportunity offered by the Exposition; and here bending, as it were, over the altar that represents the results of the struggles of your race and mine, both starting practically empty-handed three decades ago, I pledge that in your effort to work out the great and intricate problem which God has laid at the doors of the South, you shall have at all times the patient, sympathetic help of my race. Only let this be constantly in mind: that, while from representations in these buildings of the product of field, of forest, of mine, of factory, letters, and art much good will come, yet far above and beyond material benefits will be that higher good, that, let us pray God, will come, in a blotting out of sectional differences and racial animosities and suspicions, in a determination to administer absolute justice, in a willing obedience among all classes to the mandates of law. This, coupled with our material prosperity, will bring into our beloved South a new heaven and a new earth.

CROSS OF GOLD SPEECH

William Jennings Bryan   *July 8, 1896*

The United States operated on a bimetallic standard until adoption of the gold standard in 1873. The Populist movement of the 1880s and 1890s arose in part from demands to return to bimetallism after the discoveries of large silver deposits in Nevada and Arizona. Abundant currency and higher inflation favored farmers with debts and hopes for higher commodity prices.

The Populist Party was the beneficiary of a dramatic political realignment as the Democrats lost a third of their congressional seats in the 1894 election. The "silver wing" of the Democratic Party gained strength after this disaster, and at the 1896 national convention managed to win nomination of a relatively unknown congressman from Nebraska, William Jennings Bryan. Only thirty-six years old, Bryan had electrified the convention with his attack on the gold standard. The Democrats identified themselves as the free silver party and absorbed nearly all the Populists' strength in the poorer West and South, though solid middle class support assured Republi-

can victory in the electoral college. Bryan went on to run twice more for the presidency, but never again came as close as he had in 1896.

I would be presumptuous, indeed, to present myself against the distinguished gentlemen to whom you have listened if this were a mere measuring of abilities; but this is not a contest between persons. The humblest citizen in all the land, when clad in the armor of a righteous cause, is stronger than all the hosts of error. I come to speak to you in defense of a cause as holy as the cause of liberty—the cause of humanity.

When this debate is concluded, a motion will be made to lay upon the table the resolution offered in commendation of the Administration, and also, the resolution offered in condemnation of the Administration. We object to bringing this question down to the level of persons. The individual is but an atom; he is born, he acts, he dies; but principles are eternal; and this has been a contest over a principle.

Never before in the history of this country has there been witnessed such a contest as that through which we have just passed. Never before in the history of American politics has a great issue been fought out as this issue has been, by the voters of a great party. On the fourth of March 1893, a few Democrats, most of them members of Congress, issued an address to the Democrats of the nation, asserting that the money question was the paramount issue of the hour; declaring that a majority of the Democratic party has the right to control the action of the party on this paramount issue; and concluding with the request that the believers in the free coinage of silver in the Democratic party should organize, take charge of, and control the policy of the Democratic party. Three months later, at Memphis, an organization was perfected, and the silver Democrats went forth openly and courageously proclaiming their belief, and declaring that, if successful, they would crystallize into a platform the declaration which they had made. Then began the struggle. With a zeal approaching the zeal which inspired the Crusaders who followed Peter the Hermit, our silver Democrats went forth from victory unto victory until they are now assembled, not to discuss, not to debate, but to enter up the judgement already rendered by the plain people of this country. In this contest brother has been arrayed against brother, father against son. The warmest ties of love, acquaintance, and association have been disregarded; old leaders have been cast aside when they have refused to give expression to the sentiments of those whom they would lead, and new leaders have sprung up to give direction to this cause of truth. Thus has the contest been waged, and we have assembled here under as binding and solemn instructions as were ever imposed upon representatives of the people.

We do not come as individuals. As individuals we might have been glad to compliment the gentleman from New York [Senator Hill], but we know that the people for whom we speak would never be willing to put him in a position where he could thwart the will of the Democratic party. I saw it was not a question of persons; it was a question of principle, and it is not with gladness, my friends, that we find ourselves brought into conflict with those who are now arrayed on the other side. . . .

When you come before us and tell us that we are about to disturb your business interests, we reply that you have disturbed our business interests by your course.

We say to you that you have made the definition of a business man too limited in its application. The man who is employed for wages is as much a business man as his employer; the attorney in a country town is as much a business man as the corporation counsel in a great metropolis; the merchant at the cross-roads store is as much a business man as the merchant of New York; the farmer who goes forth in the morning and toils all day, who begins in the spring and toils all summer, and who by the application of brain and muscle to the natural resources of the country creates wealth, is as much a business man as the man who goes upon the Board of Trade and bets upon the price of grain; the miners who go down a thousand feet into the earth, or climb two thousand feet upon the cliffs, and bring forth from their hiding places the precious metals to be poured into the channels of trade are as much business men as the few financial magnates who, in a back room, corner the money of the world. We come to speak of this broader class of business men.

Ah, my friends, we say not one word against those who live upon the Atlantic Coast, but the hardy pioneers who have braved all the dangers of the wilderness, who have made the desert to bloom as the rose—the pioneers away out there who rear their children near to Nature's heart, where they can mingle their voices with the voices of the birds—out there where they have erected schoolhouses for the education of their young, churches where they praise their Creator, and cemeteries where rest the ashes of their dead—these people, we say, are as deserving of the consideration of our party as any people in this country. It is for these that we speak. We do not come as aggressors. Our war is not a war of conquest; we are fighting in the defense of our homes, our families, and posterity. We have petitioned, and our petitions have been scorned; we have entreated, and our entreaties have been disregarded; we have begged, and they have mocked when our calamity came. We beg no longer; we entreat no more; we petition no more. We defy them!

The gentleman from Wisconsin [Vilas] has said that he fears a Robespierre.

My friends, in this land of the free you need not fear that a tyrant will spring up from among the people. What we need is an Andrew Jackson to stand, as Jackson stood, against the encroachments of organized wealth.

They tell us that this platform was made to catch votes. We reply to them that changing conditions make new issues; that the principles upon which Democracy rests are as everlasting as the hills, but they must be applied to new conditions as they arise. Conditions have arisen, and we are here to meet those conditions. They tell us that the income tax ought not to be brought in here; that it is a new idea. They criticize us for our criticism of the Supreme Court of the United States. My friends, we have not criticized; we have simply called attention to what you already know. If you want criticisms read the dissenting opinions of the court. There you will find criticisms. They say that we passed an unconstitutional law; we deny it. The income tax was not unconstitutional when it was passed; it was not unconstitutional when it went before the Supreme Court for the first time; it did not become unconstitutional until one of the judges changed his mind, and we cannot be expected to know when a judge will change his mind. The income tax is just. It simply intends to put the burden of government justly upon the backs of the people. I am in favor of an income tax. When I find a man who is not willing to bear his share of the burdens of the government which protects him, I find a man who is unworthy to enjoy the blessings of a government like ours.

They say that we are opposing national bank currency; it is true. If you will read what Thomas Benton said, you will find he said that, in searching history, he could find but one parallel to Andrew Jackson; that was Cicero, he destroyed the conspiracy of Cataline and saved Rome. Benton said that Cicero only did for Rome what Jackson did for us when he destroyed the bank conspiracy and saved America. We say in our platform we believe that the right to coin and issue money is a function of government. We believe it. We believe that it is a part of sovereignty, and can no more with safety be delegated to private individuals than we could afford to delegate to private individuals the power to make penal statutes or levy taxes. Mr. Jefferson, who was once regarded as good Democratic authority, seems to have differed in opinion from the gentleman who has addressed us on the part of the minority. Those who are opposed to this proposition tell us that the issue of paper money is a function of the banks, and that the government ought to go out of the banking business. I stand with Jefferson rather than with them, and tell them, as he did, that the issue of money is a function of government, and that the banks ought to go out of the government business.

They complain about the plank which declares against life tenure in office. They have tried to strain it to mean that which it does not mean. What we oppose by that plank is the life tenure which is being built up in Washington, and which excludes from participation in official benefits the humbler members of society. . . .

And now, my friends, let me come to the paramount issue. If they ask us why it is that we say more on the money question than we say upon the tariff question, I reply that, if protection has slain its thousands, the gold standard has slain its tens of thousands. If they ask us why we do not embody in our platforms all the things that we believe in, we reply that when we have restored the money of the Constitution, all other necessary reform will be possible; but that until this is done, there is no other reform that can be accomplished.

Why is it that within three months such a change has come over the country? Three months ago when it was confidently asserted that those who believed in the gold standard would frame our platform and nominate our candidates, even the advocates of the gold standard did not think that we could elect a President. And they had good reason for their doubt, because there is scarcely a State here today asking for the gold standard which is not in the absolute control of the Republican Party. But note the change. Mr. McKinley was nominated at St. Louis upon a platform which declared for the maintenance of the gold standard until it can be changed into bimetallism by international agreement. Mr. McKinley was the most popular man among the Republicans, and three months ago everybody in the Republican Party prophesied his election. How is it today? Why, the man who was once pleased to think that he looked like Napoleon—that man shudders today when he remembers that he was nominated on the anniversary of the battle of Waterloo.

Not only that, but as he listens, he can hear with ever-increasing distinctness the sound of the waves as they beat upon the lonely shores of St. Helena.

Why this change? Ah, my friends, is not the reason for the change evident to any one who will look at the matter? No private character, however pure, no personal popularity, however great, can protect from the avenging wrath of an indignant people a man who will declare that he is in favor of fastening the gold standard upon this country, or who is willing to surrender the right of self-government and place the legislative control of our affairs in the hands of foreign potentates and powers.

We go forth confident that we shall win. Why? Because upon the paramount issue of this campaign there is not a spot of ground upon which the enemy will dare to challenge battle. If they tell us that the gold standard is a good thing, we shall point to their platform and tell them that their platform pledges the party to get rid of the gold standard and substitute bimetallism. If the gold standard is a good thing why try to get rid of it? I call your attention to the fact that some of the very people who are in this Convention today and who tell us that we ought to declare in favor of international bimetallism—thereby declaring that the gold standard is wrong and that the principle of bimetallism is better— these very people four months ago were open and avowed advocates of the gold standard, and were then telling us that we could not legislate two metals together, even with the aid of all the world. If the gold standard is a good thing, we ought to declare in favor of its retention and not in favor of abandoning it; and if the gold standard is a bad thing why should we wait until other nations are willing to help us to let go? Here is the line of battle, and we care not upon which issue they force the fight; we are prepared to meet them on either issue or on both. If they tell us that the gold standard is the standard of civilization, we reply to them that this, the most enlightened of all the nations of the earth, has never declared for a gold standard and that both the great parties this year are declaring against it. If the gold standard is the standard of civilization, why, my friends, should we not have it? If they come to meet us on that issue we can present the history of our nation. More than that; we can tell them that they will search the pages of history in vain to find a single instance where the common people of any land have ever declared themselves in favor of the gold standard. They can find where the holders of fixed investments have declared for a gold standard, but not where the masses have. Mr. Carlisle said in 1878 that this was a struggle between the "idle holders of idle capital" and "the struggling masses, who produce the wealth and pay the taxes of the country," and, my friends, the question we are to decide is: Upon which side will the Democratic party fight; upon the side of "the idle holders of idle capital" or upon the side of "the struggling masses"? That is the question which the party must answer first, and then it must be answered by each individual hereafter. The sympathies of the Democratic party, as shown by the platform, are on the side of the struggling masses who have ever been the foundation of the Democratic party. There are two ideas of government. There are those who believe that if you will only legislate to make the well-to-do prosperous, their prosperity will leak through on those below. The Democratic idea, however, has been that if you make the masses prosperous, their prosperity will find its way up through every class which rests upon them.

You come to us and tell us that the great cities are in favor of the gold standard; we reply that the great cities rest upon our broad and fertile prairies. Burn down your cities and leave our farms, and your cities will spring up again as if by magic; but destroy our farms and the grass will grow in the streets of every city in the country.

My friends, we declare that this nation is able to legislate for its own people on every question, without waiting for the aid or consent of any other nation on earth; and upon that issue we expect to carry every state in the Union.

I shall not slander the inhabitants of the fair state of Massachusetts nor the inhabitants of the state of New York by saying that, when they are confronted with the proposition, they will declare that this nation is not able to attend to its own business. It is the issue of 1776 over again. Our ancestors, when but three million in number, had the courage to declare their political independence of every other nation; shall we, their descendants, when we have grown to seventy millions, declare that we are less independent than our forefathers?

No, my friends, that will never be the verdict of our people. Therefore, we care not upon what lines the battle is fought. If they say bimetallism is good, but that we cannot have it until other nations help us, we reply, that instead of having a gold standard because England has, we will restore bimetallism, and then let England have bimetallism because the United States has it. If they dare to come out in the open field and defend the gold standard as a good thing, we will fight them to the uttermost. Having behind us the producing masses of this nation and the world, supported by the commercial interests, the laboring interests and the toilers everywhere, we will answer their demand for a gold standard by saying to them: You shall not press down upon the brow of labor this crown of thorns, you shall not crucify mankind upon a cross of gold.

PLESSY V. FERGUSON

Henry B. Brown   *1896*

Polling places were not the only places excluded to blacks. In the 1880s and 1890s a series of "Jim Crow" laws completed the color line in nearly all public spheres. This lawful separation was endorsed by the Supreme Court in 1896. Homer Plessy, a black man (who was in fact seven-eighths white) was arrested for sitting in a "whites only" car on a Louisiana train. The Supreme Court upheld his conviction on the grounds that "separate but equal" facilities did not violate the Fourteenth Amendment. In the lone dissenting opinion, Justice John Marshall Harlan pointed out the inconsistencies and troubling implications of legal segregation and argued against any regulation of civil liberties. The ruling was not reversed until the landmark Brown v. Board of Education of Topeka decision in 1954.

BROWN, J. This case turns upon the constitutionality of an act of the general assembly of the state of Louisiana, passed in 1890, providing for separate railway carriages for the white and colored races. . . .

The constitutionality of this act is attacked upon the ground that it conflicts both with the 13th Amendment of the Constitution, abolishing slavery, and the 14th Amendment, which prohibits certain restrictive legislation on the part of the states.

1. That it does not conflict with the 13th Amendment, which abolished slavery and involuntary servitude, except as a punishment for crime, is too clear for argument. . . .

A statute which implies merely a legal distinction between the white and colored races—a distinction which is founded in the color of the two races, and which must always exist so long as white men are distinguished from the other race by color—has no tendency to destroy the legal equality of the two races, or re-establish a state of involuntary servitude. Indeed, we do not understand that the 13th Amendment is strenuously relied upon by the plaintiff in error in this connection. . . .

The object of the amendment was undoubtedly to enforce the absolute equality of the two races before the law, but in the nature of things it could not have been intended to abolish distinctions based upon color, or to enforce social, as distinguished from political, equality, or a commingling of the two races upon terms unsatisfactory to either. Laws permitting, and even requiring their separation in places where they are liable to be brought into contact do not necessarily imply the inferiority of either race to the other, and have been generally, if not universally, recognized as within the competency of the state legislatures in the exercise of their police power. The most common instance of this is connected with the establishment of separate schools for white and colored children, which have been held to be a valid exercise of the legislative power even by courts of states where the political rights of the colored race have been longest and most earnestly enforced. . . .

It is claimed by the plaintiff in error that, in any mixed community, the reputation of belonging to the dominant race, in this instance the white race is property, in the same sense that a right of action, or of inheritance, is property. Conceding this to be so, for the purposes of this case, we are unable to see how this statute deprives him of, or in any way affects his right to, such property. If he be a white man and assigned to a colored coach, he may have his action for damages against the company for being deprived of his so-called property. Upon the other hand, if he be a colored man and be so assigned, he has been deprived of no property, since he is not lawfully entitled to the reputation of being a white man. . . .

So far, then, as a conflict with the 14th Amendment is concerned, the case reduces itself to the question whether the statute of Louisiana is a reasonable regulation, and with respect to this there must necessarily be a large discretion on the part of the legislature. In determining the question of reasonableness it is at liberty to act with reference to the established usages, customs, and traditions of the people, and with a view to the promotion of their comfort, and the preservation of the public peace and good order. Gauged by this standard, we cannot say that a law which authorizes or even requires the separation of the two races in public conveyances is unreasonable or more obnoxious to the 14th Amendment than the acts of Congress requiring separate schools for colored children in the District of Columbia, the constitutionality of which does not seem to have been questioned, or the corresponding acts of state legislatures.

We consider the underlying fallacy of the plaintiff's argument to consist in the assumption that the enforced separation of the two races stamps the colored race with a badge of inferiority. If this be so, it is not by reason of anything found in the act, but solely because the colored race chooses to put that construction upon it. The argument necessarily assumes that if, as has been more than once the case, and is not unlikely to be so again, the colored race should become the dominant power in the state legislature, and should enact a law in precisely similar terms, it would thereby relegate the white race to an inferior position. We imagine that the white race, at least, would not acquiesce in this assumption. The argument also assumes that social prejudice may be overcome by legislation, and that equal rights cannot be secured to the Negro except by an enforced commingling of the two races. We cannot accept this proposition. If the two races are to meet on terms of social equality, it must be the result of natural affinities, a mutual appreciation of each other's merits and a voluntary consent of individuals. . . . Legislation is powerless to eradicate racial instincts or to abolish distinctions based upon physical differences, and the attempt to do so can only result in accentuating the difficulties of the present situation. If the civil and political right of both races be equal, one cannot be inferior . . . to the other civilly or politically. If one race be inferior to the other socially, the Constitution of the United States cannot put them upon the same plane.

Justice Harlan, dissenting: It was said in argument that the statute of Louisiana does not discriminate against either race, but prescribes a rule applicable alike to white and colored citizens. But the argument does not meet the difficulty. Every one knows that the statute in question had its origin in the purpose, not so much to exclude white persons from railroad cars occupied by blacks, as to exclude colored people from coaches occupied by or assigned to white persons. . . .

If a State can prescribe, as a rule of civil conduct, that whites and blacks shall not travel as passengers in the same railroad coach, why may it not so regulate the use of the streets of its cities and towns as to compel white citizens to keep on one side of a street and black citizens to keep on the other? . . . Further, if this statute of Louisiana is consistent with the personal liberty of citizens, why may not the State require the separation in railroad coaches of native and naturalized citizens of the United States, or of Protestants and Roman Catholics? . . .

In respect of civil rights, common to all citizens, the Constitution of the United States does not, I think, permit any public authority to know the race of those entitled to be protected in the enjoyment of such rights. Every true man has pride of race, and under appropriate circumstances, when the rights of others, his equals before the law, are not to be affected, it is his privilege to express such pride and to take such action based upon it as to him seems proper. But I deny that any legislative body or judicial tribunal may have regard to the race of citizens when the civil rights of those citizens are involved. Indeed such legislation as that here in question is inconsistent, not only with that equality of rights which pertains to citizenship, national and state, but with the personal liberty enjoyed by every one within the United States. . . .

In my opinion, the judgment this day rendered will, in time, prove to be quite as pernicious as the decision made by this tribunal in the Dred Scott Case. It was adjudged in that case that the descendants of Africans who were imported into this country and sold as slaves were not included nor intended to be included under the word "citizens" in the Constitution, and could not claim any of the rights and privileges which that instrument provided for and secured to citizens of the United States; that at the time of the adoption of the Constitution they were "considered as a subordinate and inferior class of beings, who had been subjugated by the dominant race, and, whether emancipated or not, yet remained subject to their authority, and had no rights or privileges but such as those who held the power and the government might choose to grant them." The recent amendments of the Constitution, it was supposed, had eradicated these principles from our institutions. But it seems that we have yet, in some of the states, a dominant race, a superior class of citizens, which assumes to regulate the enjoyment of civil rights, common to all citizens, upon the basis of race. The present decision, it may well be apprehended, will not only stimulate aggressions, more or less brutal and irritating, upon the admitted rights of colored citizens, but will encourage the belief that it is possible, by means of state enactments, to defeat the beneficent purposes which the people of the United States had in view when they adopted the recent amendments of the Constitution, by one of which the blacks of this country were made citizens of the United

States and of the states in which they respectively reside and whose privileges and immunities, as citizens, the states are forbidden to abridge. Sixty millions of whites are in no danger from the presence here of eight millions of blacks. The destinies of the two races in this country are indissolubly linked together, and the interests of both require that the common government of all shall not permit the seeds of race hate to be planted under the sanction of law. What can more certainly arouse race hate, what more certainly create and perpetuate a feeling of distrust between these races, than state enactments which in fact proceed on the ground that colored citizens are so inferior and degraded that they cannot be allowed to sit in public coaches occupied by white citizens? That, as all will admit, is the real meaning of such legislation as was enacted in Louisiana. . . .

The sure guarantee of the peace and security of each race is the clear, distinct, unconditional recognition by our governments, national and state, of every right that inheres in civil freedom, and of the equality before the law of all citizens of the United States without regard to race. . . .

If evils will result from the commingling of the two races upon public highways established for the benefit of all, they will be infinitely less than those that will surely come from state legislation regulating the enjoyment of civil rights upon the basis of race. We boast of the freedom enjoyed by our people above all other peoples. But it is difficult to reconcile that boast with a state of the law which, practically, puts the brand of servitude and degradation upon a large class of our fellow citizens, our equals before the law. The thin disguise of "equal" accommodations for passengers in railroad coaches will not mislead anyone, or atone for the wrong this day done. . . .

I am of opinion that the statute of Louisiana is inconsistent with the personal liberty of citizens, white and black, in that state, and hostile to both the spirit and letter of the Constitution of the United States. If laws of like character should be enacted in the several states of the Union, the effect would be in the highest degree mischievous. Slavery as an institution tolerated by law would, it is true, have disappeared from our country, but there would remain a power in the states, by sinister legislation, to interfere with the full enjoyment of the blessings of freedom; to regulate civil rights, common to all citizens, upon the basis of race; and to place in a condition of legal inferiority a large body of American citizens, now constituting a part of the political community, called the people of the United States, for whom and by whom, through representatives, our government is administered. Such a system is inconsistent with the guarantee given by the Constitution to each state of a republican form of government, and may be stricken down by Congressional action, or by the courts in the discharge of their solemn duty to maintain the supreme law of the land, anything in the

Constitution or laws of any state to the contrary notwithstanding.

For the reasons stated, I am constrained to withhold my assent from the opinion and judgment of the majority.

Letter to Booker T. Washington

Susan B. Anthony   *December 19, 1898*

Though sometimes conflicting, the campaigns for black and women's civil rights continued their close association through the end of the nineteenth century. Following a visit by President William McKinley to the Tuskegee Institute, Susan B. Anthony wrote this letter to Booker T. Washington, praising his work, and urging him to support both women's and Asian suffrage in the newly acquired territory of Hawaii.

MY Dear Friends:—

I am despatching to you a set of my biography, both for yourself and for the library of your splendid school.

I should very much like to have been present when you were escorting the President through the different departments of your institution. It must have made him and the members of the cabinet realize something of the work you are doing for the education and elevation of the colored people of the South.

You have of course noticed the proscription of the Chinese and Japanese from citizenship in the proposed government of the new Territory of Hawaii, and I hope you have also noticed the invidious shutting out of all women from the right to vote or hold office there. Both propositions, I hope, will be repudiated by Congress, and if not I shall hope that President McKinley will veto the bill on the ground of the preliminary constitution violation of the fundamental principles of our government.

I trust that you are well, and that your family and your school are all prospering. Please accept my kind regards and Christmas greetings for all who abide with you.

Very sincerely yours,
Susan B. Anthony

OPEN DOOR CIRCULAR LETTER

John Hay   *September 6, 1899*

---

*The long decline of the Chinese Qing Dynasty became
apparent after China's defeat by the Japanese in 1895. As the
Japanese and European imperialists moved in for the final
carving up of the Middle Kingdom, Great Britain and the
United States became increasingly concerned, not as much for
the fate of China as for maintenance of British and American
trading rights. In March 1898, the British ambassador proposed
a joint action to protect the integrity of China (and, of course,
British and American interests), eventually leading to the
formulation of the famous "Open Door" policy. In September
1899, Secretary of State John Hay announced this policy in a
circular note to United States ambassadors at Berlin, London
and St. Petersburg.*

*While the replies of the various powers were far from the
support Hay hoped to obtain, he chose to interpret them as
acceptance, announcing their assent in a second circular note.
When the Boxer Rebellion broke out in 1900, the United States
joined the campaign to raise the siege of foreign legations at
Beijing, taking the opportunity to assert China's territorial
integrity. As long as an "independent" China survived, so
would United States claims to equal access to the Chinese
market.*

MR. Hay to Mr. White
Department of State

Sir: At the time when the Government of the United States was informed
by that of Germany that it had leased from His Majesty the Emperor of China the
port of Kiao-chao and the adjacent territory in the province of Shantung,
assurances were given to the ambassador of the United States at Berlin by the
Imperial German minister for foreign affairs that the rights and privileges insured
by treaties with China to citizens of the United States would not thereby suffer
or be in anywise impaired within the area over which Germany has thus obtained
control.

More recently, however, the British Government recognized by a formal agreement with Germany the exclusive right of the latter country to enjoy in said leased area and the contiguous "sphere of influence or interest" certain privileges, more especially those relating to railroads and mining enterprises; but, as the exact nature and extent of the rights thus recognized have not been clearly defined, it is possible that serious conflicts of interest may at any time arise, not only between British and German subjects within said area, but that the interests of our citizens may also be jeopardized thereby.

Earnestly desirous to remove any cause of irritation and to insure at the same time to the commerce of all nations in China the undoubted benefits which should accrue from a formal recognition by the various powers claiming "spheres of interest" that they shall enjoy perfect equality of treatment for their commerce and navigation within such "spheres," the Government of the United States would be pleased to see His German Majesty's Government give formal assurances and lend its coöperation in securing like assurances from the other interested powers that each within its respective sphere of whatever influence—

First. Will in no way interfere with any treaty port or any vested interest within any so-called "sphere of interest" or leased territory it may have in China.

Second. That the Chinese treaty tariff of the time being shall apply to all merchandise landed or shipped to all such ports as are within said "sphere of interest" (unless they be "free ports"), no matter to what nationality it may belong, and that duties so leviable shall be collected by the Chinese Government.

Third. That it will levy no higher harbor dues on vessels of another nationality frequenting any port in such "sphere" than shall be levied on vessels of its own nationality, and no higher railroad charges over lines built, controlled, or operated within its "sphere" on merchandise belonging to citizens or subjects of other nationalities transported through such "sphere" than shall be levied on similar merchandise belonging to its own nationals transported over equal distances.

The liberal policy pursued by His Imperial German Majesty in declaring Kiao-chao a free port and in aiding the Chinese Government in the establishment there of a custom-house are so clearly in line with the proposition which this Government is anxious to see recognized that it entertains the strongest hope that Germany will give its acceptance and hearty support.

The recent case of His Majesty the Emperor of Russia declaring the port of Talien-wan open during the whole of the lease under which it is held from China, to the merchant ships of all nations, coupled with the categorical assurances made to this Government by His Imperial Majesty's representative at this capital at the time, and since repeated to me by the present Russian ambassador, seem to insure the support of the Emperor to the proposed measure. Our ambassador at the Court of St. Petersburg has, in consequence, been instructed to submit it to the Russian Government and to request their early consideration of it. A copy of my instruction on the subject to Mr. Tower is herewith inclosed for your confidential information.

The commercial interests of Great Britain and Japan will be so clearly served by the desired declaration of intentions, and the views of the Governments of these countries as to the desirability of the adoption of measures insuring the benefits of equality of treatment of all foreign trade throughout China are so similar to those entertained by the United States, that their acceptance of the propositions herein outlined and their cooperation in advocating their adoption by the other powers can be confidently expected. I inclose herewith copy of the instruction which I have sent to Mr. Choate on the subject.

In view of the present favorable conditions, you are instructed to submit the above considerations to His Imperial German Majesty's minister for foreign affairs, and to request his early consideration of the subject.

Copy of this instruction is sent to our ambassadors at London and at St. Petersburg for their information.

FOURTH ANNUAL MESSAGE TO CONGRESS

Theodore Roosevelt   *December 6, 1904*

Theodore Roosevelt served two terms as president of the United States (1901–1909) and ran for a third. Roosevelt's dedication to furthering the United States' international role, especially in the Western Hemisphere, marked a departure from the isolationism of the nineteenth century. Roosevelt received a Nobel Peace Prize for his mediation of the Russo-Japanese War in 1905. His fourth annual message to Congress outlines his view of the responsibilities of the United States to keep its neighbors "stable, orderly, and prosperous." Roosevelt advocated United States military intervention and occupation when necessary to uphold the ideals of the Monroe Doctrine.

. . . IT is not true that the United States feels any land hunger or entertains any projects as regards the other nations of the Western Hemisphere save such as are for their welfare. All that this country desires is to see the neighboring countries stable, orderly, and prosperous. Any country whose people conduct themselves well can count upon our hearty friendship. If a nation shows that it knows how to act with reasonable efficiency and decency in social and political matters, if it keeps order and pays its obligations, it need fear no interference from the United States. Chronic wrongdoing, or an impotence which results in a general loosening of the ties of civilized society, may in America, as elsewhere, ultimately require intervention by some civilized nation, and in the Western Hemisphere the adherence of the United States to the Monroe Doctrine may force the United States, however reluctantly, in flagrant cases of such wrongdoing or impotence, to the exercise of an international police power. If every country washed by the Caribbean Sea would show the progress in stable and just civilization which with the aid of the Platt amendment Cuba has shown since our troops left the island, and which so many of the republics in both Americas are constantly and brilliantly showing, all question of interference by this Nation with their affairs would be at an end. Our interests and those of our southern neighbors are in reality identical. They have great natural riches, and if within their borders the reign of law and justice obtains, prosperity is sure to come to them. While they thus obey the primary laws of civilized society they may rest assured that they will be treated by us in a spirit of cordial and helpful sympathy. We would interfere with them only in the last resort, and then only if it became evident that their inability or unwillingness to do justice at home and abroad had violated the rights of the United States or had invited foreign aggression to the detriment of the entire body of American nations. It is a mere truism to say that every nation, whether in America or anywhere else, which desires to maintain its freedom, its independence, must ultimately realize that the right of such independence can not be separated from the responsibility of making good use of it.

In asserting the Monroe Doctrine, in taking such steps as we have taken in regard to Cuba, Venezuela, and Panama, and in endeavoring to circumscribe the theater of war in the Far East, and to secure the open door in China, we have acted in our own interest as well as in the interest of humanity at large. There are, however, cases in which, while our own interests are not greatly involved, strong appeal is made to our sympathies. . . . But in extreme cases action may be justifiable and proper. What form the action shall take must depend upon the circumstances of the case; that is, upon the degree of the atrocity and upon our power to remedy it. The cases in which we could interfere by force of arms as we interfered to put a stop to intolerable conditions in Cuba are necessarily very few.

SEVENTH ANNUAL MESSAGE TO CONGRESS

Theodore Roosevelt   *December 3, 1907*

Theodore Roosevelt brought the Progressive ideals of the need for government regulation with him to the White House; his efforts to control the growth of corporations earned him the nickname "Trust Buster." With his chief advisor on natural resources, Gifford Pinchot, Roosevelt implemented a program of conservation of public lands and resources for use, as opposed to preservation, and spearheaded government regulation of natural resources. In his seventh annual message to Congress, Roosevelt stated the necessity of federal government involvement to ensure the continued availability of the nation's wilderness lands and natural resources.

TO the Senate and House of Representatives:

. . . The conservation of our natural resources and their proper use constitute the fundamental problem which underlies almost every other problem of our national life. . . . As a nation we not only enjoy a wonderful measure of present prosperity but if this prosperity is used aright it is an earnest of future success such as no other nation will have. The reward of foresight for this nation is great and easily foretold. But there must be the look ahead, there must be a realization of the fact that to waste, to destroy, our natural resources, to skin and exhaust the land instead of using it so as to increase its usefulness, will result in undermining in the days of our children the very prosperity which we ought by right to hand down to them amplified and developed. For the last few years, through several agencies, the government has been endeavoring to get our people to look ahead and to substitute a planned and orderly development of our resources in place of a haphazard striving for immediate profit. Our great river systems should be developed as national water highways, the Mississippi, with its tributaries, standing first in importance, and the Columbia second, although there are many others of importance on the Pacific, the Atlantic, and the Gulf slopes. The National Government should undertake this work, and I hope a beginning will be made in the present Congress; and the greatest of all our rivers, the Mississippi, should receive special attention. From the Great Lakes to the mouth of the Mississippi there should be a deep waterway, with deep waterways leading from it to the East and the West. Such a waterway would practically mean the extension of our coastline into the very heart of our country. It would be of incalculable benefit to our people. If begun at once it can be carried through in time appreciably to relieve the congestion of our great freight-carrying lines of railroads. The work should be systematically and continuously carried forward in accordance with some well-conceived plan. The main streams should be improved to the highest point of efficiency before the improvement of the branches is attempted; and the work should be kept free from every taint of recklessness or jobbery. The inland waterways which lie just back of the whole

Theodore Roosevelt.

Eastern and Southern coasts should likewise be developed. Moreover, the development of our waterways involves many other important water problems, all of which should be considered as part of the same general scheme. The government dams should be used to produce hundreds of thousands of horse-power as an incident to improving navigation; for the annual value of the unused water-power of the United States perhaps exceeds the annual value of the products of all our mines. As an incident to creating the deep waterways down the Mississippi, the government should build along its whole lower length levees which, taken together with the control of the headwaters, will at once and forever put a complete stop to all threat of floods in the immensely fertile delta region. The territory lying adjacent to the Mississippi along its lower course will thereby become one of the most prosperous and populous, as it already is one of the most fertile, farming regions in all the world. I have appointed an inland waterways commission to study and outline a comprehensive scheme of development along all the lines indicated. Later I shall lay its report before the Congress.

Irrigation should be far more extensively developed than at present, not only in the States of the great plains and the Rocky Mountains, but in many others, as, for instance, in large portions of the South Atlantic and Gulf States, where it should go hand in hand with the reclamation of swampland. The Federal Government should seriously devote itself to this task, realizing that utilization of waterways and water-power, forestry, irrigation, and the reclamation of lands threatened with overflow, are all interdependent parts of the same problem. The work of the Reclamation Service in developing the larger opportunities of the Western half of our country for irrigation is more important than almost any other movement. The constant purpose of the government in connection with the Reclamation Service has been to use the water resources of the public lands for the ultimate greatest good of the greatest number; in other words, to put upon the land permanent home-makers, to use and develop it for themselves and for their children and children's children. . . .

The effort of the government to deal with the public land has been based upon the same principle as that of the Reclamation Service. The land law system which was designed to meet the needs of the fertile and well-watered regions of the Middle West has largely broken down when applied to the drier regions of the great plains, the mountains, and much of the Pacific slope, where a farm of 160 acres is inadequate for self-support. . . .

Some such legislation as that proposed is essential in order to preserve the great stretches of public grazing-land which are unfit for cultivation under present methods and are valuable only for the forage which they supply. These stretches amount in all to some 300,000,000 acres, and are open to the free grazing of cattle, sheep, horses, and goats, without restriction. Such a system, or lack of system, means that the range is not so much used as wasted by abuse. As the West settles, the range becomes more and more overgrazed. Much of it cannot be used to advantage unless it is fenced, for fencing is the only way by which to keep in check the owners of nomad flocks which roam hither and thither, utterly destroying the pastures and leaving a waste behind so that their presence is incompatible with the presence of home-makers. The existing fences are all illegal. . . . All these fences, those that are hurtful and those that are beneficial, are alike illegal and must come down. But it is outrage that the law should necessitate such action on the part of the Administration. The unlawful fencing of public lands for private grazing must be stopped, but the necessity which occasioned it must be provided for. The Federal Government should have control of the range, whether by permit or lease, as local necessities may determine. Such control could secure the great benefit of legitimate fencing, while at the same time securing and promoting the settlement of the country. . . . The government should part with its title only to the actual home-maker, not to the profit-maker who does not care to make a home. Our prime object is to secure the rights and guard the interests of the small ranchman, the man who ploughs and pitches hay for himself. It is this small ranchman, this actual settler and home-maker, who in the long run is most hurt by permitting thefts of the public land in whatever form.

Optimism is a good characteristic, but if carried to an excess it becomes foolishness. We are prone to speak of the resources of this country as inexhaustible; this is not so. The mineral wealth of the country, the coal, iron, oil, gas, and the like, does not reproduce itself, and therefore is certain to be exhausted ultimately; and wastefulness in dealing with it today means that our descendants will feel the exhaustion a generation or two before they otherwise would. But there are certain other forms of waste which could be entirely stopped—the waste of soil by washing, for instance, which is among the most dangerous of all wastes now in progress in the United States, is easily preventable, so that this present enormous loss of fertility is entirely unnecessary. The preservation or replacement of the forests is one of the most important means of preventing this loss. We have made a beginning in forest preservation, but . . . so rapid has been the rate of exhaustion of timber in the United States in the past, and so rapidly is the remainder being exhausted, that the country is unquestionably on the verge of a timber famine which will be felt in every household in the land. . . . The present annual consumption of lumber is certainly three times as great as the annual growth; and if the consumption and growth continue unchanged, practically all our lumber will be exhausted in another generation, while long before the limit to complete exhaustion is reached the growing scarcity will make itself felt in many blighting ways upon our national welfare. About twenty per cent of our forested territory is now reserved in national forests; but these do not include the most valuable timberlands, and in any event the proportion is too small to expect that the reserves can accomplish more than a mitigation of the trouble which is ahead for the nation. . . . We should acquire in the Appalachian and White Mountain regions all the forest-lands that it is possible to acquire for the use of the nation. These lands, because they form a national asset, are as emphatically national as the rivers which they feed, and which flow through so many States before they reach the ocean. . . .

DECLARATION OF THE
CONSERVATION CONFERENCE

U.S. Governors   *May 15, 1908*

---

*In response to President Theodore Roosevelt's 1907
address on the need for federal laws governing natural resources and national lands, a conference of United States state
and territorial governors met in 1908 to discuss the states' role*

in conservation. At this Conservation Conference, the governors issued a declaration on May 15, 1908, which called for judicious use of American lands to preserve their productivity as well as their beauty. The governors called for swift action by the United States Congress to conserve American water and land, and promised that the states themselves would also endeavor to protect the environment. In a moment of rare concert, all state and territorial governors signed the measure.

WE the Governors of the States and Territories of the United States of America, in Conference assembled, do hereby declare the conviction that the great prosperity of our country rests upon the abundant resources of the land chosen by our forefathers for their homes and where they laid the foundation of this great Nation.

We look upon these resources as a heritage to be made use of in establishing and promoting the comfort, prosperity, and happiness of the American People, but not to be wasted, deteriorated, or needlessly destroyed.

We agree that our country's future is involved in this; that the great natural resources supply the material basis on which our civilization must continue to depend, and on which the perpetuity of the Nation itself rests.

We agree, in the light of facts brought to our knowledge and from information received from sources which we can not doubt, that this material basis is threatened with exhaustion. Even as each succeeding generation from the birth of the Nation has performed its part in promoting the progress and development of the Republic, so do we in this generation recognize it as a high duty to perform our part; and this duty in large degrees lies in the adoption of measures for the conservation of the natural wealth of the country.

We declare our firm conviction that this conservation of our natural resources is a subject of transcendent importance, which should engage unremittingly the attention of the Nation, the States, and the People in earnest cooperation. These natural resources include the land on which we live and which yields our food; the living waters which fertilize the soil, supply power, and form great avenues of commerce; the forests which yield the materials for our homes, prevent erosion of the soil, and conserve the navigation and other uses of our streams; and the minerals which form the basis of our industrial life, and supply us with heat, light, and power.

We agree that the land should be so used that erosion and soil-wash shall cease; that there should be reclamation of arid and semi-arid regions by means of irrigation, and of swamp and overflowed regions by means of drainage; that the waters should be so conserved and used as to promote navigation, to enable the arid regions to be reclaimed by irrigation, and to develop power in the interests of the People; that the forests which regulate our rivers, support our industries, and promote the fertility and productiveness of the soil should be preserved and perpetuated; that the minerals found so abundantly beneath the surface should be so used as to prolong their utility; that the beauty, healthfulness, and habitability of our country should be preserved and increased; that the sources of national wealth exist for the benefit of the People, and that monopoly thereof should not be tolerated.

We commend the wise forethought of the President in sounding the note of warning as to the waste and exhaustion of the natural resources of the country, and signify our high appreciation of his action in calling this Conference to consider the same and to seek remedies therefor through cooperation of the Nation and the States.

We agree that this cooperation should find expression in suitable action by the Congress within the limits of and coextensive with the national jurisdiction of the subject, and, complementary thereto, by the legislatures of the several States within the limits of and coextensive with their jurisdiction.

We declare the conviction that in the use of the natural resources our independent States are interdependent and bound together by ties of mutual benefits, responsibilities and duties.

We agree in the wisdom of future conferences between the President, Members of Congress, and the Governors of States on the conservation of our natural resources with a view of continued cooperation and action on the lines suggested; and to this end we advise that from time to time, as in his judgment may seem wise, the President call the Governors of the States and Members of Congress and others into conference.

We agree that further action is advisable to ascertain the present condition of our natural resources and to promote the conservation of the same; and to that end we recommend the appointment by each State of a Commission on the Conservation of Natural Resources, to cooperate with each other and with any similar commission of the Federal Government.

We urge the continuation and extension of forest policies adapted to secure the husbanding and renewal of our diminishing timber supply, the prevention of soil erosion, the protection of headwaters, and the maintenance of the purity and navigability of our streams. We recognize that the private ownership of forest lands entails responsibilities in the interests of all the People, and we favor the enactment of laws looking to the protection and replacement of privately owned forests.

We recognize in our waters a most valuable asset of the People of the

United States, and we recommend the enactment of laws looking to the conservation of water resources for irrigation, water supply, power, and navigation, to the end that navigable and source streams may be brought under complete control and fully utilized for every purpose. We especially urge on the Federal Congress the immediate adoption of a wise, active, and thorough waterway policy, providing for the prompt improvement of our streams and the conservation of their watersheds required for the uses of commerce and the protection of the interests of our People.

We recommend the enactment of laws looking to the prevention of waste in the mining and extraction of coal, oil, gas, and other minerals with a view to their wise conservation for the use of the People, and to the protection of human life in the mines.

Let us conserve the foundations of our prosperity.

[SIGNATURES]

Amendment XVI
Income Tax Authorized

February 25, 1913

Proposed by Congress July 12, 1909, its ratification was completed February 25, 1913.

THE Congress shall have power to lay and collect taxes on incomes, from whatever source derived, without apportionment among the several States and without regard to any census or enumeration.

Amendment XVII
Direct Popular Election of Senators

May 31, 1913

Proposed by Congress May 16, 1912, its ratification was completed May 31, 1913.

THE Senate of the United States shall be composed of two senators from each State, elected by the people thereof, for six years; and each Senator shall have one vote. The electors in each State shall have the qualifications requisite for electors of the most numerous branch of the State legislature.

When vacancies happen in the representation of any State in the Senate, the executive authority of such State shall issue writs of election to fill such vacancies: Provided, That the legislature of any State may empower the executive thereof to make temporary appointments until the people fill the vacancies by election as the legislature may direct.

This amendment shall not be so construed as to affect the election or term of any senator chosen before it becomes valid as part of the Constitution.

VIII

TWO WARS AND A DEPRESSION

WOMEN AND WAR

Jane Addams   *May 1915*

Jane Addams was a Progressive reformer who championed the causes of peace, women's rights and social justice. In May 1915, Addams addressed the International Congress of Women at The Hague on the subject of "Women and War." Addams argued that women, by virtue of their innate devotion to the preservation of life and civilization, were the natural enemies of violence and warfare. From this congress, Addams and other women pacifists founded the Women's International League for Peace and Freedom (WILPF) in May 1919 in reaction against World War I. Addams served as the president of the WILPF from its founding to her death in 1935. Her address at The Hague served to crystallize women's opposition to war, and she became the standard bearer for the international peace movement. She shared the Nobel Peace Prize in 1931.

AT this last evening of the International Congress of Women, now drawing to its successful conclusion, its president wishes first to express her sincere admiration for the women who have come here from the belligerent nations. They have come from home at a moment when the national consciousness is so welling up from each heart and overflowing into the consciousness of others that the individual loses, not only all concern for his personal welfare, but for his convictions as well and gladly merges all he has into his country's existence.

It is a high and precious moment in human experience; war is too great a price to pay for it but it is worth almost anything else. I therefore venture to call the journey of these women, many of them heartsick and sorrowful, to this Congress, little short of an act of heroism. Even to appear to differ from those she loves in the hour of their affliction or exaltation, has ever been the supreme test of woman's conscience.

For the women coming from neutral nations there have also been supreme difficulties. In some of these countries, woman has a large measure of political responsibility and, in all of them, women for long months have been sensitive to the complicated political conditions which may also easily compromise a neutral nation and jeopardize the peace and safety of its people. At a Congress such as this, an exaggerated word may easily be spoken or reported as spoken which would make a difficult situation still more difficult; but these women have bravely taken that risk and made the moral venture. We from the United States, who have made the longest journey and are therefore freest from these entanglements, can speak out our admiration for these fine women from the neutral as well as from the fighting nations.

Why then were women from both the warring and the neutral nations ready to come to this Congress to the number of 1500? By what profound and spiritual forces were they impelled, at this moment when the spirit of Internationalism is apparently broken down, to believe that the solidarity of women would hold fast and that through them, as through a precious instrument, they would be able to declare the reality of those basic human experiences ever perpetuating and cherishing the race, and courageously to set them over against the superficial and hot impulses which have so often led to warfare.

Those great underlying forces, in response to which so many women have come here, belong to the human race as a whole and constitute a spiritual internationalism which surrounds and completes our national life, even as our national life itself surrounds and completes our family life; they do not conflict with patriotism on one side any more than family devotion conflicts with it upon the other.

We have come to this International Congress of women not only to protest from our hearts and with the utmost patience we can command, unaffrighted even by the "difficult and technical," to study this complicated modern world of ours now so sadly at war itself; but furthermore we would fain suggest ways by which this large internationalism may find itself and dig new channels through which it may flow.

At moments it appears as if the excessive nationalistic feeling expressing itself during these fateful months through the exaltation of warfare in so many of the great nations, is due to the accumulation within their own borders of those higher human affections which should have had an outlet into the larger life of the world but could not, because no international devices had been provided for such expression. No great central authority could deal with this sum of human will, as a scientist deals with the body of knowledge in his subject irrespective of its national origins, and the nations themselves became congested, as it were, and inevitably grew confused between what was legitimate patriotism and those universal emotions which have nothing to do with national frontiers.

We are happy that the Congress has met at The Hague. Thirty years ago I came to this beautiful city, full fifteen years before the plans for international organization had found expression here. If I can look back to such wonderful beginnings in my own lifetime, who shall say that the younger women on this platform may not see the completion of an international organization which shall make war impossible because good will and just dealing between nations shall have found an ordered method of expression?

We have many evidences at the present moment that, inchoate and unorganized as it is, it may be found even in the midst of this war constantly breaking through its national bounds. The very soldiers in the opposing trenches have to be moved about from time to time lest they come to know each other, not as the enemy but as individuals, and a sense of comradeship overwhelm their power to fight.

This totally unnecessary conflict between the great issues of internationalism and of patriotism rages all about us even in our own minds so that we wage a veritable civil war within ourselves. These two great affections should never have been set one against the other; it is too late in the day for war. For decades, the lives of all the peoples of the world have been revealed to us through the products of commerce, news agencies, through popular songs and novels, through photographers and cinematographs, and last of all through the interpretations of the poets and artists.

Suddenly all these wonderful agencies are applied to the hideous business of uncovering the details of warfare.

Never before has the world known so fearfully and so minutely what war means to the soldier himself, to women and children, to that civilization which is the common heritage of all mankind. All this intimate and realistic knowledge of war is recorded upon human hearts more highly sensitized than ever before in the history of man and filled with a new and avid hunger for brotherhood.

In the shadow of this intolerable knowledge, we, the women of this International Congress, have come together to make our solemn protest against that of which we know.

Our protest may be feeble but the world progresses, in the slow and halting manner in which it does progress, only in proportion to the moral energy exerted by the men and women living in it; social advance must be pushed forward by the human will and understanding united for conscious ends. The slow progress towards juster international relations may be traced to the distinguished jurist of the Netherlands, Grotius, whose honored grave is but a few miles from here; to the great German, Immanuel Kant, who lifted the subject of "Eternal Peace" high above even philosophical controversy; to Count Tolstoy, of Russia, who so trenchantly set forth in our own day, and so on from one country to another.

Each in his own time, because he placed law above force, was called a dreamer and a coward, but each did his utmost to express clearly the truth that was in him and beyond that human effort can not go.

These mighty names are but the outstanding witnesses among the host of men and women who have made their obscure contributions to the same great end.

Conscious of our own shortcomings and not without a sense of complicity in the present war, we women have met in earnestness and in sorrow to add what we may to this swelling tide of purpose.

It is possible that the appeal for the organization of the world upon peaceful lines has been made too exclusively to man's reason and sense of justice, quite as the eighteenth century enthusiasm for humanity was prematurely founded on intellectual sentiment. Reason is only a part of the human endowment; emotion and deep-set racial impulses must be utilized as well—those primitive human urgings to foster life and to protect the hopeless, of which women were the earliest custodians, and even the social and gregarious instincts that we share with the animals themselves. These universal desires must be given opportunities to expand and the most highly trained intellects must serve them rather than the technique of war and diplomacy.

They tell us that wounded lads lying in helpless pain and waiting too long for the field ambulance, call out constantly for their mothers, impotently beseeching them for help; during this Congress we have been told of soldiers who say to their hospital nurses, "We can do nothing for ourselves, but go back to the trenches again and again so long as we are able. Can not the women do something about this war? Are you kind to us only when we are wounded?"

The time may come when the exhausted survivors of the war may well reproach women for their inaction during this terrible time. It is possible they will then say that when devotion to the ideals of patriotism drove thousands of men into international warfare, the women refused to accept the challenge and in that moment of terror failed to assert clearly and courageously the sanctity of human life, the reality of things of the spirit.

For three days we have met together, so conscious of the bloodshed and desolation surrounding us, that all irrelevant and temporary matters fell away and we spoke solemnly to each other of the great and eternal issues, as do those who meet around the bedside of the dying.

We have formulated our message and given it to the world to heed when it will, confident that at last the great Court of International Opinion will pass righteous judgment upon all human affairs.

ADDRESS TO THE UNITED STATES SENATE

Woodrow Wilson   *January 22, 1917*

Woodrow Wilson was president of the United States from 1913 to 1921. As a Progressive, Wilson opposed America's entry into World War I, which he viewed as a primarily European conflict over colonial power. However, in February 1917, Germany renewed unrestricted submarine warfare and the British intercepted the "Zimmerman note," which promised Mexico the return of Texas and California in exchange for the formation of a German-Mexican alliance against the United States. These events polarized American public opinion against the Central Powers, and Wilson entered the war on the side of Britain and France. Wilson believed that United States involvement would make it possible for America to play a decisive role in the peace, in order to "make the world safe for democracy," and to ensure that World War I would be the "war to end all wars." To these ends, Wilson proposed a "peace without victory" in a 1917 address to the Senate of the United States.

GENTLEMEN of the Senate: . . .

. . . I have sought this opportunity to address you because I thought that I owed it to you, as the counsel associated with me in the final determination of our international obligations, to disclose to you without reserve the thought and purpose that have been taking form in my mind in regard to the duty of our Government in the days to come when it will be necessary to lay afresh and upon a new plan the foundations of peace among the nations.

It is inconceivable that the people of the United States should play no part in that great enterprise. . . . They cannot in honor withhold the service to which they are now about to be challenged. They do not wish to withhold it. But they owe it to themselves and to the other nations of the world to state the conditions under which they will feel free to render it.

That service is nothing less than this, to add their authority and their power to the authority and force of other nations to guarantee peace and justice throughout the world. Such a settlement cannot now be long postponed. It is right that before it comes this Government should frankly formulate the conditions upon which it would feel justified in asking our people to approve its formal and solemn adherence to a League for Peace. I am here to attempt to state those conditions.

The present war must first be ended; but we owe it to candor and to a just regard for the opinion of mankind to say that, so far as our participation in guarantees of future peace is concerned, it makes a great deal of difference in what way and upon what terms it is ended. The treaties and agreements which bring it to an end must embody terms which will create a peace that is worth guaranteeing and preserving, a peace that will win the approval of mankind, not merely a peace that will serve the several interests and immediate aims of the nations engaged. . . .

No covenant of co-operative peace that does not include the peoples of the New World can suffice to keep the future safe against war; and yet there is only one sort of peace that the peoples of America could join in guaranteeing. The elements of that peace must be elements that engage the confidence and satisfy the principles of the American governments, elements consistent with their political faith and with the practical convictions which the peoples of America have once for all embraced and undertaken to defend. . . .

It will be absolutely necessary that a force be created as a guarantor of the permanency of the settlement so much greater than the force of any nation now engaged or any alliance hitherto formed or projected that no nation, no probable combination of nations could face or withstand it. If the peace presently to be made is to endure, it must be a peace made secure by the organized major force of mankind.

The terms of the immediate peace agreed upon will determine whether it is a peace for which such a guarantee can be secured. The question upon which the whole future peace and policy of the world depends is this: Is the present war a struggle for a just and secure peace, or only for a new balance of power? If it be only a struggle for a new balance of power, who will guarantee, who can guarantee the stable equilibrium of the new arrangement? Only a tranquil Europe can be a stable Europe. There must be, not a balance of power, but a community of power; not organized rivalries, but an organized common peace.

Fortunately we have received very explicit assurances on this point. . . . I think it will be serviceable if I attempt to set forth what we understand them to be.

They imply, first of all, that it must be a peace without victory. It is not pleasant to say this. I beg that I may be permitted to put my own interpretation upon it and that it may be understood that no other interpretation was in my thought. I am seeking only to face realities and to face them without soft concealments. Victory would mean peace forced upon the loser, a victor's terms imposed upon the vanquished. It would be accepted in humiliation, under duress, at an intolerable sacrifice, and would leave a sting, a resentment, a bitter memory upon which terms of peace would rest, not permanently, but only as upon quicksand. Only a peace between equals can last. Only a peace the very principle of which is equality and a common participation in a common benefit. The right state of mind, the right feeling between nations, is as necessary for a lasting peace as is the just settlement of vexed questions of territory or of racial and national allegiance.

The equality of nations upon which peace must be founded if it is to last must be an equality of rights; the guarantees exchanged must neither recognize nor imply a difference between big nations and small, between those that are powerful and those that are weak. Right must be based upon the common strength, not upon the individual strength, of the nations upon whose concert peace will depend. Equality of territory or of resources there of course cannot be; nor any sort of equality not gained in the ordinary peaceful and legitimate development of the peoples themselves. But no one asks or expects anything more than an equality of rights. Mankind is looking now for freedom of life, not for equipoises of power.

And there is a deeper thing involved than even equality of right among organized nations. No peace can last, or ought to last, which does not recognize and accept the principle that governments derive all their just powers from the consent of the governed, and that no right anywhere exists to hand peoples about from sovereignty to sovereignty as if they were property. I take it for granted, for instance, if I may venture upon a single example, that statesmen everywhere are agreed that there should be a united, independent, and autonomous Poland, and that henceforth inviolable security of life, of worship, and of industrial and social development should be guaranteed to all peoples who have lived hitherto under the power of governments devoted to a faith and purpose hostile to their own. . . .

So far as practicable, moreover, every great people now struggling towards a full development of its resources and of its powers should be assured a direct outlet to the great highways of the sea. Where this cannot be done by the cession of territory, it can no doubt be done by the neutralization of direct rights of way under the general guarantee which will assure the peace itself. With a right comity of arrangement no nation need be shut away from free access to the open paths of the world's commerce.

And the paths of the sea must alike in law and in fact be free. The freedom of the seas is the *sine qua non* of peace, equality, and co-operation. No doubt a somewhat radical reconsideration of many of the rules of international practice hitherto thought to be established may be necessary in order to make the seas indeed free and common in practically all circumstances for the use of mankind, but the motive for such changes is convincing and compelling. There can be no trust or intimacy between the peoples of the world without them. The free, constant, unthreatened intercourse of nations is an essential part of the process of peace and of development. It need not be difficult either to define or to secure the freedom of the seas if the governments of the world sincerely desire to come to an agreement concerning it.

It is a problem closely connected with the limitation of naval armaments and the co-operation of the navies of the world in keeping the seas at once free and safe. And the question of limiting naval armaments opens the wider and perhaps more difficult question of the limitation of armies and of all programs of military preparation. Difficult and delicate as these questions are, they must be faced with the utmost candor and decided in a spirit of real accommodation if peace is to come with healing in its wings, and come to stay. Peace cannot be had without concession and sacrifice. There can be no sense of safety and equality among the nations if great preponderating armaments are henceforth to continue here and there to be built up and maintained. The statesmen of the world must plan for peace and nations must adjust and accommodate their policy to it as they have planned for war and made ready for pitiless contest and rivalry. The question of armaments, whether on land or sea, is the most immediately and intensely practical question connected with the future fortunes of nations and of mankind.

I have spoken upon these great matters without reserve and with the utmost explicitness because it has seemed to me to be necessary if the world's yearning desire for peace was anywhere to find free voice and utterance. Perhaps I am the only person in high authority amongst all the peoples of the world who is at liberty to speak and hold nothing back. I am speaking as an individual, and yet I am speaking also, of course, as the responsible head of a great government, and I feel confident that I have said what the people of the United States would wish me to say. . . .

I am proposing, as it were, that the nations should with one accord adopt the doctrine of President Monroe as the doctrine of the world: that no nation should seek to extend its polity over any other nation or people, but that every people should be left free to determine its own polity, its own way of development, unhindered, unthreatened, unafraid, the little along with the great and powerful.

I am proposing that all nations henceforth avoid entangling alliances which would draw them into competitions of power; catch them in a net of intrigue and selfish rivalry, and disturb their own affairs with influences intruded from without. There is no entangling alliance in a concert of power. When all unite to act in the same sense and with the same purpose all act in the common interest and are free to live their own lives under a common protection.

I am proposing government by the consent of the governed; that freedom of the seas which in international conference after conference representatives of the United States have urged with the eloquence of those who are the most convinced disciples of liberty; and that moderation of armaments which makes of armies and navies a power for order merely, not an instrument of aggression or of selfish violence.

These are American principles, American policies. We could stand for no others. And they are also the principles and policies of forward looking men and women everywhere, of every modern nation, of every enlightened community. They are the principles of mankind and must prevail.

THE FOURTEEN POINTS

Woodrow Wilson   *January 8, 1918*

President Woodrow Wilson presented his plan for the postwar world in the Fourteen Points that he wished to include in the Treaty of Versailles. Wilson argued for self-determination of liberated colonies, open diplomatic negotiations among all

*countries, and, most important, a League of Nations which
would enforce liberal ideals and protect the peace. Significantly,
several of Wilson's points were omitted from the Treaty of
Versailles. Georges Clemençeau, the French Premier, criticized
Wilson's Fourteen Points by saying, "Even God Almighty only
has ten." Wilson's idealism also went unappreciated at home.
Not only did the isolationist Senate refuse to allow the United
States to join the League of Nations, but it also denied ratification of the Treaty of Versailles, necessitating a separate
peace with Germany. Wilson's frantic drive to garner public
support for the treaty and the League ended when he suffered a
debilitating stroke in Pueblo, Colorado, in September 1919.*

GENTLEMEN of the Congress: . . . It will be our wish and purpose that
the processes of peace, when they are begun, shall be absolutely open and that
they shall involve and permit henceforth no secret understandings of any kind.
The day of conquest and aggrandizement is gone by; so is also the day of secret
covenants entered into in the interest of particular governments and likely at
some unlooked-for moment to upset the peace of the world. It is this happy fact,
now clear to the view of every public man whose thoughts do not still linger in
an age that is dead and gone, which makes it possible for every nation whose
purposes are consistent with justice and the peace of the world to avow now or
at any other time the objects it has in view.

We entered this war because violations of right had occurred which
touched us to the quick and made the life of our own people impossible unless
they were corrected and the world secured once for all against their recurrence.
What we demand in this war, therefore, is nothing peculiar to ourselves. It is that
the world be made fit and safe to live in; and particularly that it be made safe for
every peace-loving nation which, like our own, wishes to live its own life,
determine its own institutions, be assured of justice and fair dealing by the other
peoples of the world as against force and selfish aggression. All the peoples of
the world are in effect partners in this interest, and for our own part we see very
clearly that unless justice be done to others it will not be done to us. The program
of the world's peace, therefore, is our program; and that program, the only
possible program, as we see it, is this:

I. Open covenants of peace, openly arrived at, after which there shall be
no private international understandings of any kind but diplomacy shall proceed
always frankly and in the public view.

II. Absolute freedom of navigation upon the seas, outside territorial waters, alike in peace and in war, except as the seas may be closed in whole or in part by international action for the enforcement of international covenants.

III. The removal, so far as possible, of all economic barriers and the establishment of an equality of trade conditions among all the nations consenting to the peace and associating themselves for its maintenance.

IV. Adequate guarantees given and taken that national armaments will be reduced to the lowest point consistent with domestic safety.

V. A free, open-minded, and absolutely impartial adjustment of all colonial claims, based upon a strict observance of the principle that in determining all such questions of sovereignty the interests of the population concerned must have equal weight with the equitable claims of the government whose title is to be determined.

VI. The evacuation of all Russian territory and such a settlement of all questions affecting Russia as will secure the best and freest coöperation of the other nations of the world in obtaining for her an unhampered and unembarrassed opportunity for the independent determination of her own political development and national policy and assure her of a sincere welcome into the society of free nations under institutions of her own choosing; and, more than a welcome, assistance also of every kind that she may need and may herself desire. The treatment accorded Russia by her sister nations in the months to come will be the acid test of their good will, of their comprehension of her needs as distinguished from their own interests, and of their intelligent and unselfish sympathy.

VII. Belgium, the whole world will agree, must be evacuated and restored, without any attempt to limit the sovereignty which she enjoys in common with all other free nations. No other single act will serve as this will serve to restore confidence among the nations in the laws which they have themselves set and determined for the government of their relations with one another. Without this healing act the whole structure and validity of international law is forever impaired.

VIII. All French territory should be freed and the invaded portions restored, and the wrong done to France by Prussia in 1871 in the matter of Alsace-Lorraine, which has unsettled the peace of the world for nearly fifty years, should be righted, in order that peace may once more be made secure in the interest of all.

IX. A readjustment of the frontiers of Italy should be effected along clearly recognizable lines of nationality.

X. The peoples of Austria-Hungary, whose place among the nations we wish to see safeguarded and assured, should be accorded the freest opportunity of autonomous development.

XI. Rumania, Serbia, and Montenegro should be evacuated; occupied territories restored; Serbia accorded free and secure access to the sea; and the relations of the several Balkan states to one another determined by friendly counsel along historically established lines of allegiance and nationality; and international guaranties of the political and economic independence and territorial integrity of the several Balkan states should be entered into.

XII. The Turkish portions of the present Ottoman Empire should be assured a secure sovereignty, but the other nationalities which are now under Turkish rule should be assured an undoubted security of life and an absolutely unmolested opportunity of autonomous development, and the Dardanelles should be permanently opened as a free passage to the ships and commerce of all nations under international guaranties.

XIII. An independent Polish state should be erected which should include the territories inhabited by indisputably Polish populations, which should be assured a free and secure access to the sea, and whose political and economic independence and territorial integrity should be guaranteed by international covenant.

XIV. A general association of nations must be formed under specific covenants for the purpose of affording mutual guaranties of political independence and territorial integrity to great and small states alike.

In regard to these essential rectifications of wrong and assertions of right we feel ourselves to be intimate partners of all the governments and peoples associated together against the Imperialists. We cannot be separated in interest or divided in purpose. We stand together until the end.

For such arrangements and covenants we are willing to fight and to continue to fight until they are achieved; but only because we wish the right to prevail and desire a just and stable peace such as can be secured only by removing the chief provocations to war, which this program does not remove. We have no jealousy of German greatness, and there is nothing in this program that impairs it. We grudge her no achievement or distinction of learning or of pacific enterprise such as have made her record very bright and enviable. We do not wish to injure her or to block in any way her legitimate influence or power. We do not wish to fight her either with arms or with hostile arrangements of trade if she is willing to associate herself with us and the other peace-loving nations of the world in covenants of justice and law and fair dealing. We wish her only to accept a place of equality among the peoples of the world,—the new world in which we now live,—instead of a place of mastery.

Neither do we presume to suggest to her any alteration or modification of her institutions. But it is necessary, we must frankly say, and necessary as a preliminary to any intelligent dealings with her on our part, that we should know whom her spokesmen speak for when they speak to us, whether for the Reichstag majority or for the military party and the men whose creed is imperial domination.

We have spoken now, surely, in terms too concrete to admit of any further doubt or question. An evident principle runs through the whole program I have outlined. It is the principle of justice to all peoples and nationalities, and their right to live on equal terms of liberty and safety with one another, whether they be strong or weak. Unless this principle be made its foundation no part of the structure of international justice can stand. The people of the United States could act upon no other principle, and to the vindication of this principle they are ready to devote their lives, their honor, and everything that they possess. The moral climax of this the culminating and final war for human liberty has come, and they are ready to put their own strength, their own highest purpose, their own integrity and devotion to the test.

AMENDMENT XVIII
LIQUOR PROHIBITION

January 16, 1919

Proposed by Congress December 18, 1917, its ratification was completed January 16, 1919.

AFTER one year from the ratification of this article, the manufacture, sale or transportation of intoxicating liquors within, the importation thereof into, or the exportation thereof from the United States and all territory subject to the jurisdiction thereof for beverage purposes is hereby prohibited.

The Congress and the several States shall have concurrent power to enforce this article by appropriate legislation.

This article shall be inoperative unless it shall have been ratified as an amendment to the Constitution by the legislatures of the several States, as provided in the Constitution, within seven years from the date of the submission hereof to the States by Congress.

AMENDMENT XIX
NATIONAL WOMAN SUFFRAGE

August 26, 1920

Proposed by Congress June 4, 1919, this amendment's ratification was completed August 26, 1920. Women had won the right to vote in Wyoming in 1869 and in several other western states in the late nineteenth century. The long battle for women's right to vote nationally was finally won with the passage of the Nineteenth Amendment.

THE right of citizens of the United States to vote shall not be denied or abridged by the United States or by any States on account of sex.

The Congress shall have power by appropriate legislation to enforce the provisions of this article.

THE PHILOSOPHY OF
RUGGED INDIVIDUALISM

Herbert Hoover   *October 22, 1928*

In the course of his 1928 presidential campaign, Herbert Hoover appealed to the profound faith of most Americans in the American economy and way of life. Although a few intellectuals and farmers pointed out the precariousness of the United States economy, Americans generally saw a bright and prosperous future ahead. Hoover's definition of Liberalism appealed to this majority with the argument that government regulation could only hinder economic prosperity, and he won the election. Ironically, on October 24, 1929, one year and two days after

Hoover gave this speech in New York City, the Stock Market
Crash marked the onset of the Great Depression.

———————————

THIS campaign now draws near a close. The platforms of the two parties defining principles and offering solutions of various national problems have been presented and are being earnestly considered by our people. . . .

In my acceptance speech I endeavored to outline the spirit and ideals by which I would be guided in carrying that platform into administration. Tonight I will not deal with the multitude of issues which have been already well canvassed. I intend rather to discuss some of those more fundamental principles and ideals upon which I believe the government of the United States should be conducted. . . .

After the war, when the Republican party assumed administration of the country, we were faced with the problem of determination of the very nature of our national life. During one hundred and fifty years we have built up a form of self-government and a social system which is peculiarly our own. It differs essentially from all others in the world. It is the American system. It is just as definite and positive a political and social system as has ever been developed on earth. It is founded upon a particular conception of self-government in which decentralized local responsibility is the very base. Further than this, it is founded upon the conception that only through ordered liberty, freedom, and equal opportunity to the individual will his initiative and enterprise spur on the march of progress. And in our insistence upon equality of opportunity has our system advanced beyond all the world.

During the war we necessarily turned to the government to solve every difficult economic problem. The government having absorbed every energy of our people for war, there was no other solution. For the preservation of the state the Federal Government became a centralized despotism which undertook unprecedented responsibilities, assumed autocratic powers, and took over the business of citizens. To a large degree we regimented our whole people temporarily into a socialistic state. However justified in time of war if continued in peace-time it would destroy not only our American system but with it our progress and freedom as well.

When the war closed, the most vital of all issues both in our country and throughout the world was whether governments should continue their wartime ownership and operation of many instrumentalities of production and distribution. We were challenged with a peace-time choice between the American system of rugged individualism and a European philosophy of diametrically opposed doctrines—doctrines of paternalism and state socialism. The acceptance of these ideas would have meant the destruction of self-government through centralization of government. It would have meant the undermining of the individual initiative and enterprise through which our people have grown to unparalleled greatness. . . .

The Republican Party from the beginning resolutely turned its face away from these ideas and these war practices. . . . When the Republican Party came into full power it went at once resolutely back to our fundamental conception of the state and the rights and responsibilities of the individual. Thereby it restored confidence and hope in the American people, it freed and stimulated enterprise, it restored the government to its position as an umpire instead of a player in the economic game. For these reasons the American people have gone forward in progress while the rest of the world has halted, and some countries have even gone backwards. If anyone will study the causes of retarded recuperation in Europe, he will find much of it due to stifling of private initiative on one hand, and overloading of the government with business on the other.

There has been revived in this campaign, however, a series of proposals which, if adopted, would be a long step toward the abandonment of our American system and a surrender to the destructive operation of governmental conduct of commercial business. Because the country is faced with difficulty and doubt over certain national problems—that is prohibition, farm relief, and electrical power—our opponents propose that we must thrust government a long way into the businesses which give rise to these problems. In effect, they abandon the tenets of their own party and turn to state socialism as a solution for the difficulties presented by all three. It is proposed that we shall change from prohibition to the state purchase and sale of liquor. If their agricultural relief program means anything, it means that the government shall directly or indirectly buy and sell and fix prices of agricultural products. And we are to go into the hydroelectric power business. In other words, we are confronted with a huge program of government in business.

There is, therefore, submitted to the American people a question of fundamental principle. That is: shall we depart from the principles of our American political and economic system, upon which we have advanced beyond all the rest of the world, in order to adopt methods based on principles destructive of its very foundations? And I wish to emphasize the seriousness of these proposals. I wish to make my position clear; for this goes to the very roots of American life and progress.

I should like to state to you the effect that this projection of government in business would have upon our system of self-government and our economic system. That effect would reach to the daily life of every man and woman. It would impair the very basis of liberty and freedom not only for those left outside the fold of expanded bureaucracy but for those embraced within it.

Let us first see the effect upon self-government. When the Federal Government undertakes to go into commercial business it must at once set up the organization and administration of that business, and it immediately finds itself in a labyrinth, every alley of which leads to the destruction of self-government.

Commercial business requires a concentration of responsibility. Self-government requires decentralization and many checks and balances to safeguard liberty. Our Government to succeed in business would need to become in effect a despotism. There at once begins the destruction of self-government. . . .

It is a false liberalism that interprets itself into the government operation of commercial business. Every step of bureaucratizing of the business of our country poisons the very roots of liberalism—that is, political equality, free speech, free assembly, free press, and equality of opportunity. It is the road not to more liberty, but to less liberty. Liberalism should be found not striving to spread bureaucracy but striving to set bounds to it. True liberalism seeks all legitimate freedom first in the confident belief that without such freedom the pursuit of all other blessings and benefits is vain. That belief is the foundation of all American progress, political as well as economic.

Liberalism is a force truly of the spirit, a force proceeding from the deep realization that economic freedom cannot be sacrificed if political freedom is to be preserved. Even if Governmental conduct of business could give us more efficiency instead of less efficiency, the fundamental objection to it would remain unaltered and unabated. It would destroy political equality. It would increase rather than decrease abuse and corruption. It would stifle initiative and invention. It would undermine the development of leadership. It would cramp and cripple the mental and spiritual energies of our people. It would extinguish equality and opportunity. It would dry up the spirit of liberty and progress. For these reasons primarily it must be resisted. For a hundred and fifty years liberalism has found its true spirit in the American system, not in the European systems.

I do not wish to be misunderstood in this statement. I am defining a general policy. It does not mean that our government is to part with one iota of its national resources without complete protection to the public interest. I have already stated that where the government is engaged in public works for purposes of flood control, of navigation, of irrigation, of scientific research or national defense, or in pioneering a new art, it will at times necessarily produce power or commodities as a by-product. But they must be a by-product of the major purpose, not the major purpose itself.

Nor do I wish to be misinterpreted as believing that the United States is free-for-all and devil-take-the-hindmost. The very essence of equality of opportunity and of American individualism is that there shall be no domination by any group or combination in this republic, whether it be business or political. On the contrary, it demands economic justice as well as political and social justice. It is no system of *laissez faire*.

I feel deeply on this subject because during the war I had some practical experience with governmental operation and control. I have witnessed not only at home but abroad the many failures of government in business. I have seen its tyrannies, its injustices, its destructions of self-government, its undermining of the very instincts which carry our people forward to progress. I have witnessed the lack of advance, the lowered standards of living, the depressed spirits of people working under such a system. My objection is based not upon theory or upon a failure to recognize wrong or abuse, but I know the adoption of such methods would strike at the very roots of American life and would destroy the very basis of American progress.

Our people have the right to know whether we can continue to solve our great problems without abandonment of our American system. I know we can. . . .

And what have been the results of the American system? Our country has become the land of opportunity to those born without inheritance, not merely because of the wealth of its resources and industry but because of this freedom of initiative and enterprise. Russia has natural resources equal to ours. Her people are equally industrious, but she has not had the blessings of one hundred and fifty years of our form of government and our social system.

By adherence to the principles of decentralized self-government, ordered liberty, equal opportunity, and freedom to the individual, our American experiment in human welfare has yielded a degree of well-being unparalleled in all the world. It has come nearer to the abolition of poverty, to the abolition of fear of want, than humanity has ever reached before. Progress of the past seven years is the proof of it. This alone furnishes the answer to our opponents, who ask us to introduce destructive elements into the system by which this has been accomplished. . . .

I have endeavored to present to you that the greatness of America has grown out of a political and social system and a method of control of economic forces distinctly its own—our American system—which has carried this great experiment in human welfare farther than ever before in all history. We are nearer today to the ideal of the abolition of poverty and fear from the lives of men and women than ever before in any land. And I again repeat that the departure from our American system by injecting principles destructive to it which our opponents propose, will jeopardize the very liberty and freedom of our people, and will destroy equality of opportunity not alone to ourselves but to our children. . . .

AMENDMENT XX: BEGINNING OF PRESIDENTIAL TERMS, CONGRESSIONAL SESSIONS

January 23, 1933

Proposed by Congress March 2, 1932, its ratification was completed January 23, 1933.

SEC. 1. The terms of the President and Vice-President shall end at noon on the twentieth day of January, and the terms of Senators and Representatives at noon on the third day of January, of the years in which such terms would have ended if this article had not been ratified; and the terms of their successors shall then begin.

SEC. 2. The Congress shall assemble at least once in every year, and such meeting shall begin at noon on the third day of January, unless they shall by law appoint a different day.

SEC. 3. If, at the time fixed for the beginning of the term of the President, the President-elect shall have died, the Vice-President-elect shall become President. If a President shall not have been chosen before the time fixed for the beginning of his term, or if the President-elect shall have failed to qualify, then the Vice-President-elect shall act as President until a President shall have qualified; and the Congress may by law provide for the case wherein neither a President-elect nor a Vice-President-elect shall have qualified, declaring who shall then act as President, or the manner in which one who is to act shall be selected, and such person shall act accordingly until a President or Vice-President shall have qualified.

SEC. 4. The Congress may by law provide for the case of the death of any of the persons from whom the House of Representatives may choose a President whenever the right of choice shall have devolved upon them, and for the case of the death of any of the persons from whom the Senate may choose a Vice-President whenever the right of choice shall have devolved upon them.

SEC. 5. Sections 1 and 2 shall take effect on the 15th day of October following the ratification of this article.

SEC. 6. This article shall be inoperative unless it shall have been ratified as an amendment to the Constitution by the legislatures of three-fourths of the several States within seven years from the date of its submission.

FIRST INAUGURAL ADDRESS

Franklin Delano Roosevelt   *March 4, 1933*

———————

Franklin Delano Roosevelt was elected president of the United States for an unprecedented four terms (1933–1945) and saw the United States through the Great Depression and World War II. On the eve of his first inauguration in March 1933, the nation's banking system collapsed as millions of panicked depositors attempted to withdraw savings that banks had invested in long-term loans. Roosevelt spoke to this crisis in his inaugural address on March 4, 1933, telling Americans "the only thing we have to fear is fear itself." Soon Roosevelt closed American banks by proclamation and summoned a special session of Congress to pass emergency banking legislation. Roosevelt's response to the banking crisis marked the beginning of what was termed the "New Deal," an extensive series of social and economic programs aimed at economic recovery.

———————

PRESIDENT Hoover, Mr. Chief Justice, my friends:

This is a day of national consecration, and I am certain that my fellow-Americans expect that on my induction into the Presidency I will address them with a candor and a decision which the present situation of our nation impels.

This is pre-eminently the time to speak the truth, the whole truth, frankly and boldly. Nor need we shrink from honestly facing conditions in our country today. This great nation will endure as it has endured, will revive and will prosper.

So first of all let me assert my firm belief that the only thing we have to fear is fear itself—nameless, unreasoning, unjustified terror which paralyzes needed efforts to convert retreat into advance.

In every dark hour of our national life a leadership of frankness and vigor has met with that understanding and support of the people themselves which is essential to victory. I am convinced that you will again give that support to leadership in these critical days.

In such a spirit on my part and on yours we face our common difficulties. They concern, thank God, only material things. Values have shrunken to fantastic levels; taxes have risen; our ability to pay has fallen, government of all kinds is faced by serious curtailment of income; the means of exchange are frozen in the currents of trade; the withered leaves of industrial enterprise lie on every side; farmers find no markets for their produce; the savings of many years in thousands of families are gone.

More important, a host of unemployed citizens face the grim problem of existence, and an equally great number toil with little return. Only a foolish optimist can deny the dark realities of the moment.

Yet our distress comes from no failure of substance. We are stricken by no plague of locusts. Compared with the perils which our forefathers conquered because they believed and were not afraid, we have still much to be thankful for. Nature still offers her bounty and human efforts have multiplied it. Plenty is at our doorstep, but a generous use of it languishes in the very sight of the supply.

Primarily, this is because the rulers of the exchange of mankind's goods have failed through their own stubbornness and their own incompetence, have admitted their failure and abdicated. Practices of the unscrupulous money changers stand indicted in the court of public opinion, rejected by the hearts and minds of men.

True, they have tried, but their efforts have been cast in the pattern of an outworn tradition. Faced by failure of credit, they have proposed only the lending of more money.

Stripped of the lure of profit by which to induce our people to follow their false leadership, they have resorted to exhortations, pleading tearfully for restored confidence. They know only the rules of a generation of self-seekers.

They have no vision, and when there is no vision the people perish.

The money changers have fled from their high seats in the temple of our civilization. We may now restore that temple to the ancient truths.

The measure of the restoration lies in the extent to which we apply social values more noble than mere monetary profit.

Happiness lies not in the mere possession of money; it lies in the joy of achievement, in the thrill of creative effort.

The joy and moral stimulation of work no longer must be forgotten in the mad chase of evanescent profits. These dark days will be worth all they cost us if they teach us that our true destiny is not to be ministered unto but to minister to ourselves and to our fellow-men.

Recognition of the falsity of material wealth as the standard of success goes hand in hand with the abandonment of the false belief that public office and high political position are to be valued only by the standards of pride of place and personal profit; and there must be an end to a conduct in banking and in business which too often has given to a sacred trust the likeness of callous and selfish wrongdoing.

Small wonder that confidence languishes, for it thrives only on honesty, on honor, on the sacredness of obligations, on faithful protection, on unselfish performance. Without them it cannot live.

Restoration calls, however, not for changes in ethics alone. This nation asks for action, and action now.

Our greatest primary task is to put people to work. This is no unsolvable problem if we face it wisely and courageously.

It can be accomplished in part by direct recruiting by the government itself, treating the task as we would treat the emergency of a war, but at the same time, through this employment, accomplishing greatly needed projects to stimulate and reorganize the use of our natural resources.

Hand in hand with this, we must frankly recognize the overbalance of population in our industrial centers and, by engaging on a national scale in the redistribution, endeavor to provide a better use of the land for those best fitted for the land.

The task can be helped by definite efforts to raise the values of agricultural products and with this the power to purchase the output of our cities.

It can be helped by preventing realistically the tragedy of the growing loss, through foreclosure, of our small homes and our farms.

It can be helped by insistence that the Federal, State and local governments act forthwith on the demand that their cost be drastically reduced.

It can be helped by the unifying of relief activities which today are often scattered, uneconomical and unequal. It can be helped by national planning for and supervision of all forms of transportation and of communications and other utilities which have a definitely public character.

There are many ways in which it can be helped, but it can never be helped merely by talking about it. We must act, and act quickly.

Finally, in our progress toward a resumption of work we require two safeguards against a return of the evils of the old order; there must be a strict supervision of all banking and credits and investments; there must be an end to speculation with other people's money, and there must be provision for an adequate but sound currency.

These are the lines of attack. I shall presently urge upon a new Congress in special session detailed measures for their fulfillment, and I shall seek the immediate assistance of the several States.

Through this program of action we address ourselves to putting our own national house in order and making income balance outgo.

Our international trade relations, though vastly important, are, in point of time and necessity, secondary to the establishment of a sound national economy.

I favor as a practical policy the putting of first things first. I shall spare no effort to restore world trade by international economic readjustment, but the emergency at home cannot wait on that accomplishment.

The basic thought that guides these specific means of national recovery is not narrowly nationalistic.

It is the insistence, as a first consideration, upon the interdependence of the various elements in, and parts of, the United States—a recognition of the old and permanently important manifestation of the American spirit of the pioneer.

It is the way to recovery. It is the immediate way. It is the strongest assurance that the recovery will endure.

In the field of world policy I would dedicate this nation to the policy of the good neighbor—the neighbor who resolutely respects himself and, because he does so, respects the rights of others—the neighbor who respects his obligations and respects the sanctity of his agreements in and with a world of neighbors.

If I read the temper of our people correctly, we now realize as we have never before, our interdependence on each other; that we cannot merely take, but we must give as well; that if we are to go forward we must move as a trained and loyal army willing to sacrifice for the good of a common discipline, because, without such discipline, no progress is made, no leadership becomes effective.

We are, I know, ready and willing to submit our lives and property to such discipline because it makes possible a leadership which aims at a larger good.

This I propose to offer, pledging that the larger purposes will bind upon us all as a sacred obligation with a unity of duty hitherto evoked only in time of armed strife.

With this pledge taken, I assume unhesitatingly the leadership of this great army of our people, dedicated to a disciplined attack upon our common problems.

Action in this image and to this end is feasible under the form of government which we have inherited from our ancestors.

Our Constitution is so simple and practical that it is possible always to meet extraordinary needs by changes in emphasis and arrangement without loss of essential form.

That is why our constitutional system has proved itself the most superbly enduring political mechanism the modern world has produced. It has met every stress of vast expansion of territory, of foreign wars, of bitter internal strife, of world relations.

It is to be hoped that the normal balance of executive and legislative authority may be wholly adequate to meet the unprecedented task before us. But it may be that an unprecedented demand and need for undelayed action may call for temporary departure from that normal balance of public procedure.

I am prepared under my constitutional duty to recommend the measures that a stricken nation in the midst of a stricken world may require.

Franklin D. Roosevelt, portrait by Frank O. Salisbury.

These measures, or such other measures as the Congress may build out of its experience and wisdom, I shall seek, within my constitutional authority, to bring to speedy adoption.

But in the event that the Congress shall fail to take one of these two courses, and in the event that the national emergency is still critical, I shall not evade the clear course of duty that will then confront me.

I shall ask the Congress for the one remaining instrument to meet the crisis—broad executive power to wage a war against the emergency as great as the power that would be given me if we were in fact invaded by a foreign foe.

For the trust reposed in me I will return the courage and the devotion that befit the time. I can do no less.

We face the arduous days that lie before us in the warm courage of national unity; with the clear consciousness of seeking old and precious moral values; with the clean satisfaction that comes from the stern performance of duty by old and young alike.

We aim at the assurance of a rounded and permanent national life.

We do not distrust the future of essential democracy. The people of the United States have not failed. In their need they have registered a mandate that they want direct, vigorous action.

They have asked for discipline and direction under leadership. They have made me the present instrument of their wishes. In the spirit of the gift I take it.

In this dedication of a nation we humbly ask the blessing of God. May He protect each and every one of us! May He guide me in the days to come!

Amendment XXI
Repeal of Amendment XVIII

December 5, 1933

Proposed by Congress February 20, 1933, its ratification was completed December 5, 1933.

SEC. 1. The eighteenth article of amendment to the Constitution of the United States is hereby repealed.

SEC. 2. The transportation or importation into any State, Territory, or Possession of the United States for delivery or use therein of intoxicating liquors, in violation of the laws thereof, is hereby prohibited.

SEC. 3. This article shall be inoperative unless it shall have been ratified as an amendment to the Constitution by conventions in the several States, as provided in the Constitution, within seven years from the date of the submission hereof to the States by the Congress.

Four Freedoms Speech

Franklin Delano Roosevelt   *January 6, 1941*

As 1941 began, Nazi Germany controlled the European continent from the Arctic to the Pyrenees. From America it seemed that only Great Britain stood between Hitler and the United States. Still, the isolationism of Congress and the American public remained firm.

Franklin Roosevelt had been elected for his third term with promises to keep the United States out of the war in Europe. Despite this vow, he looked on events in Europe with great concern. On January 6, 1941, Roosevelt addressed a joint session of Congress to discuss the seriousness of the European

*situation and to draw attention to the need for Americans to
defend liberty.*

———————————

TO the Congress of the United States:

I address you, the Members of the Seventy-Seventh Congress, at a moment unprecedented in the history of the Union. I use the word "unprecedented," because at no previous time has American security been as seriously threatened from without as it is today. . . .

It is true that prior to 1914 the United States often had been disturbed by events in other Continents. We had even engaged in two wars with European nations and in a number of undeclared wars in the West Indies, in the Mediterranean and in the Pacific for the maintenance of American rights and for the principles of peaceful commerce. In no case, however, had a serious threat been raised against our national safety or our independence.

What I seek to convey is the historic truth that the United States as a nation has at all times maintained opposition to any attempt to lock us in behind an ancient Chinese wall while the procession of civilization went past. Today, thinking of our children and their children, we oppose enforced isolation for ourselves or for any part of the Americas.

Even when the World War broke out in 1914, it seemed to contain only small threat of danger to our own American future. But, as time went on, the American people began to visualize what the downfall of democratic nations might mean to our own democracy.

We need not over-emphasize imperfections in the Peace of Versailles. We need not harp on failure of the democracies to deal with problems of world deconstruction. We should remember that the Peace of 1919 was far less unjust than the kind of "pacification" which began even before Munich, and which is being carried on under the new order of tyranny that seeks to spread over every continent today. The American people have unalterably set their faces against that tyranny.

Every realist knows that the democratic way of life is at this moment being directly assailed in every part of the world—assailed either by arms, or by secret spreading of poisonous propaganda by those who seek to destroy unity and promote discord in nations still at peace. During sixteen months this assault has blotted out the whole pattern of democratic life in an appalling number of independent nations, great and small. The assailants are still on the march, threatening other nations, great and small.

Therefore, as your President, performing my constitutional duty to "give to the Congress information of the state of the Union," I find it necessary to report that the future and the safety of our country and of our democracy are overwhelmingly involved in events far beyond our borders.

Armed defense of democratic existence is now being gallantly waged in four continents. If that defense fails, all the population and all the resources of Europe, Asia, Africa and Australia will be dominated by the conquerors. The total of those populations and their resources greatly exceeds the sum total of the population and resources of the whole of the Western Hemisphere—many times over.

In times like these it is immature—and incidentally untrue—for anybody to brag that an unprepared America, single-handed, and with one hand tied behind its back, can hold off the whole world.

No realistic American can expect from a dictator's peace international generosity, or return of true independence, or world disarmament, or freedom of expression, or freedom of religion—or even good business. Such a peace would bring no security for us or for our neighbors. "Those, who would give up essential liberty to purchase a little temporary safety, deserve neither liberty nor safety." As a nation we may take pride in the fact that we are soft-hearted; but we cannot afford to be soft-hearted. We must always be wary of those who with sounding brass and a tinkling cymbal preach the "ism" of appeasement. We must especially beware of that small group of selfish men who would clip the wings of the American eagle in order to feather their own nests.

I have recently pointed out how quickly the tempo of modern warfare could bring into our very midst the physical attack which we must expect if the dictator nations win this war.

There is much loose talk of our immunity from immediate and direct invasion from across the seas. Obviously, as long as the British Navy retains its power, no such danger exists. Even if there were no British Navy, it is not probable that any enemy would be stupid enough to attack us by landing troops in the United States from across thousands of miles of ocean, until it had acquired strategic bases from which to operate. But we learn much from the lessons of the past years in Europe—particularly the lesson of Norway, whose essential seaports were captured by treachery and surprise built up over a series of years. The first phase of the invasion of this Hemisphere would not be the landing of regular troops. The necessary strategic points would be occupied by secret agents and their dupes—and great numbers of them are already here, and in Latin America.

As long as the aggressor nations maintain the offensive, they—not we—will choose the time and the place and the method of their attack. That is why the future of all American Republics is today in serious danger. That is why this Annual Message to the Congress is unique in our history. That is why every member of the Executive branch of the government and every member of the Congress face great responsibility—and great accountability.

The need of the moment is that our actions and our policy should be devoted primarily—almost exclusively—to meeting the foreign peril. For all our domestic problems are now a part of the great emergency. Just as our national policy in internal affairs has been based upon a decent respect for the rights and dignity of all our fellowmen within our gates, so our national policy in foreign affairs has been based on a decent respect for the rights and dignity of all nations, large and small. And the justice of morality must and will win in the end.

Our national policy is this.

First, by an impressive expression of the public will and without regard to partisanship, we are committed to all-inclusive national defense.

Second, by an impressive expression of the public will and without regard to partisanship, we are committed to full support of all those resolute peoples, everywhere, who are resisting aggression and are thereby keeping war away from our Hemisphere. By this support, we express our determination that the democratic cause shall prevail; and we strengthen the defense and security of our own nation.

Third, by an impressive expression of the public will and without regard to partisanship we are committed to the proposition that principles of morality and considerations for our own security will never permit us to acquiesce in a peace dictated by aggressors and sponsored by appeasers. We know that enduring peace cannot be bought at the cost of other people's freedom.

In the recent national election there was no substantial difference between the two great parties in respect to that national policy. No issue was fought out on this line before the American electorate. Today, it is abundantly evident that American citizens everywhere are demanding and supporting speedy and complete action in recognition of obvious danger. Therefore, the immediate need is a swift and driving increase in our armament production. . . .

Our most useful and immediate role is to act as an arsenal for them as well as for ourselves. They do not need man power. They do need billions of dollars worth of the weapons of defense. . . .

Let us say to the democracies: "We Americans are vitally concerned in your defense of freedom. We are putting forth our energies, our resources and our organizing powers to give you the strength to regain and maintain a free world. We shall send you, in ever-increasing numbers, ships, planes, tanks, guns. This is our purpose and our pledge." In fulfillment of this purpose we will not be intimidated by the threats of dictators that they will regard as a breach of international law and as an act of war our aid to the democracies which dare to resist their aggression. Such aid is not an act of war, even if a dictator should unilaterally proclaim it so to be. When the dictators are ready to make war upon us, they will not wait for an act of war on our part. They did not wait for Norway or Belgium or the Netherlands to commit an act of war. Their only interest is in a new one-way international law, which lacks mutuality in its observance, and, therefore, becomes an instrument of oppression.

The happiness of future generations of Americans may well depend upon how effective and how immediate we can make our aid felt. No one can tell the exact character of the emergency situations that we may be called upon to meet. The Nation's hands must not be tied when the Nation's life is in danger. We must all prepare to make the sacrifices that the emergency—as serious as war itself—demands. Whatever stands in the way of speed and efficiency in defense preparations must give way to the national need.

A free nation has the right to expect full cooperation from all groups. A free nation has the right to look to the leaders of business, of labor, and of agriculture to take the lead in stimulating effort, not among other groups but within their own groups. The best way of dealing with the few slackers and trouble makers in our midst is, first, to shame them by patriotic example, and, if that fails, to use the sovereignty of government to save government.

As men do not live by bread alone, they do not fight by armaments alone. Those who man our defenses, and those behind them who build our defenses, must have the stamina and courage which come from an unshakable belief in the manner of life which they are defending. The mighty action which we are calling for cannot be based on a disregard of all things worth fighting for.

The Nation takes great satisfaction and much strength from the things which have been done to make its people conscious of their individual stake in the preservation of democratic life in America. Those things have toughened the fibre of our people, have renewed their faith and strengthened their devotion to the institutions we make ready to protect. Certainly this is no time to stop thinking about the social and economic problems which are the root cause of the social revolution which is today a supreme factor in the world.

There is nothing mysterious about the foundations of a healthy and strong democracy. The basic things expected by our people of their political and economic systems are simple. They are: equality of opportunity for youth and for others; jobs for those who can work; security for those who need it; the ending of special privilege for the few; the preservation of civil liberties for all; the enjoyment of the fruits of scientific progress in a wider and constantly rising standard of living.

These are the simple and basic things that must never be lost sight of in the turmoil and unbelievable complexity of our modern world. The inner and abiding strength of our economic and political systems is dependent upon the degree to which they fulfill these expectations.

Many subjects connected with our social economy call for immediate improvement. As examples: We should bring more citizens under the coverage of old age pensions and unemployment insurance. We should widen the opportunities for adequate medical care. We should plan a better system by which persons deserving or needing gainful employment may obtain it.

I have called for personal sacrifice. I am assured of the willingness of almost all Americans to respond to that call. . . .

In the future days, which we seek to make secure, we look forward to a world founded upon four essential human freedoms.

The first is freedom of speech and expression—everywhere in the world.

The second is freedom of every person to worship God in his own way—everywhere in the world.

The third is freedom from want—which, translated into world terms, means economic understandings which will secure to every nation a healthy peace time life for its inhabitants—everywhere in the world.

The fourth is freedom from fear—which, translated into world terms, means a world-wide reduction of armaments to such a point and in such a thorough fashion that no nation will be in a position to commit an act of physical aggression against any neighbor—anywhere in the world.

That is no vision of a distant millenium. It is a definite basis for a kind of world attainable in our own time and generation. That kind of world is the very antithesis of the so-called new order of tyranny which the dictators seek to create with the crash of a bomb.

To that new order we oppose the greater conception—the moral order. A good society is able to face schemes of world domination and foreign revolutions alike without fear.

Since the beginning of our American history we have been engaged in change—in a perpetual peaceful revolution—a revolution which goes on steadily, quietly adjusting itself to changing conditions—without the concentration camp or the quick-lime in the ditch. The world order which we seek is the cooperation of free countries, working together in a friendly, civilized society.

This nation has placed its destiny in the hands and heads and hearts of its millions of free men and women; and its faith in freedom under the guidance of God. Freedom means the supremacy of human rights everywhere. Our support goes to those who struggle to gain those rights or keep them. Our strength is in our unity of purpose.

To that high concept there can be no end save victory.

THE ATLANTIC CHARTER

Franklin Delano Roosevelt   *August 14, 1941*
and Winston Churchill

> *In August 1941, President Roosevelt and British Prime Minister Winston Churchill met for four days off the coast of Newfoundland. At this meeting they discussed how the United States might support the British war effort and delineated war aims and the shape of the postwar world. Echoing Woodrow Wilson's Fourteen Points, the Atlantic Charter called for collective security, disarmament, self-determination, economic cooperation and freedom of the seas. It also provided the basis for the United Nations Organization, which was chartered in 1945.*

THE President of the United States of America and the Prime Minister, Mr. Churchill, representing His Majesty's Government in the United Kingdom, being met together, deem it right to make known certain common principles in the national policies of their respective countries on which they base their hopes for a better future for the world.

First, their countries seek no aggrandizement, territorial or other;

Second, they desire to see no territorial changes that do not accord with the freely expressed wishes of the peoples concerned;

Third, they respect the right of all peoples to choose the form of government under which they will live; and they wish to see sovereign rights and self government restored to those who have been forcibly deprived of them;

Fourth, they will endeavor, with due respect for their existing obligations, to further the enjoyment by all States, great or small, victor or vanquished, of access, on equal terms, to the trade and to the raw materials of the world which are needed for their economic prosperity;

Fifth, they desire to bring about the fullest collaboration between all nations in the economic field with the object of securing, for all, improved labor standards, economic advancement and social security;

Sixth, after the final destruction of the Nazi tyranny, they hope to see established a peace which will afford to all nations the means of dwelling in safety within their own boundaries, and which will afford assurance that all the men in all the lands may live out their lives in freedom from fear and want;

Seventh, such a peace should enable all men to traverse the high seas and oceans without hindrance;

Eighth, they believe that all of the nations of the world, for realistic as well as spiritual reasons must come to the abandonment of the use of force. Since no future peace can be maintained if land, sea or air armaments continue to be employed by nations which threaten, or may threaten, aggression outside of their frontiers, they believe, pending the establishment of a wider and permanent system of general security, that the disarmament of such nations is essential. They will likewise aid and encourage all other practicable measures which will lighten for peace-loving peoples the crushing burden of armaments.

Franklin D. Roosevelt
Winston S. Churchill

DECLARATION OF WAR

Franklin Delano Roosevelt   *December 8, 1941*

———————

By the fall of 1941 relations between the United States and Japan had strained to the breaking point. Protesting continued Japanese expansion in Asia as well as Japanese membership in the Rome–Berlin–Tokyo Axis, the United States froze Japanese assets in the United States and placed a trade embargo on oil shipments to Japan. America's refusal to lift the embargo convinced the Japanese government that war with the United States was inevitable. Fearing that they could not win a protracted war against the United States, the Japanese planned a massive attack on the Philippines and Hawaii to paralyze the American Pacific fleet. On the morning of December 7, 1941, Japanese planes attacked the unsuspecting American naval base at Pearl Harbor, killing more than 2,500 people, sinking several battleships and destroying aircraft.

The following day, President Franklin Delano Roosevelt captured the shock and grief of a nation in his address announcing the attack and asking for a declaration of war.

———————

YESTERDAY, December 7, 1941—a date which will live in infamy—the United States of America was suddenly and deliberately attacked by naval and air forces of the Empire of Japan.

The United States was at peace with that nation and, at the solicitation of Japan, was still in conversation with its Government and its Emperor looking toward the maintenance of peace in the Pacific. Indeed, one hour after Japanese air squadrons had commenced bombing in Oahu, the Japanese Ambassador to the United States and his colleague delivered to the Secretary of State a formal reply to a recent American message. While this reply stated that it seemed useless to continue the existing diplomatic negotiations, it contained no threat or hint of war or armed attack.

It will be recorded that the distance of Hawaii from Japan makes it obvious that the attack was deliberately planned many days or even weeks ago. During the intervening time the Japanese Government has deliberately sought to deceive the United States by false statements and expressions of hope for continued peace.

The attack yesterday on the Hawaiian Islands has caused severe damage to American naval and military forces. Very many American lives have been lost. In addition American ships have been reported torpedoed on the high seas between San Francisco and Honolulu.

Yesterday the Japanese Government also launched an attack against Malaya. Last night Japanese forces attacked Hong Kong. Last night Japanese forces attacked Guam. Last night Japanese forces attacked the Philippine Islands. Last night the Japanese attacked Wake Island. This morning the Japanese attacked Midway Island.

Japan has, therefore, undertaken a surprise offensive extending throughout the Pacific area. The facts of yesterday speak for themselves. The people of the United States have already formed their opinions and well understand the implications to the very life and safety of our nation.

As Commander-in-Chief of the Army and Navy, I have directed that all measures be taken for our defense.

Always will we remember the character of the onslaught against us.

No matter how long it may take us to overcome this premeditated invasion, the American people in their righteous might will win through to absolute victory.

I believe I interpret the will of the Congress and of the people when I assert that we will not only defend ourselves to the uttermost but will make very certain that this form of treachery shall never endanger us again.

Hostilities exist. There is no blinking at the fact that our people, our territory and our interests are in grave danger.

With confidence in our armed forces—with the unbonded determination of our people—we will gain the inevitable triumph—so help us God.

I ask that the Congress declare that since the unprovoked and dastardly attack by Japan on Sunday, December seventh, a state of war has existed between the United States and the Japanese Empire.

EXECUTIVE ORDER 9066

Franklin Delano Roosevelt   *February 19, 1942*

The shock of the Japanese attack on Pearl Harbor made deep impressions on the nation. It combined with the lack of American understanding of Japanese culture to encourage fear of all people of Japanese ancestry, and especially of those who had come to settle in the western United States. In February 1942, Japanese-Americans were stripped of their rights of citizenship and subjected to curfews, forced to abandon their property, and interned in relocation camps away from the West Coast.

Almost immediately Nisei (Japanese-Americans born in the United States) protested for their rights in the courts and attempted to prove their loyalty to America. In January 1943, Secretary of War Henry Stimson gave in to pressures from Nisei to form a Nisei fighting unit to serve in the European theater; from this came the 442nd Regimental Combat Team, the most decorated American unit in World War II, made up of Nisei volunteers and the federalized Hawaiian National Guard.

WHEREAS the successful prosecution of the war requires every possible protection against espionage and against sabotage to national-defense materials, national-defense premises, and national-defense utilities. . . .

Now, therefore, by virtue of the authority vested in me as President of the United States, and Commander in Chief of the Army and Navy, I hereby authorize and direct the Secretary of War, and the Military Commanders whom he may from time to time designate, whenever he or any designated Commander deems such action necessary or desirable, to prescribe military areas in such places and of such extent as he or the appropriate Military Commander may determine, from which any or all persons may be excluded, and with respect to which, the right of any person to enter, remain in, or leave shall be subject to whatever restrictions the Secretary of War or the appropriate Military Commander may impose in his discretion. The Secretary of War is hereby authorized to provide for residents of any such area who are excluded therefrom, such transportation, food, shelter, and other accommodations as may be necessary, in the judgment of the Secretary of War or the said Military Commander, and until other arrangements are made, to accomplish the purpose of this order. The designation of military areas in any region or locality shall supersede designations of prohibited and restricted areas by the Attorney General under the Proclamations of December 7 and 8, 1941, and shall supersede the responsibility and authority of the Attorney General under the said Proclamations in respect of such prohibited and restricted areas.

I hereby further authorize and direct the Secretary of War and the said Military Commanders to take such other steps as he or the appropriate Military Commander may deem advisable to enforce compliance with the restrictions applicable to each Military area hereinabove authorized to be designated, including the use of Federal troops and other Federal Agencies, with authority to accept assistance of state and local agencies.

I hereby further authorize and direct all Executive Departments, independent establishments and other Federal Agencies, to assist the Secretary of War or the said Military Commanders in carrying out this Executive Order, including the furnishing of medical aid, hospitalization, food, clothing, transportation, use of land, shelter, and other supplies, equipment, utilities, facilities, and services. . . .

Members of the Mochida Family awaiting evacuation bus in Hayward, California, 1942. From the records of the War Relocation Authority, photograph by Dorothea Lange.

Victory, uncontrollable exuberance displayed by men of Service Squadron 10 anchored in the western Pacific as news of Japan's willingness to surrender spread through the fleet, August 10, 1945. From the general records of the Department of the Navy, photographer unknown.

IX

THE UNITED STATES AND WORLD POWER

THE UNITED NATIONS CONFERENCE

Harry S. Truman   *June 26, 1945*

Vice President Harry S. Truman, who became president upon the death of Franklin Roosevelt, had come to prominence in the early 1940s as a senator from Missouri. After Roosevelt died unexpectedly in April 1945, Truman tried to carry on the policies of his predecessor as closely as possible in the first years of his own administration. Early in the war the Allies had discussed the formation of a new international organization. As early as the Atlantic Charter, Roosevelt and Churchill had delineated what the goals and functions of such a body should be. In 1943 at the Teheran Conference, Roosevelt had proposed an institution controlled by the "Four Policemen": the United States, Great Britain, the Soviet Union, and China. The following year at Dumbarton Oaks, representatives of the four countries approved a preliminary charter for what was then called the United Nations Organization. In April 1945 the United Nations Conference assembled in San Francisco, California, to approve a final charter. On June 26, President

Truman addressed this organization and pledged the support
promised by the late President Roosevelt.

———————————

MR. Chairman and Delegates to the United Nations Conference on International Organization:

I deeply regret that the press of circumstances when this Conference opened made it impossible for me to be here to greet you in person. I have asked for the privilege of coming today, to express on behalf of the people of the United States our thanks for what you have done here, and to wish you Godspeed on your journeys home.

Somewhere in this broad country, every one of you can find some of our citizens who are sons and daughters, or descendants in some degree of your own native land. All our people are glad and proud that this historic meeting and its accomplishments have taken place in our country. And that includes the millions of loyal and patriotic Americans who stem from the countries not represented at this Conference.

We are grateful to you for coming. We hope you have enjoyed your stay, and that you will come again.

You assembled in San Francisco nine weeks ago with the high hope and confidence of peace-loving people the world over.

Their confidence in you has been justified.

The Charter of the United Nations which you have just signed is a solid structure upon which we can build a better world. History will honor you for it. Between the victory in Europe and the final victory in Japan, in this most destructive of all wars, you have won a victory against war itself.

It was the hope of such a Charter that helped sustain the courage of stricken peoples through the darkest days of the war. For it is a declaration of great faith by the nations of the earth—faith that war is not inevitable, faith that peace can be maintained.

If we had had this Charter a few years ago—and above all, the will to use it—millions now dead would be alive. If we should falter in the future in our will to use it, millions now living will surely die.

It has already been said by many that this is only a first step to a lasting peace. That is true. The important thing is that all our thinking and all our actions be based on the realization that it is in fact only a first step. Let us all have it firmly in mind that we start today from a good beginning and, with our eye always on the final objective, let us march forward.

The Constitution of my own country came from a Convention which— like this one—was made up of delegates with many different views. Like this

Charter, our Constitution came from a free and sometimes bitter exchange of conflicting opinions. When it was adopted, no one regarded it as a perfect document. But it grew and developed and expanded. And upon it there was built a bigger, a better, a more perfect union.

This Charter, like our own Constitution, will be expanded and improved as time goes on. No one claims that it is now a final or a perfect instrument. It has not been poured into any fixed mold. Changing world conditions will require readjustments—but they will be the readjustments of peace and not of war.

That we now have this Charter at all is a great wonder. It is also a cause for profound thanksgiving to Almighty God, who has brought us so far in our search for peace through world organization.

There were many who doubted that agreement could ever be reached by these fifty countries differing so much in race and religion, in language and culture. But these differences were all forgotten in one unshakable unity of determination—to find a way to end wars. . . .

We have tested the principle of cooperation in this war and have found that it works. Through the pooling of resources, through joint and combined military command, through constant staff meetings, we have shown what united strength can do in war. That united strength forced Germany to surrender. United strength will force Japan to surrender.

The United Nations have also had experience, even while the fighting was still going on, in reaching economic agreements for times of peace. What was done on the subject of relief at Atlantic City, food at Hot Springs, finance at Bretton Woods, aviation at Chicago, was a fair test of what can be done by nations determined to live cooperatively in a world where they cannot live peacefully any other way.

What you have accomplished in San Francisco shows how well these lessons of military and economic cooperation have been learned. You have created a great instrument for peace and security and human progress in the world.

The world must now use it! . . .

There is a time for making plans—and there is a time for action. The time for action is now! Let us, therefore, each in his own nation and according to its own way, seek immediate approval of this Charter—and make it a living thing.

I shall send this Charter to the United States Senate at once. I am sure that the overwhelming sentiment of the people of my country and of their representatives in the Senate is in favor of immediate ratification.

A just and lasting peace cannot be attained by diplomatic agreement alone, or by military cooperation alone. Experience has shown how deeply the seeds of war are planted by economic rivalry and by social injustice. The Charter recognizes this fact for it has provided for economic and social cooperation as well. It has provided for this cooperation as part of the very heart of the entire compact.

It has set up machinery of international cooperation which men and nations of good will can use to help correct economic and social causes for conflict.

Harry S. Truman, portrait by Martha G. Kempton, 1947.

Artificial and uneconomic trade barriers should be removed—to the end that the standard of living of as many people as possible throughout the world may be raised. For Freedom from Want is one of the basic Four Freedoms toward which we all strive. The large and powerful nations of the world must assume leadership in this economic field as in all others.

Under this document we have good reason to expect the framing of an international bill of rights, acceptable to all the nations involved. That bill of rights will be as much a part of international life as our own Bill of Rights is a part of our Constitution. The Charter is dedicated to the achievement and observance of human rights and fundamental freedoms. Unless we can attain those objectives for all men and women everywhere—without regard to race, language or religion—we cannot have permanent peace and security.

With this Charter the world can begin to look forward to the time when all worthy human beings may be permitted to live decently as free people.

The world has learned again that nations, like individuals, must know the truth if they would be free—must read and hear the truth, learn and teach the truth.

We must set up an effective agency for constant and thorough interchange of thought and ideas. For there lies the road to a better and more tolerant understanding among nations and among peoples.

All Fascism did not die with Mussolini. Hitler is finished—but the seeds spread by his disordered mind have firm root in too many fanatical brains. It is easier to remove tyrants and destroy concentration camps than it is to kill the ideas which gave them birth and strength. Victory on the battlefield was essential, but it was not enough. For a good peace, a lasting peace, the decent peoples of the earth must remain determined to strike down the evil spirit which has hung over the world for the last decade. . . .

IRON CURTAIN SPEECH

Winston Churchill   *March 5, 1946*

After serving as Prime Minister through World War II, Churchill was replaced as British Prime Minister by Clement Atlee of the Labor Party in July 1945. President Truman invited Churchill to come to the United States and Churchill chose the small Westminister College in Fulton, Missouri, as his forum. Churchill titled his speech "The Sinews of Peace" and warned about the tyranny behind the iron curtain and the danger to the west of Soviet expansion. He introduced the concept of peace through strength. This concept, later articulated through the policy of "containment" and the idea of American and European unity, including NATO, dominated United States and western foreign policy for the next half century.

. . . LADIES and gentlemen, the United States stands at this time at the pinnacle of world power. It is a solemn moment for the American democracy. For with this primacy in power is also joined an awe-inspiring accountability to the future. As you look around you, you must feel not only the sense of duty done, but also you must feel anxiety lest you fall below the level of achievement. Opportunity is here now, clear and shining, for both our countries. To reject it or ignore it or fritter it away will bring upon us all the long reproaches of the aftertime.

It is necessary that constancy of mind, persistency of purpose, and the grand simplicity of decision shall rule and guide the conduct of the English-speaking peoples in peace as they did in war. We must—and I believe we shall—provide ourselves equal to this severe requirement. . . .

It is my duty, however—and I am sure you would not wish me not to state the facts as I see them to you—it is my duty to place before you certain facts about the present position in Europe.

From Stettin in the Baltic to Trieste in the Adriatic, an iron curtain has descended across the Continent. Behind that line lie all the capitals of the ancient states of Central and Eastern Europe. Warsaw, Berlin, Prague, Vienna, Budapest, Belgrade, Bucharest, and Sofia; all these famous cities and the populations around them lie in what I might call the Soviet sphere, and all are subject, in one form or another, not only to Soviet influence but to a very high and in some cases increasing measure of control from Moscow.

Police governments are pervading from Moscow. But Athens alone, with its immortal glories, is free to decide its future at an election under British, American, and French observation.

The Russian-dominated Polish government has been encouraged to make enormous and wrongful inroads upon Germany, and mass expulsions of millions of Germans on a scale grievous and undreamed-of are now taking place.

The Communist parties, which were very small in all these eastern states of Europe, have been raised to preeminence and power far beyond their numbers and are seeking everywhere to obtain totalitarian control. . . .

Twice in our own lifetime we have—the United States against her wishes and her traditions, against arguments the force of which it is impossible not to comprehend—twice we have seen them drawn by irresistible forces into these wars in time to secure the victory of the good cause, but only after frightful slaughter, and devastation have occurred.

Twice the United States has had to send several millions of its young men across the Atlantic to fight the wars. But now we all can find any nation, wherever it may dwell, between dusk and dawn. Surely we should work with conscious purpose for a grand pacification of Europe within the structure of the United Nations and in accordance with our Charter. . . .

If the population of the English-speaking Commonwealth be added to that of the United States, with all such cooperation implies in the air, on the sea, all over the globe, and in science and in industry, and in moral force, there will be no quivering, precarious balance of power to offer its temptation to ambition or adventure. On the contrary, there will be an overwhelming assurance of security.

If we adhere faithfully to the Charter of the United Nations and walk forward in sedate and sober strength, seeking no one's land or treasure, seeking to lay no arbitrary control upon the thoughts of men, if all British moral and material forces and convictions are joined with your own in fraternal association, the high roads of the future will be clear, no only for us but for all, not only for our time but for a century to come.

THE TRUMAN DOCTRINE

Harry S. Truman   *March 12, 1947*

Relations between the United States and the Soviet Union had begun to deteriorate in 1942 over the United States' delay in opening a second front in Europe. Conflicts over the disposition of Allied-conquered territories in Eastern Europe, and Germany especially, had led American policymakers to conclude that the Soviet Union was by nature expansionistic and that it would have to be contained.

As early as 1944 a civil war had raged in Greece between the sitting monarchist government, supported by Great Britain, and Communist rebels. President Truman saw in Greece his worst nightmare: a capitalist country threatened by what he believed to be a U.S.S.R.-sponsored Communist insurrection. In reality the Communist rebels in Greece were nationalists supported by the Yugoslavian leader, Marshal Tito, against Stalin's wishes. In 1947, in response to the spread of Soviet influence, Truman proclaimed a program of economic aid for Greece and any other nation threatened by Communist expansion or insurrection.

THE gravity of the situation which confronts the world today necessitates my appearance before a joint session of the Congress. The foreign policy and the national security of this country are involved.

One aspect of the present situation, which I wish to present to you at this time for your consideration and decision, concerns Greece and Turkey.

The United States has received from the Greek Government an urgent appeal for financial and economic assistance. Preliminary reports from the American Economic Mission now in Greece and reports from the American Ambassador in Greece corroborate the statement of the Greek Government that assistance is imperative if Greece is to survive as a free nation.

I do not believe that the American people and the Congress wish to turn a deaf ear to the appeal of the Greek Government.

The very existence of the Greek state is today threatened by the terrorist activities of several thousand armed men, led by Communists, who defy the

Government's authority at a number of points, particularly along the northern boundaries. A commission appointed by the United Nations Security Council is at present investigating disturbed conditions in Northern Greece and alleged border violations along the frontiers between Greece on the one hand and Albania, Bulgaria and Yugoslavia on the other.

Meanwhile, the Greek Government is unable to cope with the situation. The Greek Army is small and poorly equipped. It needs supplies and equipment if it is to restore the authority to the Government throughout Greek territory.

Greece must have assistance if it is to become a self-supporting and self-respecting democracy. The United States must supply this assistance. We have already extended to Greece certain types of relief and economic aid but these are inadequate. There is no other country to which democratic Greece can turn. No other nation is willing and able to provide the necessary support for a democratic Greek Government.

The British Government, which has been helping Greece, can give no further financial or economic aid after March 31. Great Britain finds itself under the necessity of reducing or liquidating its commitments in several parts of the world, including Greece.

We have considered how the United Nations might assist in this crisis. But the situation is an urgent one requiring immediate action, and the United Nations and its related organizations are not in a position to extend help of the kind that is required. . . .

Greece's neighbor, Turkey, also deserves our attention. The future of Turkey as an independent and economically sound state is clearly no less important to the freedom-loving peoples of the world than the future of Greece. The circumstances in which Turkey finds itself today are considerably different from those of Greece. Turkey has been spared the disasters that have beset Greece. And during the war, the United States and Great Britain furnished Turkey with material aid. Nevertheless, Turkey now needs our support.

Since the war Turkey has sought additional financial assistance from Great Britain and the United States for the purpose of effecting the modernization necessary for the maintenance of its national integrity. That integrity is essential to the preservation of order in the Middle East.

The British Government has informed us that, owing to its own difficulties, it can no longer extend financial or economic aid to Turkey. As in the case of Greece, if Turkey is to have the assistance it needs, the United States must supply it. We are the only country able to provide that help.

I am fully aware of the broad implications involved if the United States extends assistance to Greece and Turkey, and I shall discuss these implications with you at this time.

One of the primary objectives of the foreign policy of the United States is the creation of conditions in which we and other nations will be able to work out a way of life free from coercion. This was a fundamental issue in the war with Germany and Japan. Our victory was won over countries which sought to impose their will, and their way of life, upon other nations.

To ensure the peaceful development of nations, free from coercion, the United States has taken a leading part in establishing the United Nations. The United Nations is designed to make possible lasting freedom and independence for all its members. We shall not realize our objectives, however, unless we are willing to help free peoples to maintain their free institutions and their national integrity against aggressive movements that seek to impose on them totalitarian regimes. This is no more than a frank recognition that totalitarian regimes imposed on free peoples, by direct or indirect aggression, undermine the foundations of international peace and hence the security of the United States.

The peoples of a number of countries of the world have recently had totalitarian regimes forced upon them against their will. The Government of the United States had made frequent protests against coercion and intimidation, in violation of the Yalta Agreement, in Poland, Rumania and Bulgaria. I must also state that in a number of other countries there have been similar developments.

At the present moment in world history nearly every nation must choose between alternative ways of life. The choice is too often not a free one.

One way of life is based upon the will of the majority, and is distinguished by free institutions, representative government, free elections, guarantees of individual liberty, freedom of speech and religion, and freedom from political oppression.

The second way of life is based upon the will of the minority forcibly imposed upon the majority. It relies upon terror and oppression, a controlled press and radio, fixed elections, and the suppression of personal freedoms.

I believe that it must be the policy of the United States to support free peoples who are resisting attempted subjugation by armed minorities or by outside pressures.

I believe that we must assist free peoples to work out their own destinies in their own way.

I believe that our help should be primarily through economic and financial aid which is essential to economic stability and orderly political processes.

The world is not static, and the status quo is not sacred. But we cannot allow changes in the status quo in violation of the charter of the United Nations by such methods as coercion, or by such subterfuges as political infiltration. In helping free and independent nations to maintain their freedom, the United

States will be giving effect to the principles of the charter of the United Nations.

It is necessary only to glance at a map to realize that the survival and integrity of the Greek nation are of grave importance in a much wider situation. If Greece should fall under the control of an armed minority, the effect upon its neighbor, Turkey, would be immediate and serious. Confusion and disorder might well spread throughout the entire Middle East.

Moreover, the disappearance of Greece as an independent state would have a profound effect upon those countries in Europe whose peoples are struggling against great difficulties to maintain their freedoms and their independence while they repair the damages of war.

It would be an unspeakable tragedy if these countries, which have struggled so long against overwhelming odds, should lose that victory for which they sacrificed so much. Collapse of free institutions and loss of independence would be disastrous not only for them but for the world. Discouragement and possibly failure would quickly be the lot of neighboring peoples striving to maintain their freedom and independence.

Should we fail to aid Greece and Turkey in this fateful hour, the effect will be far-reaching to the west as well as to the east. We must take immediate and resolute action.

I therefore ask the Congress to provide authority for assistance to Greece and Turkey in the amount of $400,000,000 for the period ending June 30, 1948.

In addition to funds, I ask the Congress to authorize the detail of American civilian and military personnel to Greece and Turkey, at the request of those countries, to assist in the tasks of reconstruction, and for the purpose of supervising the use of such financial and material assistance as may be furnished. I recommend that authority also be provided for the instruction and training of selected Greek and Turkish personnel.

Finally, I ask that the Congress provide authority which will permit the speediest and most effective use, in terms of needed commodities, supplies, and equipment, of such funds as may be authorized. . . .

The seeds of totalitarian regimes are nurtured by misery and want. They spread and grow in the evil soil of poverty and strife. They reach their full growth when the hope of a people for a better life has died. We must keep that hope alive. The free peoples of the world look to us for support in maintaining their freedoms.

If we falter in our leadership, we may endanger the peace of the world— and we shall surely endanger the welfare of this nation.

Great responsibilities have been placed upon us by the swift movement of events. I am confident that the Congress will face these responsibilities squarely.

THE MARSHALL PLAN

George C. Marshall   *June 5, 1947*

George C. Marshall, who had been chief of the American staff during World War II, served as President Harry Truman's secretary of state from 1947 to 1949. Marshall realized that the economic devastation of the European continent after the war made governments there unstable and, Marshall believed, susceptible to overthrow or invasion by Communists.

In an address at Harvard University, Marshall announced the European Recovery Plan, or as it came to be called, the Marshall Plan. Marshall pledged United States economic and technical assistance to reconstruct the European economy. The Soviet Union and other Eastern European countries were also invited to take part, but they declined. Sixteen western European countries and West Germany formed the Organization of Economic Cooperation to coordinate the program, and from 1948 to 1952 the participating countries received over $12 billion in aid from the United States.

I need not tell you gentlemen that the world situation is very serious. That must be apparent to all intelligent people. I think one difficulty is that the problem is one of such enormous complexity that the very mass of facts presented to the public by press and radio make it exceedingly difficult for the man in the street to reach a clear appraisement of the situation. Futhermore, the people of this country are distant from the troubled areas of the earth and it is hard for them to comprehend the plight and consequent reactions of the long-suffering peoples, and the effect of those reactions on their governments in connection with our efforts to promote peace in the world.

In considering the requirements for the rehabilitation of Europe the physical loss of life, the visible destruction of cities, factories, mines, and railroads was correctly estimated, but it has become obvious during recent months that this visible destruction was probably less serious than the dislocation of the entire fabric of European economy. For the past ten years conditions have been highly abnormal. The feverish preparation for war and the more feverish maintenance of the war effort engulfed all aspects of national economies. Machinery has fallen into disrepair or is entirely obsolete. Under the arbitrary and destructive Nazi rule, virtually every possible enterprise was geared into the German war machine. Long-standing commercial ties, private institutions, banks, insurance companies and shipping companies disappeared, through loss of capital, absorption through nationalization or by simple destruction. In many countries, confidence in the local currency has been severely shaken. The breakdown of the business structure of Europe during the war was complete. Recovery has been seriously retarded by the fact that two years after the close of hostilities a peace settlement with Germany and Austria has not been agreed upon. But even given a more prompt solution of these difficult problems, the rehabilitation of the economic structure of Europe quite evidently will require a much longer time and greater effort than had been foreseen.

There is a phase of this matter which is both interesting and serious. The farmer has always produced the foodstuffs to exchange with the city dweller for the other necessities of life. This division of labor is the basis of modern civilization. At the present time it is threatened with breakdown. The town and city industries are not producing adequate goods to exchange with the food-producing farmer. Raw materials and fuel are in short supply. Machinery is lacking or worn out. The farmer or the peasant cannot find the goods for sale which he desires to purchase. So the sale of his farm produce for money which he cannot use seems to him an unprofitable transaction. He, therefore, has withdrawn many fields from crop cultivation and is using them for grazing. He feeds more grain to stock and finds for himself and his family an ample supply of food, however short he may be on clothing and the other ordinary gadgets of civilization. Meanwhile people in the cities are short of food and fuel. So the governments are forced to use their foreign money and credits to procure these necessities abroad. This process exhausts funds which are urgently needed for reconstruction. Thus a very serious situation is rapidly developing which bodes no good for the world. The modern system of the division of labor upon which the exchange of products is based is in danger of breaking down.

The truth of the matter is that Europe's requirements for the next three or four years of foreign food and other essential products—principally from America—are so much greater than her present ability to pay that she must have substantial additional help, or face economic, social, and political deterioration of a very grave character.

The remedy lies in breaking the vicious circle and restoring the confidence of the European people in the economic future of their own countries and of Europe as a whole. The manufacturer and the farmer throughout wide areas must be able and willing to exchange their products for currencies the continuing value of which is not open to question.

Aside from the demoralizing effect on the world at large and the possibilities of disturbances arising as a result of the desperation of the people concerned, the consequences to the economy of the United States should be apparent to all. It is logical that the United States should do whatever it is able to do to assist in the return of normal economic health in the world, without which there can be no political stability and no assured peace. Our policy is directed not against any country or doctrine but against hunger, poverty, desperation, and chaos. Its purpose should be the revival of a working economy in the world so as to permit the emergence of political and social conditions in which free institutions can exist. Such assistance, I am convinced, must not be on a piecemeal basis as various crises develop. Any assistance that this Government may render in the future should provide a cure rather than a mere palliative. Any government that is willing to assist in the task of recovery will find full cooperation, I am sure, on the part of the United States Government. Any government which maneuvers to block the recovery of other countries cannot expect help from us. Furthermore, governments, political parties, or groups which seek to perpetuate human misery in order to profit therefrom politically or otherwise will encounter the opposition of the United States.

It is already evident that, before the United States Government can proceed much further in its efforts to alleviate the situation and help start the European world on its way to recovery, there must be some agreement among the countries of Europe as to the requirements of the situation and the part those countries themselves will take in order to give proper effect to whatever action might be undertaken by this Government. It would be neither fitting nor efficacious for this Government to undertake to draw up unilaterally a program designed to place Europe on its feet economically. This is the business of the Europeans. The initiative, I think, must come from Europe. The role of this country should consist of friendly aid in the drafting of a European program and of later support of such a program so far as it may be practical for us to do so. The program should be a joint one, agreed to by a number, if not all European nations.

An essential part of any successful action on the part of the United States is an understanding on the part of the people of America of the character of the problem and the remedies to be applied. Political passion and prejudice should have no part. With foresight, and a willingness on the part of our people to face up to the vast responsibility which history has clearly placed upon our country, the difficulties I have outlined can and will be overcome.

INAUGURAL ADDRESS

Harry S. Truman   *January 19, 1949*

---

*President Harry Truman inherited his predecessor's deep
involvement in international affairs but was also very concerned with domestic matters. Truman's legacy includes the
Fair Deal as well as the desegregation of the armed forces in
1947. In foreign affairs Truman's outlook consisted mainly of
containing Soviet expansion and supporting those who opposed
the Soviet Union and rejected the Communist system. To these
ends the Truman administration presented a statement of
policy, titled NSC-68, a complete reorganization of the American defense system which formed the United States Air Force,
founded the National Security Council and created the Central
Intelligence Agency. Domestically, Truman strove to maintain
agreement on the importance of social programs in the tradition
of the New Deal. President Truman's inaugural address, given
on January 19, 1949, reflects these simultaneous concerns.*

. . . IN the coming years, our program for peace and freedom will
emphasize four major courses of action.

First, we will continue to give unfaltering support to the United Nations
and related agencies, and we will continue to search for ways to strengthen their
authority and increase their effectiveness. We believe that the United Nations will
be strengthened by the new nations which are being formed in lands now
advancing toward self-government under democratic principles.

Second, we will continue our programs for world economic recovery.

This means, first of all, that we must keep our full weight behind the
European Recovery Program. We are confident of the success of this major
venture in world recovery. We believe that our partners in this effort will achieve
the status of self-supporting nations once again.

In addition, we must carry out our plans for reducing the barriers to world
trade and increasing its volume. Economic recovery and peace itself depend on
increased world trade.

Third, we will strengthen freedom-loving nations against the dangers of
aggression.

We are now working out with a number of countries a joint agreement designed to strengthen the security of the North Atlantic area. Such an agreement would take the form of a collective defense arrangement within the terms of the United Nations Charter.

We have already established such a defense pact for the Western Hemisphere by the treaty of Rio de Janeiro.

The primary purpose of these agreements is to provide unmistakable proof of the joint determination of the free countries to resist armed attack from any quarter. Each country participating in these arrangements must contribute all it can to the common defense.

If we can make it sufficiently clear, in advance, that any armed attack affecting our national security would be met with overwhelming force, the armed attack might never occur.

I hope soon to send to the Senate a treaty respecting the North Atlantic security plan.

In addition, we will provide military advice and equipment to free nations which will cooperate with us in the maintenance of peace and security.

Fourth, we must embark on a bold new program for making the benefits of our scientific advances and industrial progress available for the improvement and growth of under-developed areas.

More than half the people of the world are living in conditions approaching misery. Their food is inadequate. They are victims of disease. Their economic life is primitive and stagnant. Their poverty is a handicap and a threat both to them and to more prosperous areas.

For the first time in history, humanity possesses the knowledge and the skill to relieve the suffering of these people.

The United States is pre-eminent among nations in the development of industrial and scientific techniques. The material resources which we can afford to use for the assistance of other peoples are limited. But our imponderable resources in technical knowledge are constantly growing and are inexhaustible.

I believe that we should make available to peace-loving peoples the benefits of our store of technical knowledge in order to help them realize their aspirations for a better life. And, in cooperation with other nations, we should foster capital investment in areas needing development.

Our aim should be to help the free peoples of the world, through their own efforts, to produce more food, more clothing, more materials for housing, and more mechanical power to lighten their burdens.

We invite other countries to pool their technological resources in this undertaking. Their contributions will be warmly welcomed. This should be a cooperative enterprise in which all nations work together through the United

Nations and its specialized agencies wherever practicable. It must be a world wide effort for the achievement of peace, plenty, and freedom.

With the cooperation of business, private capital, agriculture, and labor in this country, this program can greatly increase the industrial activity in other nations and can raise substantially their standards of living.

Such new economic developments must be devised and controlled to benefit the peoples of the areas in which they are established. Guarantees to the investor must be balanced by guarantees in the interest of the people whose resources and whose labor go into these developments.

The old imperialism—exploitation for foreign profit—has no place in our plans. What we envisage is a program of development based on the concepts of democratic fair-dealing.

All countries, including our own, will greatly benefit from a constructive program for the better use of the world's human and natural resources. Experience shows that our commerce with other countries expands as they progress industrially and economically.

Greater production is the key to prosperity and peace. And the key to greater production is a wider and more vigorous application of modern scientific and technical knowledge.

Only by helping the least fortunate of its members to help themselves can the human family achieve the decent, satisfying life that is the right of all people.

Democracy alone can supply the vitalizing force to stir the peoples of the world into triumphant action, not only against their human oppressors, but also against their ancient enemies—hunger, misery, and despair.

On the basis of these four major courses of action we hope to help create the conditions that will lead eventually to personal freedom and happiness for all mankind.

If we are to be successful in carrying out these policies, it is clear that we must have continued prosperity in this country and we must keep ourselves strong.

Slowly but surely we are weaving a world fabric of international security and growing prosperity.

We are aided by all who wish to live in freedom from fear—even by those who live today in fear under their own governments.

We are aided by all who want relief from the lies of propaganda—who desire truth and sincerity.

We are aided by all who desire self-government and a voice in deciding their own affairs.

We are aided by all who long for economic security—for the security and abundance that men in free societies can enjoy.

We are aided by all who desire freedom of speech, freedom of religion, and freedom to live their own lives for useful ends.

Our allies are the millions who hunger and thirst after righteousness.

In due time, as our stability becomes manifest, as more and more nations come to know the benefits of democracy and to participate in growing abundance, I believe that those countries which now oppose us will abandon their delusions and join with the free nations of the world in a just settlement of international differences.

Events have brought our American democracy to new influence and new responsibilities. They will test our courage, our devotion to duty, and our concept of liberty.

But I say to all men, what we have achieved in liberty, we will surpass in greater liberty.

Steadfast in our faith in the Almighty, we will advance toward a world where man's freedom is secure.

To that end we will devote our strength, our resources, and our firmness of resolve. With God's help, the future of mankind will be assured in a world of justice, harmony, and peace.

Amendment XXII
Limit Two Terms for President

February 27, 1951

Proposed by Congress March 24, 1947, its ratification was completed February 27, 1951.

SEC. 1. No person shall be elected to the office of the President more than twice, and no person who has held the office of President, or acted as President, for more than two years of a term to which some other person was elected President shall be elected to the office of the President more than once. But this Article shall not apply to any person holding the office of President when this Article was proposed by the Congress, and shall not prevent any person who may be holding the office of President, or acting as President, during the term within which this Article becomes operative from holding the office of President or acting as President during the remainder of such term.

Brown v. the Board of Education of Topeka, Kansas

Earl Warren   *1954*

Earl Warren, former governor of California, was appointed chief justice of the Supreme Court by President Dwight D. Eisenhower in 1953. Although Warren had a reputation as a staunch conservative, Warren's court handed down some of the most liberal decisions in the history of the court. Miranda v. Arizona, Gideon v. Wainwright, *and* Brown v. the Board of Education of Topeka *were the most famous of these. Warren resigned as chief justice in 1969 and was replaced by Warren Berger.*

The Brown case came before the Supreme Court in 1952 as a test case supported by the National Association for the Advancement of Colored People (NAACP). The Brown family and the NAACP challenged the 1896 Plessy v. Ferguson *decision, which held that separate but equal facilities for blacks and whites were constitutional.* Brown v. the Board of Education of Topeka *overturned the 1896 decision, and Warren, in this unanimous opinion, stated that separate but equal facilities in public education were inherently unequal. This decision marked a major victory for the American civil rights movement.*

APPEAL from the U.S. Dist. Court, District of Kansas.

Warren, C.J. These cases come to us from the States of Kansas, South Carolina, Virginia, and Delaware. They are premised on different facts and different local conditions, but a common legal question justifies their consideration together in this consolidated opinion.

In each of the cases, minors of the Negro race, through their legal representatives, seek the aid of the courts in obtaining admission to the public schools of their community on a nonsegregated basis. In each instance, they have been denied admission to schools attended by white children under laws requiring or permitting segregation according to race. This segregation was alleged to deprive the plaintiffs of the equal protection of the laws under the

Fourteenth Amendment. In each of the cases other than the Delaware case, a three-judge federal district court denied relief to the plaintiffs on the so-called "separate but equal" doctrine announced by this Court in *Plessy v. Ferguson*, 163 U.S. 537. Under that doctrine, equality of treatment is accorded when the races are provided substantially equal facilities, even though these facilities be separate. In the Delaware case, the Supreme Court of Delaware adhered to that doctrine, but ordered that the plaintiffs be admitted to the white schools because of their superiority to the Negro schools.

The plaintiffs contend that segregated public schools are not "equal" and cannot be made "equal," and that hence they are deprived of the equal protection of the laws. Because of the obvious importance of the question presented, the Court took jurisdiction. Argument was heard in the 1952 Term, and reargument was heard this Term on certain questions propounded by the Court.

Reargument was largely devoted to the circumstances surrounding the adoption of the Fourteenth Amendment in 1868. It covered exhaustively consideration of the Amendment in Congress, ratification by the states, then existing practices in racial segregation, and the views of proponents and opponents of the Amendment. This discussion and our own investigation convince us that, although these sources cast some light, it is not enough to resolve the problem with which we are faced. At best, they are inconclusive. The most avid proponents of the post-War Amendments undoubtedly intended them to remove all legal distinctions among "all persons born or naturalized in the United States." Their opponents, just as certainly, were antagonistic to both the letter and the spirit of the Amendments and wished them to have the most limited effect. What others in Congress and the state legislatures had in mind cannot be determined with any degree of certainty.

An additional reason for the inconclusive nature of the Amendment's history, with respect to segregated schools, is the status of public education at that time. In the South, the movement toward free common schools, supported by general taxation, had not yet taken hold. Education of white children was largely in the hands of private groups. Education of Negroes was almost nonexistent, and practically all of the race were illiterate. In fact, any education of Negroes was forbidden by law in some states. Today, in contrast, many Negroes have achieved outstanding success in the arts and sciences as well as in the business and professional world. It is true that public education had already advanced further in the North, but the effect of the Amendment on Northern States was generally ignored in the congressional debates. Even in the North, the conditions of public education did not approximate those existing today. The curriculum was usually rudimentary; ungraded schools were common in rural areas; the school term was but three months a year in many states; and compulsory school attendance was virtually unknown. As a consequence, it is not surprising that there should be so little in the history of the Fourteenth Amendment relating to its intended effect on public education.

In the first cases in this Court construing the Fourteenth Amendment, decided shortly after its adoption, the Court interpreted it as proscribing all state-imposed discriminations against the Negro race. The doctrine of "separate but equal" did not make its appearance in this Court until 1896 in the case of *Plessy v. Ferguson, supra,* involving not education but transportation. American courts have since labored with the doctrine for over half a century. In this Court, there have been six cases involving the "separate but equal" doctrine in the field of public education. . . .

In approaching this problem, we cannot turn the clock back to 1868 when the Amendment was adopted, or even to 1896 when *Plessy v. Ferguson* was written. We must consider public education in the light of its full development and its present place in American life throughout the Nation. Only in this way can it be determined if segregation in public schools deprives these plaintiffs of the equal protection of the laws.

Today, education is perhaps the most important function of state and local governments. Compulsory school attendance laws and the great expenditures for education both demonstrate our recognition of the importance of education to our democratic society. It is required in the performance of our most basic public responsibilities, even service in the armed forces. It is the very foundation of good citizenship. Today it is a principal instrument in awakening the child to cultural values, in preparing him for later professional training, and in helping him to adjust normally to his environment. In these days, it is doubtful that any child may reasonably be expected to succeed in life if he is denied the opportunity of an education. Such an opportunity, where the state has undertaken to provide it, is a right which must be made available to all on equal terms.

We come then to the question presented: Does segregation of children in public schools solely on the basis of race, even though the physical facilities and other "tangible" factors may be equal, deprive the children of the minority group of equal educational opportunities? We believe that it does.

In *Sweatt v. Painter, supra* [339 U.S. 629, 70 S.Ct. 850], in finding that a segregated law school for Negroes could not provide them equal educational opportunities, this Court relied in large part on "those qualities which are incapable of objective measurement but which make for greatness in a law school." In *McLaurin v. Oklahoma State Regents, supra* [339 U.S. 637, 70 S.Ct. 853], the Court, in requiring that a Negro admitted to a white graduate school be treated like all other students, again resorted to intangible considerations: ". . .

his ability to study, to engage in discussions and exchange views with other students, and, in general, to learn his profession." Such considerations apply with added force to children in grade and high schools. To separate them from others of similar age and qualifications solely because of their race generates a feeling of inferiority as to their state in the community that may affect their hearts and minds in a way unlikely ever to be undone. . . .

Whatever may have been the extent of psychological knowledge at the time of *Plessy v. Ferguson*, this finding is amply supported by modern authority. Any language in *Plessy v. Ferguson* contrary to this finding is rejected.

We conclude that in the field of public education the doctrine of "separate but equal" has no place. Separate educational facilities are inherently unequal. Therefore, we hold that the plaintiffs and others similarly situated for whom the actions have been brought are, by reason of the segregation complained of, deprived of the equal protection of the laws guaranteed by the Fourteenth Amendment. This deposition makes unnecessary any discussion whether such segregation also violates the Due Process Clause of the Fourteenth Amendment.

Because these are class actions, because of the wide applicability of this decision, and because of the great variety of local conditions, the formulation of decrees in these cases presents problems of considerable complexity. On reargument, the consideration of appropriate relief was necessarily subordinated to the primary question—the constitutionality of segregation in public education. We have now announced that such segregation is a denial of the equal protection of the laws. In order that we may have the full assistance of the parties in formulating decrees, the cases will be restored to the docket, and the parties are requested to present further argument. . . . The Attorney General of the United States is again invited to participate. The Attorneys General of the states requiring or permitting segregation in public education will also be permitted to appear as *amici curiae* upon request to do so by September 15, 1954, and submission of briefs by October 1, 1954.

It is so ordered.

FAREWELL ADDRESS

Dwight D. Eisenhower   *January 17, 1961*

---

*Dwight D. Eisenhower served as president from 1953 to
1961. During World War II, Eisenhower had been the Supreme
Commander of the Allied Expeditionary Force that landed at*

Normandy and swept through Europe in 1944 and 1945. As a result of his war experiences, Eisenhower repeatedly criticized American readiness to send United States troops abroad. His 1952 campaign stated that Eisenhower would go to Korea and bring home American soldiers involved in the war there. His farewell address, given January 17, 1961, indicates the level of Eisenhower's commitment to the prevention of serious aggression and "hot war" involving the United States. Eisenhower warned the American people against the "military-industrial complex," the conjunction of interests and the great potential influence wielded by a large military establishment together with a large arms industry.

MY fellow Americans:

Three days from now, after half a century in the service of our country, I shall lay down the responsibilities of office as, in traditional and solemn ceremony, the authority of the Presidency is vested in my successor. . . .

We now stand ten years past the midpoint of a century that has witnessed four major wars among great nations. Three of them involved our own country. Despite these holocausts America is today the strongest, the most influential and most productive nation in the world. Understandably proud of this pre-eminence we yet realize that America's leadership and prestige depend, not merely upon our unmatched material progress, riches and military strength, but on how we use our power in the interests of world peace and human betterment.

Throughout America's adventure in free government, our basic purposes have been to keep the peace; to foster progress in human achievement, and to enhance liberty, dignity and integrity among people and among nations. To strive for less would be unworthy of a free and religious people. Any failure traceable to arrogance, or our lack of comprehension or readiness to sacrifice would inflict upon us grievous hurt both at home and abroad.

Progress toward these noble goals is persistently threatened by the conflict now engulfing the world. It commands our whole attention, absorbs our very beings. We face a hostile ideology—global in scope, atheistic in character, ruthless in purpose, and insidious in method. Unhappily the danger it poses promises to be of indefinite duration. To meet it successfully, there is called for, not so much the emotional and transitory sacrifices of crisis, but rather those which enable us to carry forward steadily, surely, and without complaint the burdens of a prolonged and complex struggle—with liberty the stake. Only thus shall we remain, despite every provocation, on our charted course toward permanent peace and human betterment. . . .

A vital element in keeping the peace is our military establishment. Our arms must be mighty, ready for instant action, so that no potential aggressor may be tempted to risk his own destruction.

Our military organization today bears little relation to that known by any of my predecessors in peacetime, or indeed by the fighting men of World War II or Korea.

Until the latest of our world conflicts, the United States had no armaments industry. American makers of plowshares could, with time and as required, make swords as well. But now we can no longer risk emergency improvisation of national defense; we have been compelled to create a permanent armaments industry of vast proportions. Added to this, three and a half million men and women are directly engaged in the defense establishment. We annually spend on military security more than the net income of all United States corporations.

This conjunction of an immense military establishment and a large arms industry is new in the American experience. The total influence—economic, political, even spiritual—is felt in every city, every statehouse, every office of the federal government. We recognize the imperative need for this development. Yet we must not fail to comprehend its grave implications. Our toil, resources, and livelihood are all involved; so is the very structure of our society.

In the councils of government, we must guard against the acquisition of unwarranted influence, whether sought or unsought, by the military-industrial complex. The potential for the disastrous rise of misplaced power exists and will persist.

We must never let the weight of this combination endanger our liberties or democratic processes. We should take nothing for granted. Only an alert and knowledgeable citizenry can compel the proper meshing of the huge industrial and military machinery of defense with our peaceful methods and goals, so that security and liberty may prosper together.

Akin to, and largely responsible for the sweeping changes in our industrial-military posture, has been the technological revolution during recent decades.

In this revolution, research has become central; it also becomes more formalized, complex, and costly. A steadily increasing share is conducted for, by, or at the direction of, the federal government. . . .

The prospect of domination of the nation's scholars by federal employment, project allocations, and the power of money is ever present—and is gravely to be regarded.

Yet, in holding scientific research and discovery in respect, as we should, we must also be alert to the equal and opposite danger that public policy could itself become the captive of a scientific-technological elite.

It is the task of statesmanship to mold, to balance, and to integrate these and other forces, new and old, within the principles of our democratic system—ever aiming toward the supreme goals of our free society.

Another factor in maintaining balance involves the element of time. As we peer into society's future, we—you and I, and our government—must avoid

Dwight D. Eisenhower, portrait by J. Anthony Wills.

the impulse to live only for today, plundering, for our own ease and convenience, the precious resources of tomorrow. We cannot mortgage the material assets of our grandchildren without risking the loss also of their political and spiritual heritage. We want democracy to survive for all generations to come, not to become the insolvent phantom of tomorrow.

Down the long lane of the history yet to be written America knows that this world of ours, ever growing smaller, must avoid becoming a community of dreadful fear and hate, and be, instead, a proud confederation of mutual trust and respect.

Such a confederation must be one of equals. The weakest must come to the conference table with the same confidence as do we, protected as we are by our moral, economic, and military strength. That table, though scarred by many past frustrations, cannot be abandoned for the certain agony of the battlefield.

Disarmament, with mutual honor and confidence, is a continuing imperative. Together we must learn how to compose differences, not with arms, but with intellect and decent purpose. Because this need is so sharp and apparent I confess that I lay down my official responsibilities in this field with a definite sense of disappointment. As one who has witnessed the horror and the lingering sadness of war—as one who knows that another war could utterly destroy this civilization which has been so slowly and painfully built over thousands of years—I wish I could say tonight that a lasting peace is in sight.

Happily, I can say that war has been avoided. Steady progress toward our ultimate goal has been made. But, so much remains to be done. As a private citizen, I shall never cease to do what little I can to help the world advance along that road. . . .

INAUGURAL ADDRESS

John F. Kennedy   *January 20, 1961*

———————

*John Fitzgerald Kennedy served as president from 1961
to his assassination in 1963. Kennedy rose to political prominence as a senator from Massachusetts. In 1960 Kennedy ran
against the sitting vice president, Richard Nixon, and won with
the narrowest of margins on the strength of the great personal
charisma he showed in the presidential debates.*

*In his inaugural address on January 20, 1961, perhaps
one of the most famous in American history, Kennedy captured
the spirit of "the New Frontier." With great enthusiasm he
outlined both the rights and the responsibilities of American
citizenship in a troubled world. For many Americans, Kennedy's statement, "Ask not what your country can do for you—
ask what you can do for your country," embodied the idealism
of the early 1960s.*

———————

VICE President Johnson, Mr. Speaker, Mr. Chief Justice, President
Eisenhower, Vice President Nixon, President Truman, Reverend Clergy, Fellow
Citizens:

We observe today not a victory of party but a celebration of freedom—
symbolizing an end as well as a beginning—signifying renewal as well as change.
For I have sworn before you and Almighty God the same solemn oath our
forebears prescribed nearly a century and three-quarters ago.

The world is very different now. For man holds in his mortal hands the
power to abolish all forms of human poverty and all forms of human life. And
yet the same revolutionary beliefs for which our forebears fought are still at issue
around the globe—the belief that the rights of man come not from the generosity
of the state but from the hand of God.

We dare not forget today that we are the heirs of that first revolution. Let
the word go forth from this time and place, to friend and foe alike, that the torch
has been passed to a new generation of Americans—born in this century,
tempered by war, disciplined by a hard and bitter peace, proud of our ancient
heritage—and unwilling to witness or permit the slow undoing of those human
rights to which this nation has always been committed, and to which we are

committed today at home and around the world.

Let every nation know, whether it wishes us well or ill, that we shall pay any price, bear any burden, meet any hardship, support any friend, oppose any foe to assure the survival and the success of liberty.

This much we pledge—and more.

To those old allies whose cultural and spiritual origins we share, we pledge the loyalty of faithful friends. United, there is little we cannot do in a host of co-operative ventures. Divided, there is little we can do—for we dare not meet a powerful challenge at odds and split asunder.

To those new states whom we welcome to the ranks of the free, we pledge our word that one form of colonial control shall not have passed away merely to be replaced by a far more iron tyranny. We shall not always expect to find them supporting our view. But we shall always hope to find them strongly supporting their own freedom—and to remember that, in the past, those who foolishly sought power by riding the back of the tiger ended up inside.

To those people in the huts and villages of half the globe struggling to break the bonds of mass misery, we pledge our best efforts to help them help themselves, for whatever period is required—not because the Communists may be doing it, not because we seek their votes, but because it is right. If a free society cannot help the many who are poor, it cannot save the few who are rich.

To our sister republics south of our border, we offer a special pledge—to convert our good words into good deeds—in a new alliance for progress—to assist free men and free governments in casting off the chains of poverty. But this peaceful revolution of hope cannot become the prey of hostile powers. Let all our neighbors know that we shall join with them to oppose aggression or subversion anywhere in the Americas. And let every other power know that this hemisphere intends to remain the master of its own house.

To that world assembly of sovereign states, the United Nations, our last best hope in an age where the instruments of war have far outpaced the instruments of peace, we renew our pledge of support—to prevent it from becoming merely a forum for invective—to strengthen its shield of the new and the weak—and to enlarge the area in which its writ may run.

Finally, to those nations who would make themselves our adversary, we offer not a pledge but a request: that both sides begin anew the quest for peace, before the dark powers of destruction unleashed by science engulf all humanity in planned or accidental self-destruction.

We dare not tempt them with weakness. For only when our arms are sufficient beyond doubt can we be certain beyond doubt that they will never be employed.

But neither can two great and powerful groups of nations take comfort from our present course—both sides overburdened by the cost of modern weapons, both rightly alarmed by the steady spread of the deadly atom, yet both racing to alter that uncertain balance of terror that stays the hand of mankind's final war.

So let us begin anew—remembering on both sides that civility is not a sign of weakness, and sincerity is always subject to proof. Let us never negotiate out of fear. But let us never fear to negotiate.

Let both sides explore what problems unite us instead of belaboring those problems which divide us.

Let both sides, for the first time, formulate serious and precise proposals for the inspection and control of arms—and bring the absolute power to destroy other nations under the absolute control of all nations.

Let both sides seek to invoke the wonders of science instead of its terrors. Together let us explore the stars, conquer the deserts, eradicate diseases, tap the ocean depths, and encourage the arts and commerce.

Let both sides unite to heed in all corners of the earth the command of Isaiah—to "undo the heavy burdens . . . and let the oppressed go free."

And if a beachhead of co-operation may push back the jungle of suspicion, let both sides join in creating a new endeavor, not a new balance of power, but a new world of law, where the strong are just and the weak secure and the peace preserved.

All this will not be finished in the first one hundred days. Nor will it be finished in the first one thousand days, nor in the life of this administration, nor even perhaps in our lifetime on this planet. But let us begin.

In your hands, my fellow citizens, more than mine, will rest the final success or failure of our course. Since this country was founded, each generation of Americans has been summoned to give testimony to its national loyalty. The graves of young Americans who answered the call to service surround the globe.

Now the trumpet summons us again—not as a call to bear arms, though arms we need—not as a call to battle, though embattled we are—but a call to bear the burden of a long twilight struggle, year in and year out, "rejoicing in hope, patient in tribulation"—a struggle against the common enemies of man: tyranny, poverty, disease, and war itself.

Can we forge against these enemies a grand and global alliance, North and South, East and West, that can assure a more fruitful life for all mankind? Will you join in that historic effort?

In the long history of the world, only a few generations have been granted the role of defending freedom in its hour of maximum danger. I do not shrink from this responsibility—I welcome it. I do not believe that any of us would exchange places with any other people or any other generation. The energy, the faith, the devotion which we bring to this endeavor will light our country and all who serve it—and the glow from that fire can truly light the world.

And so, my fellow Americans: ask not what your country can do for you—ask what you can do for your country.

My fellow citizens of the world: ask not what America will do for you, but what together we can do for the freedom of man.

Finally, whether you are citizens of America or citizens of the world, ask of us here the same high standards of strength and sacrifice which we ask of you. With a good conscience our only sure reward, with history the final judge of our deeds, let us go forth to lead the land we love, asking His blessing and His help, but knowing that here on earth God's work must truly be our own.

AMENDMENT XXIII: PRESIDENTIAL VOTE FOR DISTRICT OF COLUMBIA

March 29, 1961

Proposed by Congress June 16, 1960, its ratification was completed March 29, 1961.

SEC. 1. The District constituting the seat of Government of the United States shall appoint in such manner as the Congress may direct:

A number of electors of President and Vice-President equal to the whole number of Senators and Representatives in Congress to which the District would be entitled if it were a State, but in no event more than the least populous State; they shall be in addition to those appointed by the States, but they shall be considered, for the purposes of the election of President and Vice-President, to be electors appointed by a State; and they shall meet in the District and perform such duties as provided by the twelfth article of amendment.

SEC. 2. The Congress shall have power to enforce this article by appropriate legislation.

DECLARATION OF INDIAN PURPOSE

June 1961

*In the 1960s the federal government proposed to deal
with problems of Indian poverty by a program of economic
development of the reservations. In many ways this plan simply
built upon John Collier's unrealized Indian New Deal of the
1930s.*

*In June 1961, over 450 Indian delegates representing
ninety tribes gathered at the University of Chicago to make
recommendations on the future of the Indian in America. In its
formal "Declaration of Indian Purpose," the gathering called for
ending the "so-called termination policy of the last administration," referring to the Eisenhower administration's policy of
abolishment of tribes and forced Indian assimilation.*

CREED

We believe in the inherent right of all people to retain spiritual and
cultural values, and that the free exercise of these values is necessary to the
normal development of any people. Indians exercised this inherent right to live
their own lives for thousands of years before the white man came and took their
lands. It is a more complex world in which Indians live today, but the Indian
people who first settled the New World and built the great civilizations which
only now are being dug out of the past, long ago demonstrated that they could
master complexity.

We believe that the history and development of America show that the
Indian has been subjected to duress, undue influence, unwarranted pressures,
and policies which have produced uncertainty, frustration, and despair. Only
when the public understands these conditions and is moved to take action
toward the formulation and adoption of sound and consistent policies and
programs will these destroying factors be removed and the Indian resume his
normal growth and make his maximum contribution to modern society.

We believe in the future of a greater America, an America which we were
first to love, where life, liberty, and the pursuit of happiness will be a reality. In
such a future, with Indians and all other Americans cooperating, a cultural climate

will be created in which the Indian people will grow and develop as members of a free society.

LEGISLATIVE AND REGULATORY PROPOSALS

In order that basic objectives may be restated and that action to accomplish these objectives may be continuous and may be pursued in a spirit of public dedication, it is proposed that recommendations be adopted to strengthen the principles of the Indian Reorganization Act and to accomplish other purposes. These recommendations would be comparable in scope and purpose to the Indian Trade and Intercourse Act of June 30, 1834, the Act of the same date establishing the Bureau of Indian Affairs, and the Indian Reorganization Act of June 18, 1934, which recognized the inherent powers of Indian Tribes.

The recommendations we propose would redefine the responsibilities of the United States toward the Indian people in terms of a positive national obligation to modify or remove the conditions which produce the poverty and lack of social adjustment as these prevail as the outstanding attributes of Indian life today. . . .

The basic principle involves the desire on the part of Indians to participate in developing their own programs with help and guidance as needed and requested, from a local decentralized technical and administrative staff, preferably located conveniently to the people it serves. Also in recent years certain technical and professional people of Indian descent are becoming better qualified and available to work with and for their own people in determining their own programs and needs. The Indians as responsible individual citizens, as responsible tribal representatives, and as responsible Tribal Councils want to participate, want to contribute to their own personal and tribal improvements and want to cooperate with their Government on how best to solve the many problems in a business-like, efficient and economical manner as rapidly as possible. . . .

CONCLUDING STATEMENT

To complete our Declaration, we point out that in the beginning the people of the New World, called Indians by accident of geography, were possessed of a continent and a way of life. In the course of many years, our people had adjusted to every climate and condition from the Arctic to the torrid zones. In their livelihood and family relationships, their ceremonial observances, they reflected the diversity of the physical world they occupied.

The conditions in which Indians live today reflect a world in which every basic aspect of life has been transformed. Even the physical world is no longer the controlling factor in determining where and under what conditions men may live. In region after region, Indian groups found their means of existence either totally destroyed or materially modified. Newly introduced diseases swept away or reduced regional populations. These changes were followed by major shifts in the internal life of tribe and family.

The time came when the Indian people were no longer the masters of their situation. Their life ways survived subject to the will of a dominant sovereign power. This is said, not in a spirit of complaint; we understand that in the lives of all nations of people, there are times of plenty and times of famine. But we do speak out in a plea for understanding.

When we go before the American people, as we do in this Declaration, and ask for material assistance in developing our resources and developing our opportunities, we pose a moral problem which cannot be left unanswered. For the problem we raise affects the standing which our nation sustains before world opinion.

Our situation cannot be relieved by appropriated funds alone, though it is equally obvious that without capital investment and funded services, solutions will be delayed. Nor will the passage of time lessen the complexities which beset a people moving toward new meaning and purpose.

The answers we seek are not commodities to be purchased, neither are they evolved automatically through the passing of time.

The effort to place social adjustment on a money-time interval scale which has characterized Indian administration, has resulted in unwanted pressure and frustration.

When Indians speak of the continent they yielded, they are not referring only to the loss of some millions of acres in real estate. They have in mind that the land supported a universe of things they knew, valued, and loved.

With that continent gone, except for the few poor parcels they still retain, the basis of life is precariously held, but they mean to hold the scraps and parcels as earnestly as any small nation or ethnic group was ever determined to hold to identity and survival.

What we ask of America is not charity, not paternalism, even when benevolent. We ask only that the nature of our situation be recognized and made the basis of policy and action.

In short, the Indians ask for assistance, technical and financial, for the time needed, however long that may be, to regain in the America of the space age some measure of the adjustment they enjoyed as the original possessors of their native land.

SILENT SPRING

Rachel Carson   *1962*

---

*Perhaps the most important book of the last half of the
20th century is marine and genetic biologist Rachel Carson's*
Silent Spring. *Its influence matches that of* Walden, *more than a
century earlier. At Thoreau's time, an educated individual was
expected to understand science, but for most of this century,
Americans have had a tendency to leave science to scientists.
After all, American science helped to win the war and later
brought health and prosperity to most Americans. But Carson
pointed out that we are all part of the planet, sharing it with
other beings, and that we had to understand the results of our
conduct, including our scientific actions.*

With the publishing of Silent Spring, *the concepts of
environmentalism, ecology and the general issue of being
responsible for this planet moved to the forefront of national
discussion. Legislative actions include the Clean Water Act
(1965), the Clean Air Act (1972), the Wilderness Act (1964), the
Rare and Endangered Species Act (1966), the Toxic Substance
Control Act (1976), the 1985 Farm Act and the development of
the Environmental Protection Agency (EPA). Equally important,
citizens and government leaders alike believed that they should
have a voice in many issues previously discussed only by
scientists and other experts. These include nuclear power plants,
hazardous waste, asbestos, lead, tobacco products, nuclear
waste storage, weapons testing, oil exploration and off-shore
drilling.*

. . . THROUGH all these new, imaginative, and creative approaches to the
problem of sharing our earth with other creatures there runs a constant theme,
the awareness that we are dealing with life—with living populations and all their
pressures and counter-pressures, their surges and recessions. Only by taking
account of such life forces and by cautiously seeking to guide them into channels
favorable to ourselves can we hope to achieve a reasonable accommodation
between the insect hordes and ourselves.

The current vogue for poisons has failed utterly to take into account these most fundamental considerations. As crude a weapon as the cave man's club, the chemical barrage has been hurled against the fabric of life—a fabric on the one hand delicate and destructible, on the other miraculously tough and resilient, and capable of striking back in unexpected ways. These extraordinary capacities of life have been ignored by the practitioners of chemical control who have brought to their task no "high-minded orientation," no humility before the vast forces with which they tamper.

The "control of nature" is a phrase conceived in arrogance, born of the Neanderthal age of biology and philosophy, when it was supposed that nature exists for the convenience of man. The concepts and practices of applied entomology for the most part date from that Stone Age of science. It is our alarming misfortune that so primitive a science has armed itself with the most modern and terrible weapons, and that in turning them against the insects it has also turned them against the earth.

ICH BIN EIN BERLINER

John F. Kennedy   *June 26, 1963*

> *On August 13, 1961, more than seventeen years after Winston Churchill talked of the formation of an ideological barrier in Eastern Europe, the East Germans began the construction of a wall through the city of Berlin to restrict the flood of refugees from east to west, which had reached 200,000 in the prior year. Families were separated as the "iron curtain" became a physical reality, an act that further heightened United States–Soviet tensions. In June 1963, President Kennedy stood in the shadow of the wall and gave the following speech. Almost three decades later, in December 1989, the wall came down and the two Germanys were reunited.*

I am proud to come to this city as the guest of your distinguished mayor, who has symbolized throughout the world the fighting spirit of West Berlin. And I am proud to visit the Federal Republic with your distinguished chancellor, who for so many years has committed Germany to democracy and freedom and progress, and to come here in the company of my fellow American General Clay, who has been in this city during its great moments of crisis and will come again if ever needed.

Two thousand years ago the proudest boast was *Civis Romanus sum.* Today, in the world of freedom, the proudest boast is *Ich bin ein Berliner.*

There are many people in the world who really don't understand, or say they don't, what is the great issue between the free world and the Communist world. Let them come to Berlin. There are some who say that communism is the wave of the future. Let them come to Berlin. And there are some who say in Europe and elsewhere we can work with the Communists. Let them come to Berlin. And there are even a few who say that it is true that communism is an evil system, but it permits us to make economic progress. *Lass' sie nach Berlin kommen.* Let them come to Berlin.

Freedom has many difficulties and democracy is not perfect, but we have never had to put a wall up to keep our people in, to prevent them from leaving us. I want to say, on behalf of my countrymen, who live many miles away on the other side of the Atlantic, who are far distant from you, that they take the greatest pride that they have been able to share with you, even from a distance, the story of the last eighteen years. I know of no town, no city, that has been besieged for eighteen years that still lives with the vitality and the force, and the hope and the determination of the city of West Berlin. While the wall is the most obvious and vivid demonstration of the failures of the Communist system, for all the world to see, we take no satisfaction in it, for it is, as your mayor has said, an offense not only against history but an offense against humanity, separating families, dividing husbands and wives and brothers and sisters, and dividing a people who wish to be joined together.

What is true of this city is true of Germany—real, lasting peace in Europe can never be assured as long as one German out of four is denied the elementary right of free men, and that is to make a free choice. In eighteen years of peace and good faith, this generation of Germans has earned the right to be free, including the right to unite their families and their nation in lasting peace, with good will to all people. You live in a defended island of freedom, but your life is part of the main. So let me ask you, as I close, to lift your eyes beyond the dangers of today, to the hopes of tomorrow, beyond the freedom merely of this city of Berlin, or your country of Germany, to the advance of freedom everywhere, beyond the wall to the day of peace with justice, beyond yourselves and ourselves to all mankind.

Freedom is indivisible, and when one man is enslaved, all are not free. When all are free, then we can look forward to that day when this city will be joined as one and this country and this great continent of Europe in a peaceful and hopeful globe. When that day finally comes, as it will, the people of West Berlin can take sober satisfaction in the fact that they were in the front lines for almost two decades.

All free men, wherever they may live, are citizens of Berlin, and therefore, as a free man, I take pride in the words *Ich bin ein Berliner.*

CIVIL RIGHTS SPEECH

Martin Luther King, Jr.   *August 28, 1963*

> *Martin Luther King, Jr., first came to national promi-*
> *nence as the spokesman for the Selma bus boycott in 1955. The*
> *son of a Baptist minister and an ordained minister himself,*
> *King advocated nonviolent civil disobedience on the part of*
> *black Americans to overcome segregation. In 1960 King became*
> *president of the Southern Christian Leadership Conference*
> *(SCLC), a position he held until his assassination in 1968.*
>
> *In August 1963, King, the SCLC and several other civil*
> *rights groups organized a march on Washington, which*
> *culminated in a mass meeting on August 28. There on the steps*
> *of the Lincoln Memorial, at the feet of the statue of the "Great*
> *Emancipator," civil rights activists addressed the crowd of more*
> *than 200,000 people. At the end of the program King rose to*
> *give what was to be a brief address. In his "I Have a Dream"*
> *speech, he "subpoenaed the conscience of the nation before the*
> *judgment seat of morality."*

FIVESCORE years ago, a great American, in whose symbolic shadow we stand today, signed the Emancipation Proclamation. This momentous decree came as a great beacon light of hope to millions of Negro slaves who had been seared in the flames of withering injustice. It came as a joyous daybreak to end the long night of their captivity.

But one hundred years later, the Negro still is not free; one hundred years later, the life of the Negro is still sadly crippled by the manacles of segregation and the chains of discrimination; one hundred years later, the Negro lives on a lonely island of poverty in the midst of a vast ocean of material prosperity; one hundred years later, the Negro is still languished in the corners of American society and finds himself in exile in his own land.

So we've come here today to dramatize a shameful condition. In a sense we've come to our nation's capital to cash a check. When the architects of our republic wrote the magnificent words of the Constitution and the Declaration of Independence, they were signing a promissory note to which every American was to fall heir. This note was the promise that all men, yes, black men as well as white men, would be guaranteed the unalienable rights of life, liberty, and the pursuit of happiness.

It is obvious today that America has defaulted on this promissory note in so far as her citizens of color are concerned. Instead of honoring this sacred obligation, America has given the Negro people a bad check; a check which has come back marked "insufficient funds." We refuse to believe that there are insufficient funds in the great vaults of opportunity of this nation. And so we've come to cash this check, a check that will give us upon demand the riches of freedom and the security of justice.

We have also come to this hallowed spot to remind America of the fierce urgency of now. This is no time to engage in the luxury of cooling off or to take the tranquilizing drug of gradualism. Now is the time to make real the promises of democracy; now is the time to rise from the dark and desolate valley of segregation to the sunlit path of racial justice; now is the time to lift our nation from the quicksands of racial injustice to the solid rock of brotherhood; now is the time to make justice a reality for all God's children. It would be fatal for the nation to overlook the urgency of the moment. This sweltering summer of the Negro's legitimate discontent will not pass until there is an invigorating autumn of freedom and equality.

Nineteen sixty-three is not an end, but a beginning. And those who hope that the Negro needed to blow off steam and will now be content, will have a rude awakening if the nation returns to business as usual.

There will be neither rest nor tranquility in America until the Negro is granted his citizenship rights. The whirlwinds of revolt will continue to shake the foundations of our nation until the bright day of justice emerges.

But there is something that I must say to my people who stand on the warm threshold which leads into the palace of justice. In the process of gaining our rightful place we must not be guilty of wrongful deeds.

Let us not seek to satisfy our thirst for freedom by drinking from the cup of bitterness and hatred. We must forever conduct our struggle on the high plane of dignity and discipline. We must not allow our creative protest to degenerate into physical violence. Again and again we must rise to the majestic heights of meeting physical force with soul force.

The marvelous new militancy which has engulfed the Negro community must not lead us to a distrust of all white people, for many of our white brothers, as evidenced by their presence here today, have come to realize that their destiny is tied up with our destiny and they have come to realize that their freedom is inextricably bound to our freedom. This offense we share mounted to storm the battlements of injustice must be carried forth by a biracial army. We cannot walk alone.

Martin Luther King, Jr., artist unknown.

And as we walk, we must make the pledge that we shall always march ahead. We cannot turn back. There are those who are asking the devotees of civil rights, "When will you be satisfied?" We can never be satisfied as long as the Negro is the victim of the unspeakable horrors of police brutality.

We can never be satisfied as long as our bodies, heavy with fatigue of travel, cannot gain lodging in the motels of the highways and the hotels of the cities. We cannot be satisfied as long as the Negro's basic mobility is from a smaller ghetto to a larger one.

We can never be satisfied as long as our children are stripped of their selfhood and robbed of their dignity by signs stating "for whites only." We cannot be satisfied as long as a Negro in Mississippi cannot vote and a Negro in New York believes he has nothing for which to vote. No, we are not satisfied, and we will not be satisfied until justice rolls down like waters and righteousness like a mighty stream.

I am not unmindful that some of you have come here out of excessive trials and tribulation. Some of you have come fresh from narrow jail cells. Some of you have come from areas where your quest for freedom left you battered by the storms of persecution and staggered by the winds of police brutality. You have been the veterans of creative suffering. Continue to work with the faith that unearned suffering is redemptive.

Go back to Mississippi; go back to Alabama; go back to South Carolina; go back to Georgia; go back to Louisiana; go back to the slums and ghettos of the northern cities, knowing that somehow this situation can, and will be changed. Let us not wallow in the valley of despair.

So I say to you, my friends, that even though we must face the difficulties of today and tomorrow, I still have a dream. It is a dream deeply rooted in the American dream that one day this nation will rise up and live out the true meaning of its creed—we hold these truths to be self-evident, that all men are created equal.

I have a dream that one day on the red hills of Georgia, sons of former slaves and sons of former slave-owners will be able to sit down together at the table of brotherhood.

I have a dream that one day, even the state of Mississippi, a state sweltering with the heat of injustice, sweltering with the heat of oppression, will be transformed into an oasis of freedom and justice.

I have a dream my four little children will one day live in a nation where they will not be judged by the color of their skin but by the content of their character. I have a dream today!

I have a dream that one day, down in Alabama, with its vicious racists, with its governor having his lips dripping with the words of interposition and nullification, that one day, right there in Alabama, little black boys and black girls will be able to join hands with little white boys and white girls as sisters and brothers. I have a dream today!

I have a dream that one day every valley shall be exalted, every hill and mountain shall be made low, the rough places shall be made plain, and the crooked places shall be made straight and the glory of the Lord will be revealed and all flesh shall see it together.

This is our hope. This is the faith that I go back to the South with.

With this faith we will be able to hew out of the mountain of despair a stone of hope. With this faith we will be able to transform the jangling discords of our nation into a beautiful symphony of brotherhood.

With this faith we will be able to work together, to pray together, to struggle together, to go to jail together, to stand up for freedom together, knowing that we will be free one day. This will be the day when all of God's children will be able to sing with new meaning—"my country 'tis of thee; sweet land of liberty; of thee I sing; land where my fathers died, land of the pilgrim's pride; from every mountain side, let freedom ring"—and if America is to be a great nation, this must become true.

So let freedom ring from the prodigious hilltops of New Hampshire.

Let freedom ring from the mighty mountains of New York.

Let freedom ring from the heightening Alleghenies of Pennsylvania.

Let freedom ring from the snow-capped Rockies of Colorado.

Let freedom ring from the curvaceous slopes of California.

But not only that.

Let freedom ring from Stone Mountain of Georgia.

Let freedom ring from Lookout Mountain of Tennessee.

Let freedom ring from every hill and molehill of Mississippi, from every mountainside, let freedom ring.

And when we allow freedom to ring, when we let it ring from every village and hamlet, from every state and city, we will be able to speed up that day when all of God's children—black men and white men, Jews and Gentiles, Catholics and Protestants—will be able to join hands and to sing in the words of the old Negro spiritual, "Free at last, free at last; thank God Almighty, we are free at last."

ADDRESS TO A
JOINT SESSION OF CONGRESS

Lyndon Baines Johnson   *November 27, 1963*

Lyndon Baines Johnson became president in 1963 upon the assassination of President John F. Kennedy. Before becoming Kennedy's vice president in 1961, Johnson had served as Senate majority leader and senator and congressman from Texas.

As the nation grieved over the shocking death of President Kennedy, Johnson addressed Congress for the first time as president on November 27. He stressed the Kennedy legacy and asked Congress to pass the pending civil rights legislation in memoriam to the dead president.

MR. Speaker, Mr. President, Members of the House, Members of the Senate, My Fellow Americans:

All I have I would have given gladly not to be standing here today.

The greatest leader of our time has been struck down by the foulest deed of our time. Today John Fitzgerald Kennedy lives on in the immortal words and works that he left behind. He lives on in the mind and memories of mankind. He lives on in the hearts of his countrymen.

No words are sad enough to express our sense of loss. No words are strong enough to express our determination to continue the forward thrust of America that he began.

The dream of conquering the vastness of space—the dream of partnership across the Atlantic, and across the Pacific as well—the dream of a Peace Corps in less-developed nations—the dream of education for all of our children—the dream of jobs for all who seek them and need them—the dream of care for our elderly—the dream of an all-out attack on mental illness—and, above all, the dream of equal rights for all Americans, whatever their race or color—these and other American dreams have been vitalized by his drive and by his dedication.

Now the ideas and ideals which he so nobly represented must and will be translated into effective action.

Under John Kennedy's leadership, this nation has demonstrated that it has the courage to seek peace and it has the fortitude to risk war. We have proved that we are a good and reliable friend to those who seek peace and freedom. We have shown that we can also be a formidable foe to those who reject the path of peace and those who seek to impose upon us or our allies the yoke of tyranny.

This nation will keep its commitments from South Vietnam to West Berlin. We will be unceasing in the search for peace; resourceful in our pursuit of areas of agreement, even with those with whom we differ; and generous and loyal to those who join with us in common cause.

In this age, when there can be no losers in peace and no victors in war, we must recognize the obligation to match national strength with national restraint. We must be prepared at one and the same time for both the confrontation of power and the limitation of power. We must be ready to defend the national interest and to negotiate the common interest. This is the path that we shall continue to pursue. Those who test our courage will find it strong and those who seek our friendship will find it honorable. We will demonstrate anew that the strong can be just in the use of strength—and the just can be strong in the defense of justice. And let all know we will extend no special privilege and impose no persecution.

We will carry on the fight against poverty and misery, ignorance and disease—in other lands and in our own. We will serve all of the nation, not one section or one sector, or one group, but all Americans. These are the United States—a united people with a united purpose.

Lyndon B. Johnson, portrait by Elizabeth Shoumatoff, 1968.

Our American unity does not depend upon unanimity. We have differences; but now, as in the past, we can derive from those differences strength, not weakness, wisdom, not despair. Both as a people and as a government we can unite upon a program, a program which is wise, just, enlightened, and constructive.

For thirty-two years Capitol Hill has been my home. I have shared many moments of pride with you—pride in the ability of the Congress of the United States to act; to meet any crisis; to distill from our differences strong programs of national action.

An assassin's bullet has thrust upon me the awesome burden of the presidency. I am here today to say I need your help, I cannot bear this burden alone. I need the help of all Americans, in all America. This nation has experienced a profound shock, and in this critical moment it is our duty—yours and mine—as the government of the United States—to do away with uncertainty and doubt and delay and to show that we are capable of decisive action—that from the brutal loss of our leader we will derive not weakness but strength, that we can and will act and act now.

From this chamber of representative government let all the world know, and none misunderstand, that I rededicate this government to the unswerving support of the United Nations, to the honorable and determined execution of our commitments to our allies, to the maintenance of military strength second to none, to the defense of the strength and the stability of the dollar, to the expansion of our foreign trade, to the reinforcement of our programs of mutual assistance and cooperation in Asia and Africa, and to our Alliance for Progress in this hemisphere.

On the 20th day of January, in 1961, John F. Kennedy told his countrymen that our national work would not be finished "in the first thousand days, nor in the life of this administration, nor even perhaps in our lifetime on this planet. But"—he said—"let us begin." Today in this moment of new resolve, I would say to all my fellow Americans, let us continue.

This is our challenge—not to hesitate, not to pause, not to turn about and linger over this evil moment, but to continue on our course so that we may fulfill the destiny that history has set for us. Our most immediate tasks are here on this Hill.

First, no memorial oration or eulogy could more eloquently honor President Kennedy's memory than the earliest possible passage of the Civil Rights Bill for which he fought so long. We have talked long enough in this country about equal rights. We have talked for 100 years or more. It is time now to write the next chapter—and to write it in the books of law.

I urge you again, as I did in 1957 and again in 1960, to enact a civil rights law so that we can move forward to eliminate from this nation every trace of discrimination and oppression that is based upon race or color. There could be no greater source of strength to this nation both at home and abroad.

And, second, no act of ours could more fittingly continue the work of President Kennedy than the early passage of the tax bill for which he fought all this long year. This is a bill designed to increase our national income and federal revenues, and to provide insurance against recession. That bill, if passed without delay, means more security for those now working, more jobs for those now without them, and more incentive for our economy.

In short, this is no time for delay. It is time for action—strong, forward-looking action on the pending education bills to help bring the light of learning to every home and hamlet in America; strong, forward-looking action on youth employment opportunities; strong, forward-looking action on the pending foreign aid bill, making clear that we are not forfeiting our responsibilities to this hemisphere or to the world, nor erasing executive flexibility in the conduct of our foreign affairs; and strong, prompt, and forward-looking action on the remaining appropriation bills.

In this new spirit of action, the Congress can expect the full cooperation and support of the executive branch. And in particular I pledge that the expenditures of your government will be administered with the utmost thrift and frugality. I will insist that the government get a dollar's value for a dollar spent. The government will set an example of prudence and economy. This does not mean that we will not meet our unfilled needs or that we will not honor our commitments. We will do both.

As one who has long served in both houses of the Congress, I firmly believe in the independence and the integrity of the legislative branch. I promise you that I shall always respect this. It is deep in the marrow of my bones. With equal firmness, I believe in the capacity and I believe in the ability of the Congress, despite the divisions of opinion which characterize our nation, to act— to act wisely, to act vigorously, to act speedily when the need arises.

The need is here. The need is now.

We meet in grief; but let us also meet in renewed dedication and renewed vigor. Let us meet in action, in tolerance, and in mutual understanding.

John Kennedy's death commands what his life conveyed—that America must move forward. The time has come for Americans of all races and creeds and political beliefs to understand and to respect one another. So let us put an end to the teaching and the preaching of hate and evil and violence. Let us turn away from the fanatics of the far left and the far right, from the apostles of bitterness and bigotry, from those defiant of law and those who pour venom into our nation's bloodstream.

I profoundly hope that the tragedy and the torment of these terrible days will bind us together in new fellowship, making us one people in our hour of sorrow. So let us here highly resolve that John Fitzgerald Kennedy did not live—or die—in vain. And on this Thanksgiving Eve, as we gather together to ask the Lord's blessing and give Him our thanks, let us unite in those familiar and cherished words:

> America, America,
> God shed His grace on thee,
> And crown thy good
> With brotherhood
> From sea to shining sea.

X

THE UNITED STATES IN THE MODERN WORLD

AMENDMENT XXIV
BANNED POLL TAX IN FEDERAL ELECTIONS

January 23, 1964

Proposed by Congress August 27, 1962, its ratification was completed January 23, 1964.

SEC. 1. The right of citizens of the United States to vote in any primary or other election for President or Vice-President, for electors for President or Vice-President, or for Senator or Representative in Congress, shall not be denied or abridged by the United States or any State by reason of failure to pay any poll tax or other tax.

SEC. 2. The Congress shall have power to enforce this article by appropriate legislation.

THE CIVIL RIGHTS ACT

July 2, 1964

---

*When Lyndon Johnson came to the presidency following
the assassination of John F. Kennedy, he made civil rights a top
priority. "No memorial oration or eulogy," he told a joint session
of Congress on November 27, "could more eloquently honor
President Kennedy's memory than the earliest possible passage
of the Civil Rights Bill." The 1964 Civil Rights Bill passed just
months later outlawed not only segregation in all public
accommodations, but also job discrimination on the basis of
race or national origin. As an enforcement measure, the act
authorized the federal government to withhold funding from
public agencies that discriminated on the basis of race, and
gave the attorney general specific powers to guarantee voting
rights and to end school segregation.*

AN Act to enforce the constitutional right to vote, to confer jurisdiction
upon the district courts of the United States to provide injunctive relief against
discrimination in public accommodations, to authorize the Attorney General to
institute suits to protect constitutional rights in public facilities and public
education, to extend the Commission on Civil Rights, to prevent discrimination
in federally assisted programs, to establish a Commission on Equal Opportunity,
and for other purposes.

TITLE I—VOTING RIGHTS
(2) No person acting under color of law shall—
  (A) in determining whether any individual is qualified under State law or
laws to vote in any Federal election, apply any standard, practice, or procedure
different from the standards, practices, or procedures applied under such law or
laws to other individuals within the same county, parish, or similar political
subdivision who have been found by State officials to be qualified to vote. . . .
  (C) employ any literacy test as a qualification for voting in any Federal
election unless (i) such test is administered to each individual and is conducted
wholly in writing; and (ii) a certified copy of the test and of the answers given
by the individual is furnished to him within twenty-five days of the submission
of his request. . . .

TITLE II—INJUNCTIVE RELIEF AGAINST DISCRIMINATION IN PLACES OF PUBLIC ACCOMMODATION

SEC. 201. (a) All persons shall be entitled to the full and equal enjoyment of the goods, services, facilities, privileges, advantages, and accommodations of any place of public accommodation, as defined in this section, without discrimination or segregation on the ground of race, color, religion, or national origin.

(b) Each of the following establishments which serves the public is a place of public accommodation within the meaning of this title if its operations affect commerce, or if discrimination or segregation by it is supported by State action:

(1) any inn, hotel, motel or other establishment which provides lodging to transient guests, other than an establishment located within a building which contains not more than five rooms for rent or hire and which is actually occupied by the proprietor of such establishment as his residence;

(2) any restaurant, cafeteria, lunchroom, lunch counter, soda fountain, or other facility principally engaged in selling food for consumption on the premises. . . .

(3) any motion picture house, theater, concert hall, sports arena, stadium or other place of exhibition or entertainment. . . .

SEC. 202. All persons shall be entitled to be free, at any establishment or place, from discrimination or segregation of any kind on the ground of race, color, religion, or national origin, if such discrimination or segregation is or purports to be required by any law, statute, ordinance, regulation, rule, or order of a State or any agency or political subdivision thereof. . . .

SEC. 206. (a) Whenever the Attorney General has reasonable cause to believe that any person or group of persons is engaged in a pattern or practice of resistance to the full enjoyment of any of the rights secured by this title, . . . the Attorney General may bring a civil action in the appropriate district court of the United States. . . .

TITLE VI—NONDISCRIMINATION IN FEDERALLY ASSISTED PROGRAMS

SEC. 601. No person in the United States shall, on the ground of race, color, or national origin, be excluded from participation in, be denied the benefits of, or be subjected to discrimination under any program or activity receiving Federal financial assistance. . . .

GULF OF TONKIN RESOLUTION

August 24, 1964

On August 5, 1964, President Lyndon Johnson requested congressional authorization of broad presidential powers to allow the executive to respond directly to attacks on American forces. This measure, the Gulf of Tonkin Resolution, became the basis for deepening United States involvement in the war in Vietnam, and ultimately served as the "declaration of war" in the undeclared war there. The resolution was passed by both houses of Congress two days later with only two no votes, from Senators Wayne Morse and Ernest Gruening. The measure responded to attacks earlier in August on the United States ships C. Turner Joy *and* Maddox *by North Vietnamese torpedo boats in the Gulf of Tonkin.*

As Congress became critical of the conduct of the war in Vietnam, dissatisfaction over the passage of the resolution grew. Its main supporter in 1964, Senator J. William Fulbright, became one of its most vocal critics in the late 1960s. In 1967 Fulbright, as head of the Senate Foreign Relations Committee, launched a full-scale investigation of the circumstances leading to the passage of the measure. In 1970 Congress repealed the Gulf of Tonkin Resolution.

WHEREAS naval units of the Communist regime in Vietnam, in violation of the principles of the Charter of the United Nations and of international law, have deliberately and repeatedly attacked United States naval vessels lawfully present in international waters, and have thereby created a serious threat to international peace; and

Whereas those attacks are part of a deliberate and systematic campaign of aggression that the Communist regime in North Vietnam has been waging against its neighbors and the nations joined with them in the collective defense of their freedom; and

Whereas the United States is assisting the peoples of Southeast Asia to protect their freedom and has no territorial, military or political ambitions in that area, but desires only that these peoples should be left in peace to work out their own destinies in their own way: Now, therefore, be it

Resolved by the Senate and House of Representatives of the United States of American in Congress assembled, That the Congress approves and supports the determination of the President, as Commander in Chief, to take all necessary measures to repel any armed attack against the forces of the United States and to prevent further aggression.

SEC. 2. The United States regards as vital to its national interest and to world peace the maintenance of international peace and security in southeast Asia. Consonant with the Constitution of the United States and the Charter of the United Nations and in accordance with its obligations under the Southeast Asia Collective Defense Treaty, the United States is, therefore, prepared, as the President determines, to take all necessary steps, including the use of armed force, to assist any member [Britain, France, Australia, New Zealand, the Philippines, Thailand and Pakistan] or protocol state [South Vietnam, Laos and Cambodia] of the Southeast Asia Collective Defense Treaty requesting assistance in defense of its freedom.

SEC. 3. This resolution shall expire when the President shall determine that the peace and security of the area is reasonably assured by international conditions created by action of the United Nations or otherwise, except that it may be terminated earlier by concurrent resolution of the Congress.

AMENDMENT XXV
PRESIDENTIAL DISABILITY AND SUCCESSION

February 10, 1967

Proposed by Congress July 6, 1965, its ratification was completed February 10, 1967.

SEC. 1. In case of the removal of the President from office or of his death or resignation, the Vice-President shall become President.

SEC. 2. Whenever there is a vacancy in the office of the Vice-President, the President shall nominate a Vice-President who shall take office upon confirmation by a majority vote of both houses of Congress.

SEC. 3. Whenever the President transmits to the President *pro tempore* of the Senate and the Speaker of the House of Representatives his written declaration that he is unable to discharge the powers and duties of his office, and until he transmits to them a written declaration to the contrary, such powers and duties shall be discharged by the Vice-President as Acting President.

SEC. 4. Whenever the Vice-President and a majority of either the principal officers of the executive departments, or of such other body as Congress may by law provide, transmit to the President *pro tempore* of the Senate and the Speaker of the House of Representatives their written declaration that the President is unable to discharge the powers and duties of his office, the Vice-President shall immediately assume the powers and duties of the office as Acting President.

Thereafter, when the President transmits to the President *pro tempore* of the Senate and the Speaker of the House of Representatives his written declaration that no inability exists, he shall resume the powers and duties of his office unless the Vice-President and a majority of either the principal officers of the executive department, or of such other body as Congress may by law provide, transmit within four days to the President *pro tempore* of the Senate and the Speaker of the House of Representatives their written declaration that the President is unable to discharge the powers and duties of his office. Thereupon Congress shall decide the issue, assembling within forty-eight hours for that purpose if not in session. If the Congress, within twenty-one days after receipt of the latter written declaration, or, if Congress is not in session, within twenty-one days after Congress is required to assemble, determines by two-thirds vote of both houses that the President is unable to discharge the powers and duties of his office, the Vice-President shall continue to discharge the same as Acting President; otherwise, the President shall resume the powers and duties of his office.

Amendment XXVI
Lowered Voting Age to Eighteen Years

July 1, 1971

Proposed by Congress March 8, 1971, its ratification was completed July 1, 1971.

SEC. 1. The right of citizens of the United States, who are eighteen years of age or older, to vote shall not be denied or abridged by the United States or by any State on account of age.

SEC. 2. The Congress shall have power to enforce this article by appropriate legislation.

THE EQUAL RIGHTS AMENDMENT

March 22, 1972

Proposed by Congress March 22, 1972, this amendment was never ratified. After women won the right to vote with the Nineteenth Amendment in 1920, many suffragists claimed that the vote was not enough to end what they saw as the repression of women. As a result, Alice Paul, leader of the National Woman's Party, wrote an Equal Rights Amendment in 1922. The proposed amendment, which called for an end to discrimination on the basis of sex, included an enforcement clause that required the federal government to act to uphold equal rights. During the 1930s and 1940s, the ERA ratification had effectively failed.

The ERA came back to life in 1966 with the founding of the National Organization for Women (NOW), inspired in part by Betty Friedan's book, The Feminine Mystique *(1963). Friedan argued that women in the home had lost their identities outside of their roles as mothers and wives. Working women, it was argued, faced job discrimination, unequal pay for equal work and a lack of professional opportunities. An Equal Rights Amendment would allow them to fight these handicaps in the courts and in Congress. In 1972, after a large-scale campaign by NOW and other feminist groups, Congress passed the Equal Rights Amendment and sent it to the states for ratification. At the state level the ERA campaign encountered strong opposition from several groups, especially the antifeminist or "profamily" movement. After passing through thirty-five state legislatures in the late 1970s, in 1982 the ERA faltered three votes short of the required three-fourths majority.*

———————

RESOLVED by the Senate and House of Representatives of the United States of America in Congress assembled (two-thirds of each House concurring therein), That the following article is proposed as an amendment to the Constitution of the United States, which shall be valid to all intents and purposes as part of the Constitution when ratified by the legislatures of three-fourths of the several States within seven years from the date of its submission by the Congress:

SEC. 1. Equality of rights under the law shall not be denied or abridged by the United States or by any State on account of sex.

SEC. 2. The Congress shall have the power to enforce, by appropriate legislation, the provisions of this article.

SEC. 3. This amendment shall take effect two years after the date of ratification.

ROE ET AL. V. WADE

Harry Blackmun   *1973*

———————

In the early 1970s American women argued that control over their bodies and their reproductive capacities was a basic right guaranteed them in the Constitution. They argued that state and federal statutes that limited women's access to abortions abrogated this right. In 1972, two tests challenged state governments' abilities to restrict women's legal access to abortion: Roe et al. v. Wade *and* Doe v. Bolton.

On January 22, 1973, Justice Harry Blackmun read the majority decision of the Supreme Court in the case of Roe et al. v. Wade. *The court ruled that state laws that criminalized abortion were unconstitutional, as they violated women's right to privacy and impinged upon women's decisions whether or not to enter pregnancy. As a result abortion became legal through the second trimester of pregnancy. In the dissenting opinion, Justice William Rehnquist argued that although one plaintiff could argue for his or her own constitutional rights,*

"he may not seek vindication for the rights of others."
    The Roe et al. v. Wade *decision was one of the court's most controversial decisions in the 1970s; it remains controversial in the 1980s and 1990s, as it continues to be addressed in cases before the Supreme Court.*

MR. Justice Blackmun delivered the opinion of the Court.

This Texas federal appeal [presents a constitutional challenge] to state criminal abortion legislation. The Texas statutes under attack here are typical of those that have been in effect in many States for approximately a century. The Georgia statutes, in contrast, have a modern cast and are a legislative product that, to an extent at least, obviously reflects the influences of recent attitudinal change, of advancing medical knowledge and techniques, and of new thinking about an old issue.

We forthwith acknowledge our awareness of the sensitive and emotional nature of the abortion controversy, of the vigorous opposing views, even among physicians, and of the deep and seemingly absolute convictions that the subject inspires. One's philosophy, one's experiences, one's exposure to the raw edges of human existence, one's religious training, one's attitudes toward life and family and their values, and the moral standards one establishes and seeks to observe, are all likely to influence and to color one's thinking and conclusions about abortion.

In addition, population growth, pollution, poverty, and racial overtones tend to complicate and not to simplify the problem.

Our task, of course, is to resolve the issue by constitutional measurement, free of emotion and of predilection. We seek earnestly to do this, and, because we do, we have inquired into, and in this opinion place some emphasis upon, medical and medical-legal history and what that history reveals about man's attitudes toward the abortion procedure over the centuries. We bear in mind, too, Mr. Justice Holmes's admonition in his now-vindicated dissent in *Lochner v. New York,* 198 U.S. 45, 76 (1905):

"[The Constitution] is made for people of fundamentally differing views, and the accident of our finding certain opinions natural and familiar or novel and even shocking ought not to conclude our judgment upon the question whether statutes embodying them conflict with the Constitution of the United States."

I. The Texas statutes that concern us here are Arts. 1191-1194 and 1196 of the State's Penal Code. These make it a crime to "procure an abortion," as therein defined, or to attempt one, except with respect to "an abortion procured or attempted by medical advice for the purpose of saving the life of the mother."

Similar statutes are in existence in a majority of the States. . . .

II. Jane Roe, a single woman who was residing in Dallas County, Texas, instituted this federal action in March 1970 against the District Attorney of the county. She sought a declaratory judgment that the Texas criminal abortion statutes were unconstitutional on their face, and an injunction restraining the defendant from enforcing the statutes.

Roe alleged that she was unmarried and pregnant; that she wished to terminate her pregnancy by an abortion "performed by a competent, licensed physician, under safe, clinical conditions"; that she was unable to get a "legal" abortion in Texas because her life did not appear to be threatened by the continuation of her pregnancy; and that she could not afford to travel to another jurisdiction in order to secure a legal abortion under safe conditions. She claimed that the Texas statutes were unconstitutionally vague and that they abridged her right of personal privacy, protected by the First, Fourth, Fifth, Ninth, and Fourteenth Amendments. . . .

V. The principal thrust of appellant's attack on the Texas statutes is that they improperly invade a right, said to be possessed by the pregnant woman, to choose to terminate her pregnancy. Appellant would discover this right in the concept of personal "liberty" embodied in the Fourteenth Amendment's Due Process Clause; or in personal, marital, familial, and sexual privacy said to be protected by the Bill of Rights. . . . Before addressing this claim, we feel it desirable briefly to survey, in several aspects, the history of abortion, for such insight as that history may afford us, and then to examine the state purposes and interests behind the criminal abortion laws.

VI. It perhaps is not generally appreciated that the restrictive criminal abortion laws in effect in a majority of States today are of relatively recent vintage. Those laws, generally proscribing abortion or its attempt at any time during pregnancy except when necessary to preserve the pregnant woman's life, are not of ancient or even of common-law origin. Instead, they derive from statutory changes effected, for the most part, in the latter half of the 19th century. . . . [There follows a review of ancient attitudes on abortion, the Hippocratic Oath, the English common law, the English statutory law, the American law, and the positions of the American Medical Association, the American Public Health Association, and the American Bar Association.]

VII. . . . The prevalence of high mortality rates at illegal "abortion mills" strengthens, rather than weakens, the State's interest in regulating the conditions under which abortions are performed. Moreover, the risk to the woman increases as her pregnancy continues. Thus, the State retains a definite interest in protecting the woman's own health and safety when an abortion is proposed at a late stage of pregnancy.

The third reason is the State's interest—some phrase it in terms of duty—in protecting prenatal life. Some of the argument for this justification rests on the theory that a new human life is present from the moment of conception. The State's interest and general obligation to protect life then extends, it is argued, to prenatal life. Only when the life of the pregnant mother herself is at stake, balanced against the life she carries within her, should the interest of the embryo or fetus not prevail. Logically, of course, a legitimate state interest in this area need not stand or fall on acceptance of the belief that life begins at conception or at some other point prior to live birth. In assessing the State's interest, recognition may be given to the less rigid claim that as long as at least potential life is involved, the State may assert interests beyond the protection of the pregnant woman alone.

Parties challenging state abortion laws have sharply disputed in some courts the contention that a purpose of these laws, when enacted, was to protect prenatal life. Pointing to the absence of legislative history to support the contention, they claim that most state laws were designed solely to protect the woman. Because medical advances have lessened this concern, at least with respect to abortion in early pregnancy, they argue that with respect to such abortions the laws can no longer be justified by any state interest. . . .

It is with these interests, and the weight to be attached to them, that this case is concerned.

VIII. The Constitution does not explicitly mention any right of privacy. In a line of decisions, however, going back perhaps as far as *Union Pacific R. Co. v. Botsford*, 141 U.S. 250, 251 (1891), the Court has recognized that a right of personal privacy, or a guarantee of certain areas or zones of privacy, does exist under the Constitution. . . .

This right of privacy, whether it be founded in the Fourteenth Amendment's concept of personal liberty and restrictions upon state action, as we feel it is, or, as the District Court determined, in the Ninth Amendment's reservation of rights to the people, is broad enough to encompass a woman's decision whether or not to terminate her pregnancy. The detriment that the State would impose upon the pregnant woman by denying this choice altogether is apparent. Specific and direct harm medically diagnosable even in early pregnancy may be involved. Maternity, or additional offspring, may force upon the woman a distressful life and future. Psychological harm may be imminent. Mental and physical health may be taxed by child care. There is also the distress, for all concerned, associated with the unwanted child, and there is the problem of bringing a child into a family already unable, psychologically and otherwise, to care for it. In other cases, as in this one, the additional difficulties and continuing stigma of unwed motherhood may be involved. All these are factors the woman and her responsible physician necessarily will consider in consultation.

On the basis of elements such as these, appellant and some *amici* argue that the woman's right is absolute and that she is entitled to terminate her pregnancy at whatever time, in whatever way, and for whatever reason she alone chooses. With this we do not agree. Appellant's arguments that Texas either has no valid interest at all in regulating the abortion decision, or no interest strong enough to support any limitation upon the woman's sole determination, are unpersuasive. The Court's decisions recognizing a right of privacy also acknowledge that some state regulation in areas protected by that right is appropriate. As noted above, a State may properly assert important interests in safeguarding health, in maintaining medical standards, and in protecting potential life. At some point in pregnancy, these respective interests become sufficiently compelling to sustain regulation of the factors that govern the abortion decision. The privacy right involved, therefore, cannot be said to be absolute. In fact, it is not clear to us that the claim asserted by some *amici* that one has an unlimited right to do with one's body as one pleases bears a close relationship to the right of privacy previously articulated in the Court's decisions. . . .

We, therefore, conclude that the right of personal privacy includes the abortion decision, but that this right is not unqualified and must be considered against important state interests in regulation.

We note that those federal and state courts that have recently considered abortion law challenges have reached the same conclusion. . . . Although the results are divided, most of these courts have agreed that the right of privacy, however based, is broad enough to cover the abortion decision; that the right, nonetheless, is not absolute and is subject to some limitations, and that at some point the state interests as to protection of health, medical standards, and prenatal life, become dominant. We agree with this approach. . . .

XI. To summarize and to repeat:

1. A state criminal abortion statute of the current Texas type, that excepts from criminality only a lifesaving procedure on behalf of the mother, without regard to pregnancy stage and without recognition of the interests involved, is violative of the Due Process Clause of the Fourteenth Amendment.

(a) For the stage prior to approximately the end of the first trimester, the abortion decision and its effectuation must be left to the medical judgment of the pregnant woman's attending physician.

(b) For the stage subsequent to approximately the end of the first trimester, the State, in promoting its interest in the health of the mother, may, if it chooses, regulate the abortion procedure in ways that are reasonably related to maternal health.

(c) For the stage subsequent to viability, the State in promoting its interest in the potentiality of human life may, if it chooses, regulate, and even proscribe, abortion except where it is necessary, in appropriate medical judgment, for the preservation of the life or health of the mother. . . .

This holding, we feel, is consistent with the relative weights of the respective interests involved, with the lessons and examples of medical and legal history, with the lenity of the common law, and with the demands of the profound problems of the present day. The decision leaves the State free to place increasing restrictions on abortion as the period of pregnancy lengthens, so long as these restrictions are tailored to the recognized state interests. . . .

Mr. Justice Rehnquist, dissenting:

The Court's opinion brings to the decision of this troubling question both extensive historical fact and a wealth of legal scholarship. While the opinion commands my respect, I find myself nonetheless in fundamental disagreement with those parts of it that invalidate the Texas statute in question, and therefore dissent. . . .

Speech in House Judiciary Committee

Barbara Jordan   *July 25, 1974*

In 1972, Barbara Jordan (D–Texas) became the first African-American woman from the South elected to the U.S. House of Representatives. She was a member of the House Judiciary Committee that considered the impeachment of President Nixon. On July 30, 1974, the Judiciary Committee adopted three articles of impeachment charging the President with obstruction of justice, failure to uphold laws and refusal to produce material subpoenaed by the committee. The matter was referred to the entire House of Representatives for a vote.

EARLIER today we heard the beginning of the Preamble to the Constitution of the United States, "We, the people." It is a very eloquent beginning. But when that document was completed, on the seventeenth of September in 1787, I was not included in that "We, the people." I felt somehow for many years that

George Washington and Alexander Hamilton just left me out by mistake. But through the process of amendment, interpretation, and court decision I have finally been included in "We, the people."

Today, I am an inquisitor. I believe hyperbole would not be fictional and would not overstate the solemness that I feel right now. My faith in the Constitution is whole, it is complete, it is total. I am not going to sit here and be an idle spectator to the diminution, the subversion, the destruction of the Constitution.

"Who can so properly be the inquisitors for the nation as the representatives of the nation themselves?" (*Federalist,* no. 65.) The subject of its jurisdiction are those offenses which proceed from the misconduct of public men. That is what we are talking about. In other words, the jurisdiction comes from the abuse of violation of some public trust. It is wrong, I suggest, it is a misreading of the Constitution for any member here to assert that for a member to vote for an article of impeachment means that member must be convinced that the president should be removed from office. The Constitution doesn't say that. The powers relating to impeachment are an essential check in the hands of this body, the legislature, against and upon the encroachment of the executive. In establishing the division between the two branches of the legislature, the House and the Senate, assigning to the one the right to accuse and to the other the right to judge, the framers of this Constitution were very astute. They did not make the accusers and the judges the same person. . . .

Common sense would be revolted if we engaged upon this process for petty reasons. Congress has a lot to do. Appropriations, tax reform, health insurance, campaign finance reform, housing, environmental protection, energy sufficiency, mass transportation. Pettiness cannot be allowed to stand in the face of such overwhelming problems. So today we are not being petty. We are trying to be big because the task we have before us is a big one. . . .

James Madison again at the Constitutional Convention: "A president is impeachable if he attempts to subvert the Constitution."

The Constitution charges the president with the task of taking care that the laws be faithfully executed, and yet the president has counseled his aides to commit perjury, willfully disregarded the secrecy of grand jury proceedings, concealed surreptitious entry, attempted to compromise a federal judge while publicly displaying his cooperation with the processes of criminal justice.

"A president is impeachable if he attempts to subvert the Constitution."

If the impeachment provision in the Constitution of the United States will not reach the offenses charged here, then perhaps that eighteenth-century Constitution should be abandoned to a twentieth-century paper shredder. Has the president committed offenses and planned and directed and acquiesced in a course of conduct which the Constitution will not tolerate? That is the question. We know that. We know the question. We should now forthwith proceed to answer the question. It is reason, and not passion, which must guide our deliberations, guide our debate, and guide our decision.

RESIGNATION SPEECH

Richard M. Nixon   *August 8, 1974*

In the 1972 presidential election, President Richard M. Nixon swept to an overwhelming victory over his Democratic challenger, Senator George McGovern. Almost immediately, however, the Nixon presidency faced charges of criminality. During the campaign, a group working for the Committee to Re-elect the President broke into Democratic National Committee headquarters at the Watergate office building in Washington, D.C., apparently in search of political intelligence. Attempts by the White House to stop or frustrate the ensuing investigations ultimately failed when Nixon's own White House tape recordings revealed that the president and his assistants had repeatedly discussed the matter. As revelations mounted, Nixon became preoccupied with preserving his presidency. The Supreme Court, in a unanimous decision, required Nixon to supply Special Prosecutor Leon Jaworski with tape recordings of conversations with his advisors. In response to the content of these tapes, the House Judiciary Committee voted to recommend approval by the full House of three articles of impeachment against President Nixon. Nine days later, on August 9, 1974, Nixon resigned his office and was succeeded by Vice President Gerald Ford. One month later Ford pardoned Nixon; Nixon accepted the pardon, but maintained that his mistakes were personal and political, not criminal.

GOOD evening.

This is the 37th time I have spoken to you from this office, where so many decisions have been made that shaped the history of this Nation. Each time I have done so to discuss with you some matter that I believe affected the national interest.

In all the decisions I have made in my public life, I have always tried to do what was best for the Nation. Throughout the long and difficult period of Watergate, I have felt it was my duty to persevere, to make every possible effort to complete the term of office to which you elected me.

In the past few days, however, it has become evident to me that I no longer have a strong enough political base in the Congress to justify continuing that effort. As long as there was such a base, I felt strongly that it was necessary to see the constitutional process through to its conclusion, that to do otherwise would be unfaithful to the spirit of that deliberately difficult process and a dangerously destabilizing precedent for the future.

But with the disappearance of that base, I now believe that the constitutional purpose has been served, and there is no longer a need for the process to be prolonged.

I would have preferred to carry through to the finish whatever the personal agony it would have involved, and my family unanimously urged me to do so. But the interest of the Nation must always come before any personal considerations.

From the discussions I have had with Congressional and other leaders, I have concluded that because of the Watergate matter I might not have the support of the Congress that I would consider necessary to back the very difficult decisions and carry out the duties of this office in the way the interests of the Nation would require.

I have never been a quitter. To leave office before my term is completed is abhorrent to every instinct in my body. But as President, I must put the interest of America first. America needs a full-time President and a full-time Congress, particularly at this time with the problems we face at home and abroad.

To continue to fight through the months ahead for my personal vindication would almost totally absorb the time and attention of both the President and the Congress in a period when our entire focus should be on the great issues of peace abroad and prosperity without inflation at home.

Therefore, I shall resign the Presidency effective at noon tomorrow. Vice President Ford will be sworn in as President at that hour in this office.

As I recall the high hopes for America with which we began this second term, I feel a great sadness that I will not be here in this office working on your behalf to achieve those hopes in the next 2 1/2 years. But in turning over direction of the Government to Vice President Ford, I know, as I told the Nation when I nominated him for that office 10 months ago, that the leadership of America will be in good hands.

In passing this office to the Vice President, I also do so with the profound sense of the weight of responsibility that will fall on his shoulders tomorrow and, therefore, of the understanding, the patience, the cooperation he will need from all Americans.

As he assumes that responsibility, he will deserve the help and the support of all of us. As we look to the future, the first essential is to begin healing the wounds of this Nation, to put the bitterness and the divisions of the recent past behind us, and to rediscover those shared ideals that lie at the heart of our strength and unity as a great and as a free people.

By taking this action, I hope that I will have hastened the start of that process of healing which is so desperately needed in America.

I regret deeply any injuries that may have been done in the course of the events that led to this decision. I would say only that if some of my judgments were wrong, and some were wrong, they were made in what I believed at the time to be the best interest of the Nation.

To those who have stood with me during these past difficult months, to my family, my friends, to many others who joined in supporting my cause because they believed it was right, I will be eternally grateful for your support.

And to those who have not felt able to give me your support, let me say I leave with no bitterness toward those who have opposed me, because all of us, in the final analysis, have been concerned with the good of the country, however our judgments might differ.

So, let us all now join together in affirming that common commitment and in helping our new President succeed for the benefit of all Americans.

I shall leave this office with regret at not completing my term, but with gratitude for the privilege of serving as your President for the past 5 1/2 years. These years have been a momentous time in the history of our Nation and the world. They have been a time of achievement in which we can all be proud, achievements that represent the shared efforts of the Administration, the Congress, and the people.

But the challenges ahead are equally great, and they, too, will require the support and the efforts of the Congress and the people working in cooperation with the new Administration.

We have ended America's longest war, but in the work of securing a lasting peace in the world, the goals ahead are even more far-reaching and more difficult. We must complete a structure of peace so that it will be said of this generation, our generation of Americans, by the people of all nations, not only that we ended one war but that we prevented future wars.

We have unlocked the doors that for a quarter of a century stood between the United States and the People's Republic of China.

We must now ensure that the one quarter of the world's people who live in the People's Republic of China will be and remain not our enemies but our friends.

In the Middle East, 100 million people in the Arab countries, many of whom have considered us their enemy for nearly 20 years, now look on us as their friends. We must continue to build on that friendship so that peace can settle at last over the Middle East and so that the cradle of civilization will not become its grave.

Together with the Soviet Union we have made the crucial breakthroughs that have begun the process of limiting nuclear arms. But we must set as our goal not just limiting but reducing and finally destroying these terrible weapons so that they cannot destroy civilization and so that the threat of nuclear war will no longer hang over the world and the people.

We have opened the new relation with the Soviet Union. We must continue to develop and expand that new relationship so that the two strongest nations of the world will live together in cooperation rather than confrontation.

Around the world, in Asia, in Africa, in Latin America, in the Middle East, there are millions of people who live in terrible poverty, even starvation. We must keep as our goal turning away from production for war and expanding production for peace so that people everywhere on this earth can at least look forward in their children's time, if not in our own time, to having the necessities for a decent life.

Here in America, we are fortunate that most of our people have not only the blessings of liberty, but also the means to live full and good and, by the world's standards, even abundant lives. We must press on, however, to a goal of not only more and better jobs, but of full opportunity for every American and of what we are striving so hard right now to achieve, prosperity without inflation.

For more than a quarter of a century in public life I have shared in the turbulent history of this era. I have fought for what I believed in. I have tried to the best of my ability to discharge those duties and meet those responsibilities that were entrusted to me.

Sometimes I have succeeded and sometimes I have failed, but always I have taken heart from what Theodore Roosevelt once said about the man in the arena, "whose face is marred by dust and sweat and blood, who strives valiantly, who errs and comes short again and again because there is not effort without error and shortcoming, but who does actually strive to do the deed, who knows the great enthusiasms, the great devotions, who spends himself in a worthy cause, who at the best knows in the end the triumphs of high achievements and who at the worst, if he fails, at least fails while daring greatly."

I pledge to you tonight that as long as I have a breath of life in my body, I shall continue in that spirit. I shall continue to work for the great causes to which I have been dedicated throughout my years as a Congressman, a Senator, a Vice President, and President, the cause of peace not just for America but among all nations, prosperity, justice, and opportunity for all of our people.

There is one cause above all to which I have been devoted and to which I shall always be devoted for as long as I live.

When I first took the oath of office as President 5 1/2 years ago, I made this sacred commitment, to "consecrate my office, my energies, and all the wisdom I can summon to the cause of peace among nations."

I have done my very best in all these days since to be true to that pledge. As a result of these efforts, I am confident that the world is a safer place today, not only for the people of America, but for the people of all nations, and that all of our children have a better chance than before of living in peace rather than dying in war.

This, more than anything, is what I hoped to achieve when I sought the Presidency. This, more than anything, is what I hope will be my legacy to you, to our country, as I leave the Presidency.

To have served in this office is to have felt a very personal sense of kinship with each and every American. In leaving it, I do so with this prayer: May God's grace be with you in all the days ahead.

FIRST INAUGURAL ADDRESS

Ronald Wilson Reagan   *January 20, 1981*

In 1980, Ronald Reagan, the two-term Governor of California, was elected the fortieth President of the United States over Jimmy Carter in a landslide. His inaugural speech specified his philosophy of a more restricted and less active role of government, especially on the domestic side. His speech repudiated Presidents Kennedy and Johnson's idea of big government. Reagan laid out a new economic course based on supply-side theories and decreased taxation on individuals and corporations.

. . . WE are a nation that has a government—not the other way around. And this makes us special among the nations of the earth.

Our government has no power except that granted it by the people. It is time to check and reverse the growth of government which shows signs of having grown beyond the consent of the governed.

It is my intention to curb the size and influence of the Federal establishment and to demand recognition of the distinction between the powers granted to the Federal Government and those reserved to the states or to the people.

All of us—all of us need to be reminded that the Federal Government did not create the states; the states created the Federal Government.

Now, so there will be no misunderstanding, it's not my intention to do away with government.

It is rather to make it work—work with us, not over us; to stand by our side, not ride on our back. Government can and must provide opportunity, not smother it; foster productivity, not stifle it.

If we look to the answer as to why for so many years we achieved so much, prospered as no other people on earth, it was because here in this land we unleashed the energy and individual genius of man to a greater extent than has ever been done before.

Freedom and the dignity of the individual have been more available and assured here than in any other place on earth. The price for this freedom at times has been high, but we have never been unwilling to pay that price.

It is no coincidence that our present troubles parallel and are proportionate to the intervention and intrusion in our lives that result from unnecessary and excessive growth of Government.

It is time for us to realize that we are too great a nation to limit ourselves to small dreams. We're not, as some would have us believe, doomed to an inevitable decline. I do not believe in a fate that will fall on us no matter what we do. I do believe in a fate that will fall on us if we do nothing.

So, with all the creative energy at our command let us begin an era of national renewal. Let us renew our determination, our courage and our strength. And let us renew our faith and our hope. We have every right to dream heroic dreams. . . .

Your dreams, your hopes, your goals are going to be the dreams, the hopes and the goals of this Administration, so help me God.

We shall reflect the compassion that is so much a part of your makeup.

How can we love our country and not love our countrymen? And loving them reach out a hand when they fall, heal them when they're sick and provide opportunity to make them self-sufficient so they will be equal in fact and not just in theory?

Can we solve the problems confronting us? Well the answer is an unequivocal and emphatic yes.

To paraphrase Winston Churchill, I did not take the oath I've just taken with the intention of presiding over the dissolution of the world's strongest economy.

In the days ahead I will propose removing the roadblocks that have slowed our economy and reduced productivity.

Steps will be taken aimed at restoring the balance between the various levels of government. Progress may be slow—measured in inches and feet, not miles—but we will progress.

It is time to reawaken this industrial giant, to get government back within its means and to lighten our punitive tax burden.

And these will be our first priorities, and on these principles there will be no compromise.

On the eve of our struggle for independence a man who might've been one of the greatest among the Founding Fathers, Dr. Joseph Warren, president of the Massachusetts Congress, said to his fellow Americans, "Our country is in danger, but not to be despaired of. On you depend the fortunes of America. You are to decide the important question upon which rest the happiness and the liberty of millions yet unborn. Act worthy of yourselves."

Well I believe we the Americans of today are ready to act worthy of ourselves, ready to do what must be done to insure happiness and liberty for ourselves, our children, and our children's children.

And as we renew ourselves here in our own land we will be seen as having greater strength throughout the world. We will again be the exemplar of freedom and a beacon of hope for those who do not now have freedom.

To those neighbors and allies who share our freedom, we will strengthen our historic ties and assure them of our support and firm commitment.

We will match loyalty with loyalty. We will strive for mutually beneficial relations. We will not use our friendship to impose on their sovereignty, for our own sovereignty is not for sale.

As for the enemies of freedom, those who are potential adversaries, they will be reminded that peace is the highest aspiration of the American people. We will negotiate for it, sacrifice for it; we will not surrender for it—now or ever.

Our forbearance should never be misunderstood. Our reluctance for conflict shold not be misjudged as a failure of will.

When action is required to preserve our national security, we will act. We will maintain sufficient strength to prevail if need be, knowing that if we do so we have the best chance of never having to use that strength.

Above all we must realize that no arsenal or no weapon in the arsenals of the world is so formidable as the will and moral courage of free men and women.

It is a weapon our adversaries in today's world do not have.

It is a weapon that we as Americans do have. . . .

It does require, however, our best effort, and our willingness to believe in ourselves and to believe in our capacity to perform great deeds; to believe that together with God's help we can and will resolve the problems which now confront us.

And after all, why shouldn't we believe that? We are Americans.

ADDRESS TO THE
UNITED NATIONS GENERAL ASSEMBLY

George Herbert Walker Bush   *October 1, 1990*

In 1988, George Bush became the forty-first President of the United States, the first sitting Vice President elected President in over 150 years. This speech relates to several earlier documents: President Truman's speech at the United Nations Conference in 1945, which was a time of great optimism for international cooperation, and the speeches of Churchill, Truman, Kennedy and Reagan that dealt with the difficulties of relations with the Soviet Union.

Throughout the 1970s and 1980s relations between the Soviets and the United States were strained as the two countries continued arms escalation and strong rhetoric. However, in the late 1980s, the situation changed dramatically. Under Mikhail Gorbachev, the Soviet Union made strides toward democratic reform. Beginning with Poland's changing politics in the 1980s, Eastern Europe became more independent. After the Berlin wall came down in 1989, the rest of Eastern Europe emerged from under the direct control of the Soviet Union, Czechoslovakia, Hungary, Bulgaria, Rumania and Albania. Finally the fifteen Republics of the Soviet Union began to splinter, starting with the Baltic Republics of Estonia, Latvia and Lithuania. In the midst of these changes, the United States found itself in a territorial crisis involving Iraq, but now the United States and the Soviet Union were on the same side of a United Nations' resolution. A new world order was at hand.

. . . FORTY-FIVE years ago, while the fires of an epic war still raged across two oceans and two continents, a small group of men and women began a search for hope amid the ruins, and they gathered in San Francisco, stepping back from the haze and horror, to try to shape a new structure that might support an ancient dream. Intensely idealistic, and yet tempered by war, they sought to build a new kind of bridge—a bridge between nations, a bridge that might help carry humankind from its darkest hour to its brightest day.

The founding of the United Nations embodied our deepest hopes for a peaceful world. And during the past year, we've come closer than ever before to realizing those hopes. We've seen a century sundered by barbed threats and barbed wire, give way to a new era of peace and competition and freedom.

The revolution of '89 swept the world almost with a life of its own, carried by a new breeze of freedom that transformed the political climate from Central Europe to Central America, and touched almost every corner of the globe. That breeze has been sustained by a now almost universal recognition of a simple, fundamental truth: The human spirit cannot be locked up forever.

The truth is, people everywhere are motivated in much the same ways, and people everywhere want much the same things: the chance to live a life of purpose, the chance to choose a life in which they and their children can learn and grow healthy, worship freely and prosper through the work of their hands and their hearts and their minds.

We're not talking about the power of nations, but the power of individuals—the power to choose, the power to risk, the power to succeed. This is a new and different world.

Not since 1945 have we seen the real possibility of using the United Nations as it was designed, as a center for international collective security.

The changes in the Soviet Union have been critical to the emergence of a stronger United Nations. The U.S.–Soviet relationship is finally beyond containment and confrontation, and now we seek to fulfill the promise of mutually shared understanding. The long twilight struggle that for 45 years has divided Europe, our two nations and much of the world has come to an end. Much has changed over the last two years. The Soviet Union has taken many dramatic and important steps to participate fully in the community of nations, and when the Soviet Union agreed with so many of us here in the United Nations to condemn the aggression of Iraq, there could be no doubt, no doubt then, that we had indeed put four decades of history behind us.

We are hopeful that the machinery of the United Nations will no longer be frozen by the divisions that plagued us during the cold war, that at last, long last, we can build new bridges and tear down old walls; that at long last we will be able to build a new world based on an event for which we have all hoped, an end to the cold war. . . .

Last year's General Assembly showed how we can make greater progress toward a more pragmatic and successful United Nations. And for the first time, the U.N. Security Council is beginning to work as it was designed to work. And now is the time to set aside old and counterproductive debates and procedures and controversies and resolutions. It's time to replace polemic attacks with pragmatic action.

And we've shown that the U.N. can count on the collective strength of the international community. We've shown that the U.N. can rise to the challenge of aggression, just as its founders hoped that it would. And now is the time of testing.

We must also show that the United Nations is the place to build international support and consensus for meeting the other challenges we face. The world remains a dangerous place, and our security and well-being often depends, in part, on events occurring far away. We need serious international cooperative efforts to make headway on the threats to the environment, on terrorism, on managing the debt burden, on fighting the scourge of international drug trafficking and on refugees and peacekeeping efforts around the world.

But the world also remains a hopeful place. Calls for democracy and human rights are being reborn everywhere, and these calls are an expression of support for the values enshrined in the United Nations Charter. They encourage our hopes for a more stable, more peaceful, more prosperous world. Free elections are the foundation of democratic government and can produce dramatic successes, as we've seen in Namibia and Nicaragua . . .

The world must know and understand, from this hour, from this day, from this hall, we step forth with a new sense of purpose, a new sense of possibilities. We stand together, prepared to swim upstream, to march uphill, to tackle the tough challenges as they come, not only as the United Nations, but as the nations of the world united.

And so let it be said of the final decade of the 20th century, this was a time when humankind came into its own, when we emerged from the grit and the smoke of the industrial age to bring about a revolution of the spirit and the mind and began a journey into a new day, a new age and a new partnership of nations. The U.N. is now fulfilling its promise as the world's parliament of peace. And I congratulate you. I support you. And I wish you godspeed in the challenges ahead.

ADDRESS TO THE
ECONOMIC CLUB OF NEW YORK

Carlos Salinas de Gortari   *December 13, 1991*

In the late twentieth century, the world's conflicts and
battles shifted from the military to the economic sphere. This
does not mean that military conflicts have disappeared, but
generally they are limited to civil wars or small-scale wars
between neighboring states. Wars between the superpowers
appear far less likely than they did earlier this century.

But there are increasing problems and opportunities on the
economic front. International economic ties and trading partners
are changing and becoming more important. Economic pressures
and disagreements exist between the United States and Japan, and
among Western Europe, Japan and the United States. One of the
more important actions in the 1990s was the development of the
North American Free Trade Agreement. This speech by the Presi-
dent of Mexico, Carlos Salinas, exhibits optimism as the three
nations of North America become closer.

. . . THE international scene is increasingly surprising, and increasingly
uncertain as well. Only two years ago we were celebrating the new adventure
of freedom and democracy in Central Europe and also in Latin America. Today
we are witnessing the resurgence of regional conflicts and war, and the
threatened breakup of nations that just a short time ago seemed rock-solid. The
world economic trend is toward more intense interdependence, leading more
countries to become active members of the world economy and creating growing
hopes for a world more open to trade and to the transfer of technology. But we
are also seeing rising competition for capital—increasingly scarce, given the
demands of the one-time socialist countries and those of Latin America—
uncertainty in the markets, risks of new forms of protectionism and obstacles to
the success of GATT agreements.

Mexico, a country neighboring on your own, has been the cradle of
magnificent civilizations and has a history forged by dint of determination and
love of freedom. It is also a nation of more than 83 million inhabitants, whose

number grows by an additional 2 million each year. To us, the pursuit of economic growth and increased opportunities is not only good policy, but a vital, immediate need. We recognize that this cannot be done without making profound changes in our internal life and without establishing new links with other nations and particularly, given the importance of our trade relations, with the United States.

Within our borders, we Mexicans are taking a new approach in dealing with national and global realities. Sustained by 3,000 years of culture and by our country's laws, we launched a process of far-reaching change in our economic structures and a renovation of our political practices as a society. We have maintained a strategy aimed at providing growth with stability, creating new employment opportunities and taking in-depth measures to combat poverty. . . .

We have recovered growth in the last three years at rates of almost 4 percent, which is almost double our population growth. We have carried out a unilateral trade opening of great consequence; in just a few years, our economy has been transformed from one of the most closed into one of the most open. We have deregulated and promoted foreign investment, which can now count on legal certainty and access to more areas of our economy. We have promoted technological innovation, technology transfers and exports.

We have also sought new linkages with the world to give us access to markets, technology and capital. We are convinced that only our own internal efforts can ensure the country's development, but also that it is essential for us to participate and broaden our presence in the world so that those efforts do not encounter obstacles in their path and will therefore prosper. Hence, we have diversified our relations with Europe, with the countries of the Pacific Rim and with Latin America. With Chile, we signed the first free trade agreement between two Latin American countries, and we are making solid progress toward the establishment of similar agreements with the countries of Central America and with Columbia and Venezuela. . . .

I am convinced that these negotiations do not merely involve adding or subtracting amounts and figures. We are also talking about a vision for the future of this region at the end of this century and the beginning of the 21st. We must bring the agreement to a satisfactory conclusion because it is the only means of facing the future, which we are already witnessing today. Europe has the resources, the technology and the market needed to become a powerful agent of the world economy at the end of 1992. Furthermore, as a result of the autumn revolution of 1989 in Central Europe, the European Community now has the possibility of gaining access to abundant skilled labor. Japan has not only built up a powerful economy, but also has entered into partnership with other countries of the Asian Pacific, distributing productive processes and resources and thereby generating a great overall capacity for exports. In addition, the countries of the Asian Pacific have access, both as consumers and producers, to a market made up of nearly 3 billion people in Asia. Both blocs, Europe and the Asian Pacific, are formidable competitors that are increasing their capacity to gain access to markets day by day. It is in this context that the significance of the Free Trade Agreement should be viewed.

Although the United States still has the largest national economy in the world and has increased its potential together with Canada, its complementariness with Mexico could significantly raise its competitive capacity. Let us remember that 35 percent of Japanese manufactures are produced in conjunction with other Asian countries, whereas only 5 percent of U.S. manufactures are produced in a similar fashion. Hence the great potential of a Free Trade Agreement with Mexico: It means greater competitiveness for your country as well as for Mexico.

In our case it would also act as an instrument of our own economic project that could give us the impetus needed to reach new levels of development. Resources, technologies and a young, energetic population structure could be brought together to make each country, and the region as a whole, more competitive and therefore more successful in dealing with competition from Europe and Japan. . . .

By changing, Mexico has strengthened its presence in the world. It is now better prepared to meet the demands and challenges of an increasingly active economic interrelationship with the world. We have confidence in our 3,000-year-old culture and in the enormous creativity of our people. We view encounters with other cultures as an opportunity to enrich our understanding and our sensibility. I urge you to become better acquainted with my country and to support the efforts of both governments to pave the way for an era of exchanges and cooperation, similar to the relationship already being shown by many families along our common border. Let us make our condition as neighbors a reason to deepen our friendship.

INAUGURAL ADDRESS

William Jefferson Clinton   *January 20, 1993*

In 1992, William Clinton was elected the forty-second president of the United States. Clinton's election marked a watershed, as he was the first president from the "baby boomers," a generation tempered by the idealism of Kennedy, the problems of Vietnam and the social upheavals of the 1960s. President Clinton harked back to the idealism of Kennedy and the activism of President Johnson, seeking a more active role for government in domestic affairs.

MY fellow citizens, today we celebrate the mystery of American renewal. This ceremony is held in the depth of winter, but by the words we speak and the faces we show the world, we force the spring. A spring reborn in the world's oldest democracy that brings forth the vision and courage to reinvent America.

When our Founders boldly declared America's independence to the world and our purposes to the Almighty, they knew that America to endure would have to change. Not change for change sake but change to preserve America's ideals—life, liberty, the pursuit of happiness. Though we march to the music of our time, our mission is timeless. Each generation of Americans must define what it means to be an American. . . .

Raised in unrivaled prosperity, we inherit an economy that is still the world's strongest but it is weakened by business failures, stagnant wages, increasing inequality and deep divisions among our own people. . . .

We earn our livelihood in America today in peaceful competition with people all across the earth. Profound and powerful forces are shaking and remaking our world. And the urgent question of our time is whether we can make change our friend and not our enemy. . . .

Though our challenges are fearsome, so are our strengths. Americans have ever been a restless, questing, hopeful people, and we must bring to our task today the vision and will of those who came before us. From our Revolution to the Civil War, to the Great Depression, to the civil rights movement, our people have always mustered the determination to construct from these crises the pillars of our history.

Thomas Jefferson believed that to preserve the very foundations of our nation we would need dramatic change from time to time. Well my fellow Americans, this is our time. Let us embrace it.

Our democracy must be not only the envy of the world but the engine of our own renewal. There is nothing wrong with America that cannot be cured by what is right with America. And so today we pledge an end to the era of deadlock and drift, and a new season of American renewal has begun.

To renew American we must be bold. We must do what no generation has had to do before. We must invest more in our own people—in their jobs and in their future—and at the same time cut our massive debt. And we must do so in a world in which we must compete for every opportunity. It will not be easy. It will require sacrifice. But it can be done and done fairly. Not choosing sacrifice for its own sake, but for our own sake. We must provide for our nation the way a family provides for its children.

Our founders saw themselves in the light of posterity. We can do no less. Anyone who has ever watched a child's eyes wander into sleep knows what posterity is. Posterity is the world to come. The world for whom we hold our ideals, from whom we have borrowed our planet and to whom we bear sacred responsibility. We must do what America does best: offer more opportunity to all and demand more responsibility from all.

It is time to break the bad habit of expecting something for nothing from our Government or from each other. Let us all take more responsibility not only for ourselves and our families but for our communities and our country.

To renew America we must revitalize our democracy. This beautiful capital, like every capital since the dawn of civilization, is often a place of intrigue and calculation. Powerful people maneuver for position and worry endlessly about who is in and who is out, who is up and who is down, forgetting those people whose toil and sweat sends us here and pays our way. . . .

Let us put aside personal advantage so that we can feel the pain and see the promise of America. Let us resolve to make our Government a place for what Franklin Roosevelt called bold, persistent experimentation, a Government for our tomorrows, not our yesterdays. Let us give this capital back to the people to whom it belongs. . . .

While America rebuilds at home, we will not shrink from the challenges nor fail to seize the opportunities of this new world. Together with our friends and allies we will work to shape change lest it engulf us. When our vital interests are challenged or the will and conscience of the international community is defied, we will act, with peaceful diplomacy whenever possible, with force when necessary. . . .

But our greatest strength is the power of our ideas, which are still new in many lands. Across the world we see them embraced and we rejoice. Our hopes, our hearts, our hands are with those on every continent who are building democracy and freedom. Their cause is America's cause.

The American people have summoned the change we celebrate today. You have raised your voices in an unmistakable chorus, you have cast your votes in historic numbers, and you have changed the face of Congress, the Presidency and the political process itself. Yes, you, my fellow Americans, have forced the spring.

Today we do more than celebrate America, we rededicate ourselves to the very idea of America: an idea born in revolution and renewed through two centuries of challenge; an idea tempered by the knowledge that but for fate we, the fortunate and the unfortunate, might have been each other; an idea ennobled by the faith that our nation can summon from its myriad diversity the deepest measure of unity; an idea infused with the conviction that America's long, heroic journey must go forever upward.

And so, my fellow Americans, as we stand at the edge of the 21st century, let us begin anew with energy and hope, with faith and discipline. And let us work until our work is done. The Scripture says, "And let us not be weary in well-doing, for in due season we shall reap if we faint not."

From this joyful mountain top of celebration we hear a call to service in the valley. We have heard the trumpets, we have changed the guard. And now each in our own way, and with God's help, we must answer the call.

SOURCES

Full texts of the documents included in *Soul of America* can be found in the following sources.

VI. CIVIL WAR

"House Divided" Speech. Alonzo T. Jones, ed., *Political Speeches and Debates of Abraham Lincoln and Stephen A. Douglas, 1854–1861* (Battle Creek, Mich.: International Tract Society, 1895).

Address to the Virginia Court. John D. Lawson, ed., *American State Trials* (17 vols.; St. Louis: Thomas Law Book Co., 1914–36), vol. 6.

South Carolina Ordinance and Declaration of Causes of Secession. Frank Moore, ed., *The Rebellion Record* (11 vols.; New York: G. P. Putnam and D. Van Nostrand, 1861–68), vol. 1.

First Inaugural Address. *Messages and Papers*, vol. 7.

The Battle Hymn of the Republic. *Atlantic Monthly*, February 1862.

The Homestead Act. *U.S. Statutes at Large*, 37th Cong., 2d sess., 1862, vol. 12.

The Morrill Act. Ibid.

The Emancipation Proclamation. Roy P. Basler, ed., *The Collected Works of Abraham Lincoln* (8 vols.; New Brunswick: Rutgers University Press, 1953), vol. 6.

Address at Gettysburg. Ibid., vol. 7.

Second Inaugural Address. Ibid., vol. 8.

Farewell to His Army. Armistead L. Long, *Memoirs of Robert E. Lee* (New York: J.M. Stoddart and Co., 1886).

Amendment XIII: Slavery Abolished. Corwin, *The Constitution*.

The Impeachment and Trial of President Andrew Johnson. Benjamin P. Poore, ed., *Trial of Andrew Johnson* (Washington, D.C.: Government Printing Office, 1868).

Amendment XIV: Citizenship Rights Not to Be Abridged. Corwin, *The Constitution*.

Amendment XV: Race No Bar to Voting Rights. Ibid.

VII. AMERICA COMES OF AGE

On Woman's Right to Suffrage. Ida Harper, *The Life and Work of Susan B. Anthony* (3 vols.; Indianapolis: Bowen–Merrill, 1898–1908), vol. 1.

Report on the Lands of the Arid Region. John Wesley Powell, *Report on the Lands of the Arid Region of the United States* (Washington, D.C.: Government Printing Office, 1878).

Narrative. Virginia Irving Armstrong, ed., *I Have Spoken: American History through the Voices of the Indians* (Chicago: Swallow Press, 1971).

The New Colossus. *The Poems of Emma Lazarus* (New York: Houghton Mifflin, 1889).

The Sherman Anti-Trust Act. *U.S. Statutes at Large*, 51st Cong., 1st sess., 1890, vol. 26.

America the Beautiful. Helen K. Johnson and Frederic Dean, eds., *Famous Songs and Those Who Made Them* (New York: Bryan, Taylor and Co., 1895).

Atlanta Exposition Speech. Booker T. Washington, *Up from Slavery: An Autobiography* (New York: Doubleday and Page, 1901).

Cross of Gold Speech. William Jennings Bryan, *The First Battle* (Chicago: W. B. Conkey Co., 1896).

Plessy v. Ferguson. *Supreme Court Reports*, 163 U.S. 537 (1896).

Letter to Booker T. Washington. Louis R. Harlan, et al., eds., *The Booker T. Washington Papers* (14 vols.; Urbana: University of Illinois Press, 1972–88), vol. 4.

Open Door Circular Letter. Malloy, ed., *Treaties, Conventions, International Acts*, vol. 1.

Fourth Annual Message to Congress. *Messages and Papers*, vol. 15.

Seventh Annual Message to Congress. Ibid.

Declaration of the Conservation Conference. *Proceedings of a Conference of Governors in the White House, Washington, D.C., May 13–15, 1908* (Washington, D.C.: Government Printing Office, 1909).

Amendment XVI: Income Tax Authorized. Corwin, *The Constitution*.

Amendment XVII: Direct Popular Election of Senators. Ibid.

VIII. Two Wars and a Depression

Women and War. Jane Addams, *Peace and Bread in Time of War* (New York: Macmillan, 1922).

Address to the United States Senate. 64th Cong., 2d sess., 1917, S. Doc. 685.

The Fourteen Points. *Messages and Papers,* vol. 18.

Amendment XVIII: Liquor Prohibition. Corwin, *The Constitution*.

Amendment XIX: National Woman Suffrage. Ibid.

The Philosophy of Rugged Individualism. *The New Day: Campaign Speeches of Herbert Hoover* (Palo Alto: Stanford University Press, 1928).

Amendment XX: Beginning of Presidential Terms, Congressional Sessions. Corwin, *The Constitution*.

First Inaugural Address. *Congressional Record*, 73d Cong., Special Session of the Senate, 1933.

Amendment XXI: Repeal of Amendment XVIII. Corwin, *The Constitution*.

Four Freedoms Speech. *Congressional Record*, 77th Cong., 1st sess., 1941.

The Atlantic Charter. 77th Cong., 1st sess., 1941, H. Doc. 358.

Declaration of War. *Congressional Record*, 77th Cong., 1st sess., 1941.

Executive Order 9066. *Federal Register*, vol. 7, 1942.

IX. The United States and World Power

The United Nations Conference. *Public Papers of the Presidents of the United States: Harry S. Truman . . . 1945* (Washington, D.C.: Government Printing Office, 1961).

Iron Curtain Speech. Robert Rhodes James, ed. *Winston Churchill: His Complete Speeches 1897–1963*. Vol. VII, 1943–1949 (New York: RR Bowker & Co.).

The Truman Doctrine. *Congressional Record*, 80th Cong., 1st sess., 1947.

The Marshall Plan. *Congressional Record*, 80th Cong., 1st sess., 1947, Appendix.

Inaugural Address. *Public Papers of the Presidents of the United States: Harry S. Truman . . . 1949* (Washington, D.C.: Government Printing Office, 1964).

Amendment XXII: Limit Two Terms for President. Corwin, *The Constitution*.

Brown v. the Board of Education of Topeka, Kansas. *Supreme Court Reports*, 347 U.S. 483 (1954).

Farewell Address. *Department of State Bulletin*, February 6, 1961.

Inaugural Address. *Public Papers of the Presidents of the United States: John F. Kennedy . . . 1961* (Washington, D.C.: Government Printing Office, 1962).

Amendment XXIII: Presidential Vote for District of Columbia. Corwin, *The Constitution*.

Declaration of Indian Purpose. Francis Paul Prucha, ed., *Documents of United States Indian Policy* (Lincoln: University of Nebraska Press, 1975).

Silent Spring. Rachel Carson (Boston: Houghton Mifflin, 1962), 296–297.

Ich Bin Ein Berliner Speech. *Public Papers of the Presidents of the United States: John F. Kennedy . . . 1963*. (Washington, D.C.: Government Printing Office, 1964).

Civil Rights Speech. Coretta Scott King, comp., *The Words of Martin Luther King, Jr.* (New York: Newmarket Press, 1987).

Address to a Joint Session of Congress. *Public Papers of the Presidents of the United States: Lyndon B. Johnson . . . 1963–64* (Washington, D.C.: Government Printing Office, 1965).

X. The United States in the Modern World

Amendment XXIV: Banned Poll Tax in Federal Elections. Corwin, *The Constitution*.

The Civil Rights Act. *U.S. Statutes at Large*, 1964, vol. 78, Public Law 88–352.

Gulf of Tonkin Resolution. *Department of State Bulletin*, August 24, 1964.

Amendment XXV: Presidential Disability and Succession. Corwin, *The Constitution*.

Amendment XXVI: Lowered Voting Age to Eighteen Years. Ibid.

The Equal Rights Amendment. Leslie F. Goldstein, *The Constitutional Rights of Women: Cases in Law and Social Change* (Madison: University of Wisconsin Press, 1988).

Roe et al. v. Wade. *Supreme Court Reports*, 410 U.S. 113 (1973).

Speech in House Judiciary Committee. *Debate on Articles of Impeachment: Hearings of the Committee on the Judiciary, House of Representatives*. 93rd Cong., 2nd Sess., 1974.

Resignation Speech. *Public Papers of the Presidents of the United States: Richard Nixon . . . 1974* (Washington, D.C.: Government Printing Office, 1975).

First Inaugural Address. *Public Papers of the Presidents of the United States, Ronald Reagan,* 1981 (Washington, D.C.: Government Printing Office, 1991).

Address to the Members of the Economic Club of New York. Mexican Embassy, Washington, D.C., December 13, 1991.

Inaugural Address. *New York Times,* January 21, 1993.

BIBLIOGRAPHY

COLLECTIONS OF DOCUMENTS

The Annals of America. 22 vols. Chicago: Encyclopedia Britannica, 1968–.

Barrett, Edward L., Jr., and William Cohen. *Constitutional Law: Cases and Materials.* 7th ed. Mineola, N.Y.: Foundation Press, 1985.

Commager, Henry Steele, ed. *Documents of American History.* 9th ed. New York: Meredith Corporation, 1973.

A Compilation of the Messages and Papers of the Presidents. 20 vols. New York: Bureau of National Literature, 1897–1917.

Documentary History of the Constitution of the United States of America, 1787–1870. 5 vols. Washington, D.C.: Department of State, 1894–1905.

Glusker, Irwin, and Richard M. Ketchum, eds. *American Testament: Fifty Great Documents in American History.* New York: American Heritage Publishing Co., 1971.

Historical Statistics of the United States: Colonial Times to 1970. 2 vols. Washington, D.C.: U.S. Department of Commerce, 1975.

Israel, Fred L. *State of the Union Messages of the Presidents, 1790–1966.* 3 vols. New York: Chelsea House Publishers, 1967.

MacDonald, H. Malcolm, et al. *Outside Readings in American Government.* New York: Crowell, 1957.

MacDonald, William, ed. *Select Documents Illustrative of the History of the United States, 1776–1861.* 1898. Reprint. New York: Burt Franklin, 1968.

Malloy, William M., ed. *Treaties, Conventions, International Acts, Protocols, and Agreements between the United States of America and Other Powers.* 2 vols. Washington, D.C.: Government Printing Office, 1910.

Meltzer, Milton, ed. *Milestones to American Liberty: The Foundations of the Republic.* New York: Crowell, 1961.

Millett, Stephen M. *A Selected Bibliography of American Constitutional History.* Santa Barbara: Clio Books, 1975.

Moquin, Wayne, and Charles van Doren, comps. *Great Documents in American Indian History.* New York: Praeger, 1973.

Morris, Richard B., ed. *Basic Documents in American History.* Princeton: D. Van Nostrand Co., 1965.

Morris, Richard B., and Jeffrey B. Morris, eds. *Great Presidential Decisions: State Papers That Changed the Course of History, from Washington to Reagan.* Rev. ed. New York: Richardson, Steirman and Black, 1988.

O'Callaghan, E. B., ed. *Documents Relative to the Colonial History of the State of New-York.* 15 vols. Albany: Weed and Parsons, 1853–87.

Poore, Benjamin P., comp. *The Federal and State Constitutions, Colonial Charters, and Other Organic Laws of the United States.* 2 vols. Washington, D.C.: Government Printing Office, 1877.

Romero, Patricia W., comp. *I Too Am America: Documents from 1619 to the Present.* New York: Publishers Co., 1968.

Tansill, C. C., ed. *Documents Illustrative of the Formation of the Union of the American States.* Washington, D.C.: Government Printing Office, 1927.

Thorpe, Francis N., ed. *The Federal and State Constitutions, Colonial Charters, and Other Organic Laws of the States, Territories, and Colonies Now or Heretofore Forming the United States of America.* 7 vols. Washington, D.C.: Government Printing Office, 1909.

ADDITIONAL READING

VI. Civil War

Basler, Roy P., ed. *The Collected Works of Abraham Lincoln.* 8 vols. New Brunswick: Rutgers University Press, 1953.

Catton, Bruce. *A Stillness at Appomattox.* Garden City: Doubleday, 1953.

Catton, Bruce. *The Centennial History of the Civil War.* 3 vols. Garden City: Doubleday, 1961–65.

Foner, Eric. *Reconstruction: America's Unfinished Revolution, 1863–1877.* New York: Harper and Row, 1988.

Foote, Shelby. *The Civil War: A Narrative.* 3 vols. New York: Random House, 1958–74.

Freeman, Douglas S. *Lee's Lieutenants: A Study in Command.* 3 vols. New York: Charles Scribner's Sons, 1942–44.

Freeman, Douglas S. *Robert E. Lee.* 4 vols. New York: Charles Scribner's Sons, 1934–35.

McPherson, James M. *Battle Cry of Freedom: The Civil War Era.* New York: Oxford University Press, 1988.

Myers, Robert Manson, ed. *The Children of Pride: A True Story of Georgia and the Civil War.* New Haven: Yale University Press, 1972.

Nevins, Allan. *Ordeal of the Union.* New York: Charles Scribner's Sons, 1947.

Sandburg, Carl. *Abraham Lincoln: The War Years.* 4 vols. New York: Harcourt, Brace, 1939.

Williams, T. Harry. *Lincoln and His Generals.* New York: Random House, 1967.

Woodward, C. Vann, ed. *Mary Chesnut's Civil War.* New Haven: Yale University Press, 1981.

VII. America Comes of Age

Beale, Howard K. *Theodore Roosevelt and the Rise of America to World Power.* Baltimore: Johns Hopkins University Press, 1956.

Boorstin, Daniel J. *The Americans: The Democratic Experience.* New York: Random House, 1973.

Commager, Henry Steele. *The American Mind.* New Haven: Yale University Press, 1950.

Du Bois, W. E. B. *Black Reconstruction in America: 1860–1880.* 1935. Reprint. New York: Russell and Russell, 1962.

Goodwyn, Lawrence. *Democratic Promise: The Populist Movement in America.* New York: Oxford University Press, 1976.

Handlin, Oscar. *The Uprooted: The Epic Story of the Great Migrations That Made the American People.* Boston: Little, Brown, 1951.

Hofstadter, Richard. *The Age of Reform: From Bryan to F.D.R.* New York: Knopf, 1955.

Josephson, Matthew. *Robber Barons: The Great American Capitalists, 1861–1901.* New York: Harcourt, Brace, 1934.

Link, Arthur S. *Woodrow Wilson and the Progressive Era, 1910–1917.* New York: Harper and Row, 1954.

McPherson, James M. *The Abolitionist Legacy: From Reconstruction to the N.A.A.C.P.* Princeton: Princeton University Press, 1975.

Turner, Frederick Jackson. *The Frontier in American History.* 1920. Reprint. Tucson: University of Arizona Press, 1985.

Washington, Booker T. *Up from Slavery: An Autobiography.* New York: Doubleday and Page, 1901.

Williams, William A. *The Tragedy of American Diplomacy.* New York: Dell Publishing, 1959.

VIII. Two Wars and a Depression

Allen, Frederick Lewis. *Only Yesterday: An Informal History of the Nineteen Twenties.* New York: Harper and Brothers, 1931.

Blum, John Morton. *V Was for Victory: Politics and American Culture During World War II.* Orlando: Harcourt, Brace, Jovanovich, 1977.

Brinkley, Alan. *Voices of Protest: Huey Long, Father Coughlin, and the Great Depression.* New York: Alfred E. Knopf, 1982.

Cook, Blanche Wiesen. *Eleanor Roosevelt: Volume 1, 1884–1933.* New York: Viking, 1992.

Cott, Nancy. *The Grounding of Modern Feminism.* New Haven: Yale University Press, 1987.

Eisenhower, Dwight D. *Crusade in Europe.* Garden City: Doubleday, 1948.

Gaddis, John Lewis. *The U.S. and the Origins of the Cold War, 1941–1947.* New York: Columbia University Press, 1972.

Hoover, Herbert. *The Ordeal of Woodrow Wilson.* New York: McGraw-Hill, 1958.

Hurt, R. Douglas. *The Dust Bowl: An Agricultural and Social History.* Chicago: Nelson–Hall, 1981.

Irons, Peter. *Justice at War: The Inside Story of the Japanese–American Internment.* New York: Oxford University Press, 1983.

Kennedy, David. *Over Here: The First World War and American Society.* New York: Oxford University Press, 1980.

Leuchtenburg, William E. *Franklin D. Roosevelt and the New Deal, 1932–1940.* New York: Harper and Row, 1963.

Link, Arthur S. *American Epoch: A History of the United States Since the 1890s*. 5th ed. New York: Knopf, 1980.

Schlesinger, Arthur M., Jr. *The Age of Roosevelt: The Crisis of the Old Order*. Boston: Houghton Mifflin, 1957.

Schlesinger, Arthur M., Jr. *The Age of Roosevelt: The Coming of the New Deal*. Boston: Houghton Mifflin, 1958.

Schlesinger, Arthur M., Jr. *The Age of Roosevelt: The Politics of Upheaval*. Boston: Houghton Mifflin, 1960.

Schulzinger, Robert D. *American Diplomacy in the Twentieth Century*. New York: Oxford University Press, 1984.

Soule, George. *Prosperity Decade: From War to Depression, 1917–1929*. New York: Rinehart, 1947.

Terkel, Studs. *"The Good War": An Oral History of World War II*. New York: Pantheon Books, 1984.

IX. *The United States and World Power*

Acheson, Dean. *Present at the Creation: My Years in the State Department*. New York: Norton, 1969.

Alexander, Charles C. *Holding the Line: The Eisenhower Era, 1952–1961*. Bloomington: Indiana University Press, 1975.

Branch, Taylor. *Parting the Waters: America in the King Years 1954–63*. New York: Simon & Schuster, 1988.

Cox, Archibald. *The Court and the Constitution*. Boston: Houghton Mifflin, 1987.

Gilbert, James. *Another Chance: Postwar America, 1945–1968*. Philadelphia: Temple University Press, 1981.

Goldman, Eric. *The Crucial Decade: America, 1945–1955*. New York: Knopf, 1956.

Herring, George C. *America's Longest War: The United States in Vietnam, 1950–1975*. New York: Knopf, 1979.

Hodgson, Godfrey. *America in Our Time: From World War II to Nixon*. Garden City: Doubleday, 1976.

McCullough, David. *Truman*. New York: Simon & Schuster, 1992.

Miller, Merle. *Plain Speaking: An Oral Biography of Harry S. Truman*. New York: Berkeley Publishing Corp., 1974.

Navasky, Victor. *Naming Names*. New York: Viking, 1980.

Oates, Stephen B. *Let the Trumpet Sound: The Life of Martin Luther King, Jr.* New York: Harper and Row, 1982.

O'Neill, William L. *Coming Apart: An Informal History of the 1960s*. New York: Quadrangle, 1971.

Pollak, Louis H. *The Constitution and the Supreme Court: A Documentary History*. Cleveland: World Publishing Co., 1966.

Prucha, Francis Paul. *The Indians in American Society: From the Revolutionary War to the Present*. Berkeley: University of California Press, 1985.

Schlesinger, Arthur M., Jr. *A Thousand Days: John F. Kennedy in the White House*. Boston: Houghton Mifflin, 1965.

White, Theodore H. *America in Search of Itself: The Making of the President, 1956–1980*. New York: Harper and Row, 1982.

X. The United States in the Modern World

Halberstam, David. *The Best and The Brightest*. New York: Random House, 1972.

Karnow, Stanley. *Vietnam: A History*. Annapolis: Naval Institute Press, 1983.

Mansbridge, Jane. *Why We Lost the ERA*. Chicago: University of Chicago Press, 1986.

Matusow, Allen J. *The Unraveling of America: A History of Liberalism in the 1960's*. New York: Harper and Row, 1985.

Terry, Wallace. *Bloods: An Oral History of the Vietnam War by Black Veterans*. New York: Random House, 1984.

INDEX